IMAGES
of America

ASSYRIANS OF EASTERN MASSACHUSETTS

On the cover: please see page 64, top photograph. (Courtesy of the Perch and Saffer families.)

IMAGES
of America

ASSYRIANS OF EASTERN MASSACHUSETTS

Sargon Donabed and Ninos Donabed

ARCADIA
PUBLISHING

ISBN 978-0-7385-4480-9

Published by Arcadia Publishing
Charleston, South Carolina

Printed in the United States of America

Library of Congress Catalog Card Number: 2005937496

For all general information contact Arcadia Publishing at:
Telephone 843-853-2070
Fax 843-853-0044
E-mail sales@arcadiapublishing.com
For customer service and orders:
Toll-Free 1-888-313-2665

Visit us on the Internet at www.arcadiapublishing.com

This book is dedicated to all Assyrians who continue to struggle for survival despite continued attempts to eradicate them and their ancient culture from the world. Also, we would like to dedicate this specifically to our parents, George and Elsie Donabed, for teaching us that Assyria is not just a dream but a living breathing reality. We now know this all too well. We love you.

Contents

ACKNOWLEDGMENTS

First and foremost, we would like to thank our parents George and Elsie Donabed for their hours of phone calls and visits to the homes of Massachusetts Assyrians. Without all that work, this book would not have been possible. Truth be told, there is no way we can thank you enough for everything you have done. Also much love and thanks to all the Assyrians of Massachusetts—first, second, and third generations—for all their help and support. Thanks go particularly to the first settlers of Assyrians who fled ethno-cultural genocide in their homeland to arrive on the shores of Massachusetts and their adopted country. Thanks to Harold and Mary Perch and family; Phyllis Saffer and daughters Pamela and Leslie; and *Malfono* Ninos Aho, Mansoura Aho and family. God Bless you all. This work would never have happened were it not for your meticulous care for your heritage. We thank you with all our hearts and express our great pleasure to have had you as our role models from childhood.

Many thanks and appreciation to Shamiran Mako, analyst and liaison for the Council for Assyrian Research and Development (CARD), Ninos Hanna of the United Assyrian Association of Massachusetts (UAAM), and Heather Snow and Steve Batiuk from the University of Toronto for their painstaking research. Much gratitude must also be given to the Kurkjy clan (whose ancestors stem from Edessa/Urfa) Sandy, Samantha, and Mark, for their tireless efforts in keeping the UAAM a working institution. Special thanks to the Hanna, Bet-Shlimon, Soloman, Stifo, Lahdo, and Dawlabani families. To Erin Stone and everyone at Arcadia Publishing for giving us the chance to present this rich and wonderful history to the world, we can only say thanks for the opportunity. You dealt with our many questions with patience and kindness.

Finally, to our family and friends all over the world, thanks for putting up with us and all our mischievous behavior from childhood—and for being there for us. God bless.

INTRODUCTION

To speak about the Assyrian people is to tell a story that begins over 6,700 years ago in northern Mesopotamia (today's north Iraq, southeast Turkey, northwest Iran, and northeast Syria). Ancient Assyria was a topographically beautiful area, resplendent with a variety of flora and fauna, as well as breathtaking mountains and rolling fertile plains. Indigenous to these mountains and valleys, the Assyrian people date their current year, 6755, to the founding of the first temple of Ashur (the ancient god of the Assyrians) from whom they received their name and land. Despite some Old Testament biblical misinformation, Assyrians were an extremely cultured people who built the first libraries, wrote the first code of laws, established roads throughout the entire Middle East (proto-postal system), wrote philosophy, poetry, and literature, and established what some have called the first zoos or wildlife sanctuaries in the world.

The highland Assyrians in the north and the Akkadian/Babylonian tribes in the south were of the same stock (as much as Athenians and Spartans were both Greek). Throughout their history, the power shifted from Nineveh in the north to the city of Babylon in the south. Assyrians were not above enriching their culture with those of other peoples close in culture such as the ancient Sumerians. For example, they adopted the cuneiform script and even many words from their neighbors to the south. Assyrians even began to (officially) speak, read, and write a closely related language (Aramaic) during the later stages of their empire. In fact, the so-called Aramaic-speaking people were absorbed into the Assyrian culture by the 8th century BC.

Assyrians lived for many years under the rule of their kings and queens until the fall of their capital of Nineveh in 612 BC and then their capital of Harran in 608 BC. Their Babylonian cousins lasted until 529 BC, but they, too, soon fell to outside forces. Despite the fall of these empires, Assyrians continued to inhabit the cities and towns of their ancestors for centuries. Persian royal archives record several failed uprisings by Assyrians in the following centuries.

Ashur and his people continued to survive until the dawn of the Christian era when they began to convert to the new religion of Jesus Christ. Ashurism (ancient Assyrian religion) continued to be practiced to the 2nd century, but eventually was eclipsed by the faster growing Christianity. Despite being the first people to adopt Christianity during the reign of King Abgar of Edessa, Assyrians continued to practice many of their ancient customs. One of which, the Akitu (or New Year) festival is celebrated to this day by Assyrians worldwide. It extends from the Vernal Equinox to April 1, on which a gala is held celebrating the return of spring. (This idea was also borrowed by the Persian people who called it Nowruz.)

Edessa and Adiabene with its capital at Arbela (modern Arbil in north Iraq), two famous Assyrian kingdoms who retained semi-autonomy, flourished in the centuries following their conversion to the Christian faith. They became centers for philosophy, theology, science, medicine, and music. Their various schools such as the first university in the world at Nisibis (in modern Turkey) were centers of learning for centuries. In fact, it was the Assyrian scholars who, during the reign of Islam and the Abbasid Caliphate in south Mesopotamia, translated many works from Greek into Assyrian (so-called Syriac) and then into Arabic. The work found its way into Spain through the Moors and then into the Latin tongue, which helped the literature spread throughout Europe.

Throughout the following centuries, the Assyrians established the Church of the East (so-called Nestorian), the first missionary church in history. Its influence reached as far as Mongolia and China passing through India where there are still those who belong to this ancient sect sometimes called St. Thomas Christians. Other Assyrians (due to theological politics) were members of the Church of Antioch (so-called Jacobite). These churches produced many writers including Bardaisan, St. Ephrem, St. Narsai, St. Michael the Great, Abdisho of Suba, and many others who wrote chronicles, poetry, philosophy, and many other works, some which survive today.

Due to the Islamic religion of the rulers of the Middle East, Assyrians were not identified as such, but increasingly became divided among their ecclesiastical denominations; the so-called Nestorian and, in AD 1551, the Chaldean (former members of the Church of the East who came to acknowledge the supremacy of the pope) and the so-called Jacobite. These names, Nestorian, Chaldean, and Jacobite, are misnomers created by antagonists to further divide and demean the ethno-cultural Assyrian heritage. Though the name Assyrian has become synonymous solely with members of the Church of the East it is a well known fact that it was from among the so-called Jacobite and Chaldean Church communities (Syrian Orthodox/Catholic) that most of the original Assyrian American organizations sprung. This issue finds its roots during the massacre of Simele when ethnic Assyrians were singled out for death by the Kurdish led Iraqi army. Local members of the Chaldean and Jacobite sects began strict identification with their religious name so as to avoid further persecution due to their Assyrian ethnicity. These ecclesiastic divisions have unfortunately been exploited by both church leaders and Assyrian opponents since that time in order to continue the division and subjugation of this ancient people.

During the Ottoman Empire period, Assyrians lived throughout their mountains and valleys in Harput, Omid (Diarbekir), Mardin, Urfa, Tur Abdin, Bohtan, Hakkari, Urmia, and the plains of Nineveh (Mosul). Assyrians in urban regions felt the brunt of various waves of persecution throughout the centuries. Those in the mountainous regions were more cautious and equipped for the perils of the Ottoman era after the plunder and destruction caused by the Tartar Timurlane (1336–1405).

The years following were a dark age of Assyrian history. They found themselves bloodied and beaten from constant attacks cumulating with the Kurdish Amir Bedr Khan Beg in 1840. Beg and his people, who enjoy press in today's post–Saddam Hussein Iraq, first began moving into these Assyrian territories during the Ottoman period. They were always at odds with the Assyrians.

Finally, the momentous event that began with the assassination of the Archduke Franz Ferdinand had arrived. World War I was now in full swing and would mark a milestone in the history of the Assyrian people, for they would not survive the ordeal unscathed.

For the first time in their 6,000 year history as a culture, the Assyrians faced the threat of complete and utter annihilation by force. Under the Ottomans, they lived in their mountainous country in semi-independence from the Sultans. This changed forever when armed Kurdish forces led a campaign to eradicate the Assyrians from their homeland and take it for their own. It was during this time that the Assyrians lost two-thirds of their entire population. This second genocide of the 20th century followed the Herero Genocide in Nambia by the Germans from 1904 through 1908. The Assyrians have come to identify this time period from 1914 to 1919 as the time of the sword, or *Sayfo/Saypa*. Despite the murder of the Assyrian patriarch of the Church of the East, Mar Benyamin Shimun, by the Kurdish thug Simko, the death marches from Urmia, modern Iran to Baquba, modern Iraq, and the murder of Assyrian intellectuals such as Professor Ashur Yousef of Euphrates College, some Assyrians managed to unite against the odds and enter the war on the side of the Allied Forces. They fought with great renown and were compared to the Gurkhas in their tactical brilliance and courage in battle. Indeed, were it not for the Assyrian forces, the Ottoman Campaign of the British, French, and Russians would never have succeeded.

This period was awash with murder and betrayal of the Assyrians. Those who were not slaughtered fled to Russia, Lebanon, Greece, and a mass of other countries including the United States. Despite being the only Middle Eastern community to fight on the side of the Allied Forces and promised a country of their own, the Assyrians were betrayed by their comrades and forced to become residents of the new countries that made up the map of the Anglo-French Middle East.

Assyrians suffered at the hands of their Muslim neighbors, yet the betrayal of their English allies left them devastated. Instead of assisting their comrades, the English used the newly formed Iraqi army under the hand of Kurdish brute Badr Sidqi to massacre the Assyrians of Simele and Deirabon, north Iraq (Assyrian Heartland), in 1933.

On the other side of the Atlantic, the Assyrians who managed to immigrate to the United States began to settle in various centers. As early as the 1870s and perhaps earlier, Assyrians were found dwelling in the United States. Most arrived in trickles from 1890 to 1910, and the largest influx came after the Assyrian Genocide from 1914–1922. Many established themselves in Chicago, Detroit, New Britain, Connecticut, and Massachusetts. A sizeable population found new homes in eastern Massachusetts, settling in the industrial cities of Boston, Lowell, and Worcester in strength. Thus begins the establishment of the Assyrian community in eastern Massachusetts, whose earliest settlers from Harput (also spelled Harpoot, Kharput, and various other ways) gravitated toward New England for industrial work while others brought their carpentry and shoe-making trades with them and established themselves as master craftsmen.

Assyrians reveled in their culture despite being in diaspora. New immigrants arriving after the 1960s, emigrating mainly from Tur Abdin (in northern Assyria) and Qamishli (the ancient Assyrian city of Nisibin), reintroduced more careful observance of traditional Assyrian fasts and festivals such as the Fast of the Ninevites, an ancient holiday (based on pre-Christian Assyrian religion and later incorporated into the book of Jonah and Assyrian church tradition) and the Akitu Festival or Assyrian New Year (observed on April 1).

Assyrians of eastern Massachusetts have changed greatly from their humble beginnings over 100 years ago. Many second and third generation Assyrians have assimilated into mainstream American society and retain little if any contact with their people and heritage. Despite this occurrence, many continue to strive for their rights both in the United States and in the Middle East, as well as for a free and independent Assyria. Through the various organizations like the United Assyrian Association of Massachusetts (UAAM), the Assyrian Aid Society, Assyrian Academic Society of the East Coast, and others, young Assyrians have a chance to express their cultural heritage at a local and national level. Many young men and women have gone on to graduate degrees and continue to work for this noble cause.

Assyrian stores and restaurants still dot the Massachusetts landscape, but less in numbers. New immigrants have also made a renewal of strength for these people and added new blood to an old body. Though St. Mary's Assyrian Church has been moved to Shrewsbury, and forced to change its rightful name, Assyrian families have started a second congregation in Grafton, declaring themselves the body of St. Mary's Assyrian National Church.

In retrospect, Assyrians have enriched the cultural mosaic that is New England. Their rich cultural traditions, music, food, and work ethic made, and continue to make them a cornerstone of ethnic community ideals in Massachusetts.

One

Leaving the Ottoman Empire

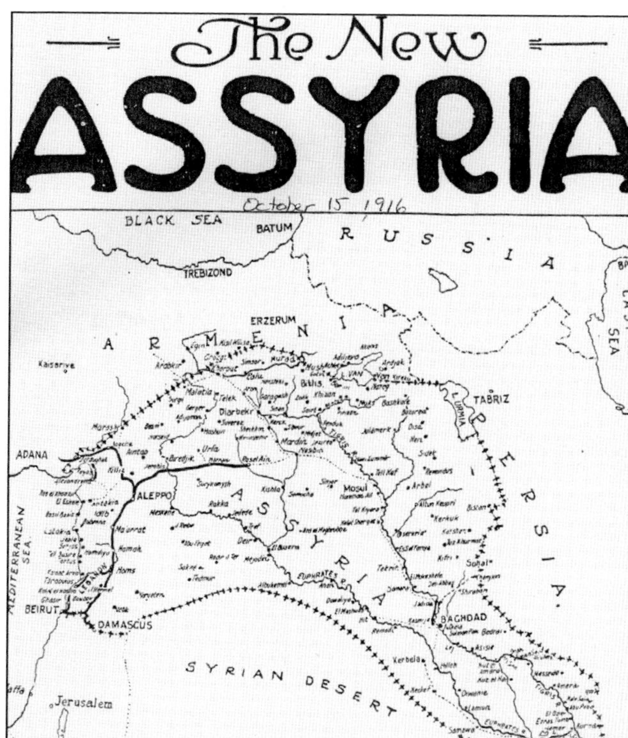

Seen here is a map of historic Greater Assyria taken from the cover of the first issue of *The New Assyria* periodical published October 15, 1916. The periodical was printed monthly by the New Assyria Publishing Company located at 1089 Summit Avenue in Jersey City, New Jersey. The publication had a large reader base with Massachusetts Assyrians.

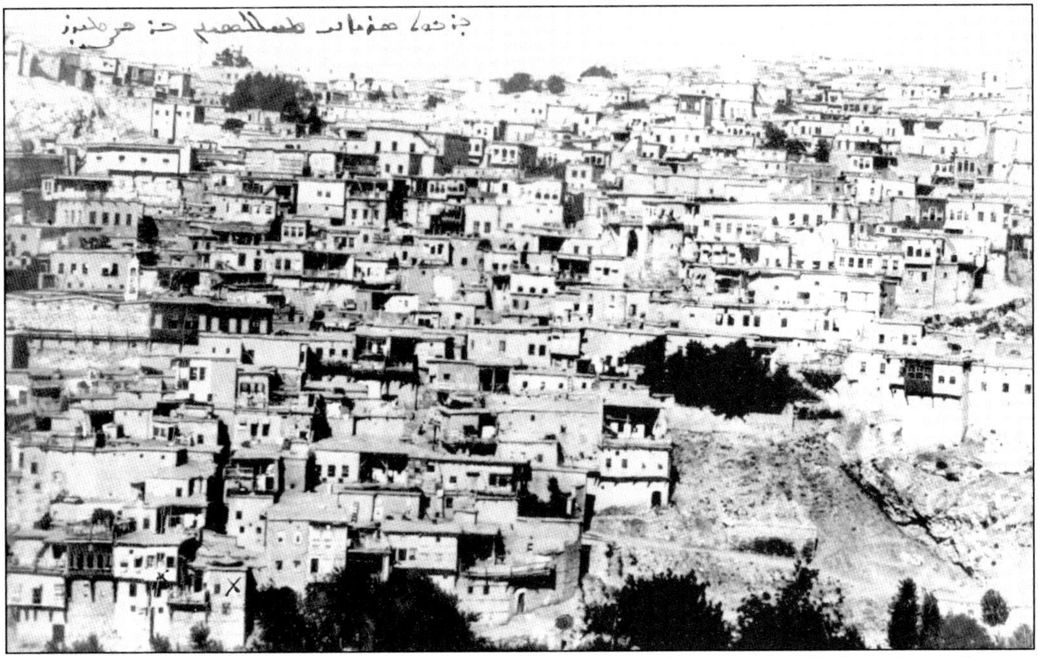

The Assyrian town of Harput is seen here, near Elazig in today's eastern Turkey. According to missionary and consulate approximations, approximately 30,000 people lived in Harput and its surrounding villages on the nearby plain. Though far from other Assyrian centers, it had constant travelers from the Assyrian centers in Omid (Diarbekir), Merde (Mardin), and Tur Abdin.

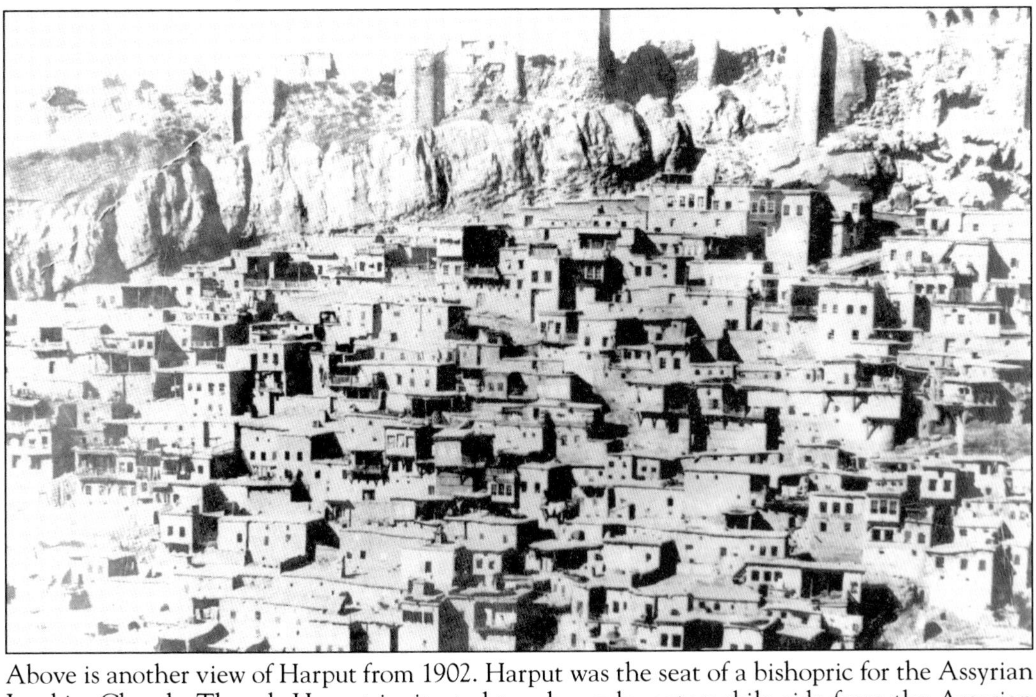

Above is another view of Harput from 1902. Harput was the seat of a bishopric for the Assyrian Jacobite Church. Though Harput is situated two hours by automobile ride from the Assyrian city of Omid (Diarbekir), pilgrims did travel to and fro, peddling goods and services as well as visiting relatives.

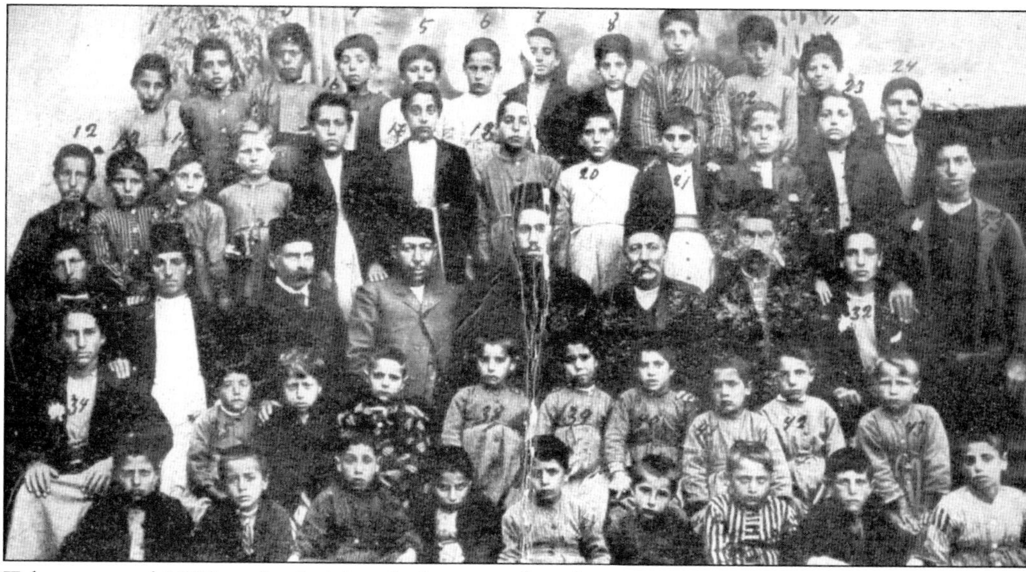

Taken around 1908 at the height of educational endeavor among Assyrians across Turkey and Iran, this typical formal photograph shows students and teachers with local intellectuals. The young David Barsum Perley stands just below Ashur Yousef. Many such children continued their studies at Euphrates College, which was established by the New England based American Board of Commissioners of Foreign Missions. Among the teachers was Theresa Huntington Ziegler (Wellesley College) and others from New England's elite schools. By 1903, Euphrates College was serving approximately 1,000 students.

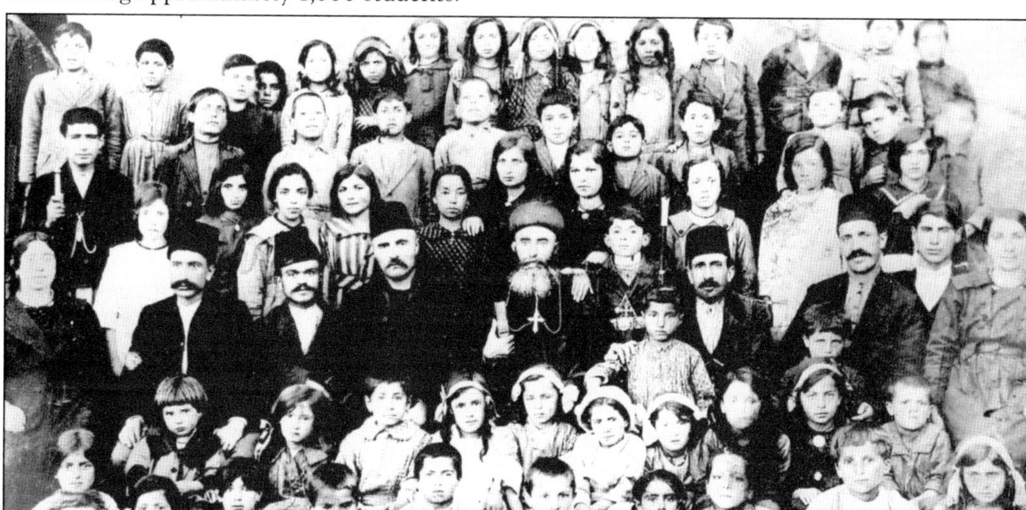

Those Assyrians that survived the Assyrian Genocide in Harput, and who did not flee to the United States, Lebanon, or Greece managed to rebuild the school in Harput. This photograph, taken in 1921, illustrates, "Assyrian directors, teachers and students, Harput, *Beth Nahrain* (Mesopotamia)." Of the known students, Elia Donabed is first on the left in the second row from the top, standing with a candle. The bishop is seated in the center. Professor Ashur Yousef, author of *The Assyrian Guide* (*Murshid Athurion*), was one of the various intellectuals who was arrested and tortured under the Ottomans and Kurds during a series of massacres and deportations occurring in 1915, and therefore never saw the reopening of his beloved school.

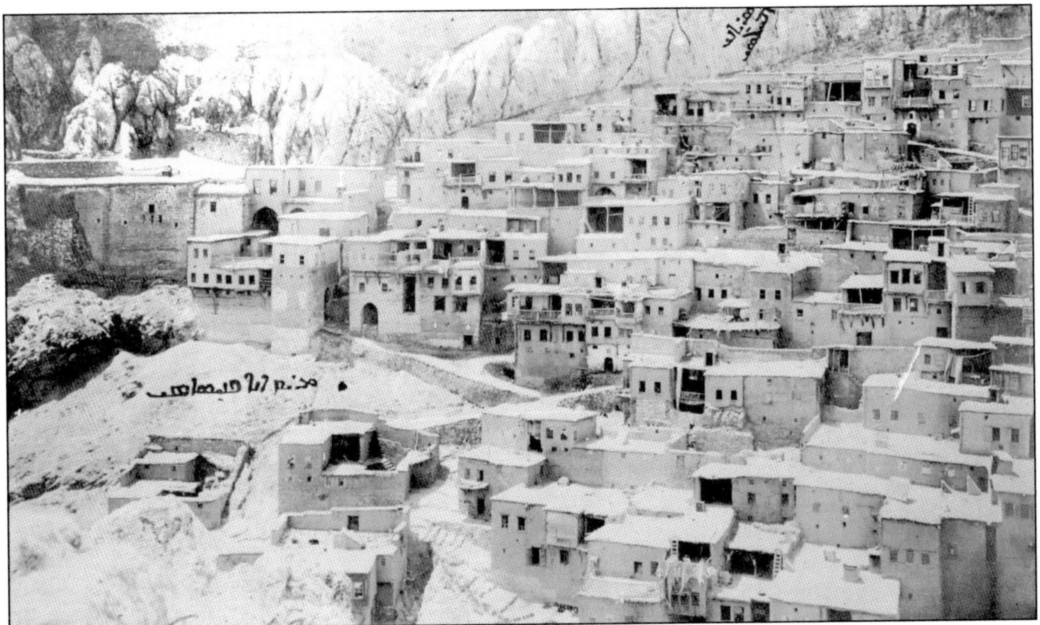

Built into the mountainside, the Church of the Virgin Mary AD 179 (Mort Maryam), is one of the earliest Assyrian churches. Over the course of nearly two millennia, it was often sacked. Those who plundered the church included the armies of Timurlane in 1404. The pulpit once held a manuscript of the gospels dating to AD 1581. After being forced to close its doors for nearly a century, the recently renovated church now conducts services during important Christian holidays.

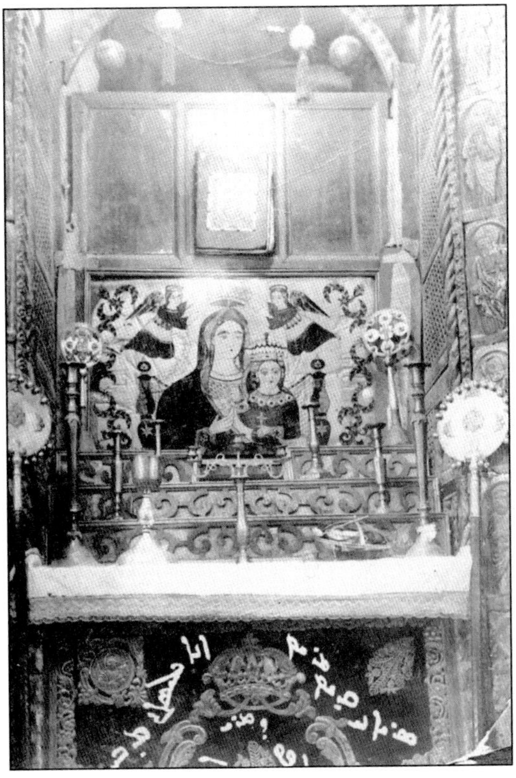

As one of the last pictures of the altar of St. Mary's church in Harput, many Assyrian homes in Massachusetts displayed copies of this photograph as a memento. Many of the vestibules were stolen when the church was sacked in 1914, and again in 1915. What is seen here is all that was salvaged and taken to the church of St. George located in nearby Elazig.

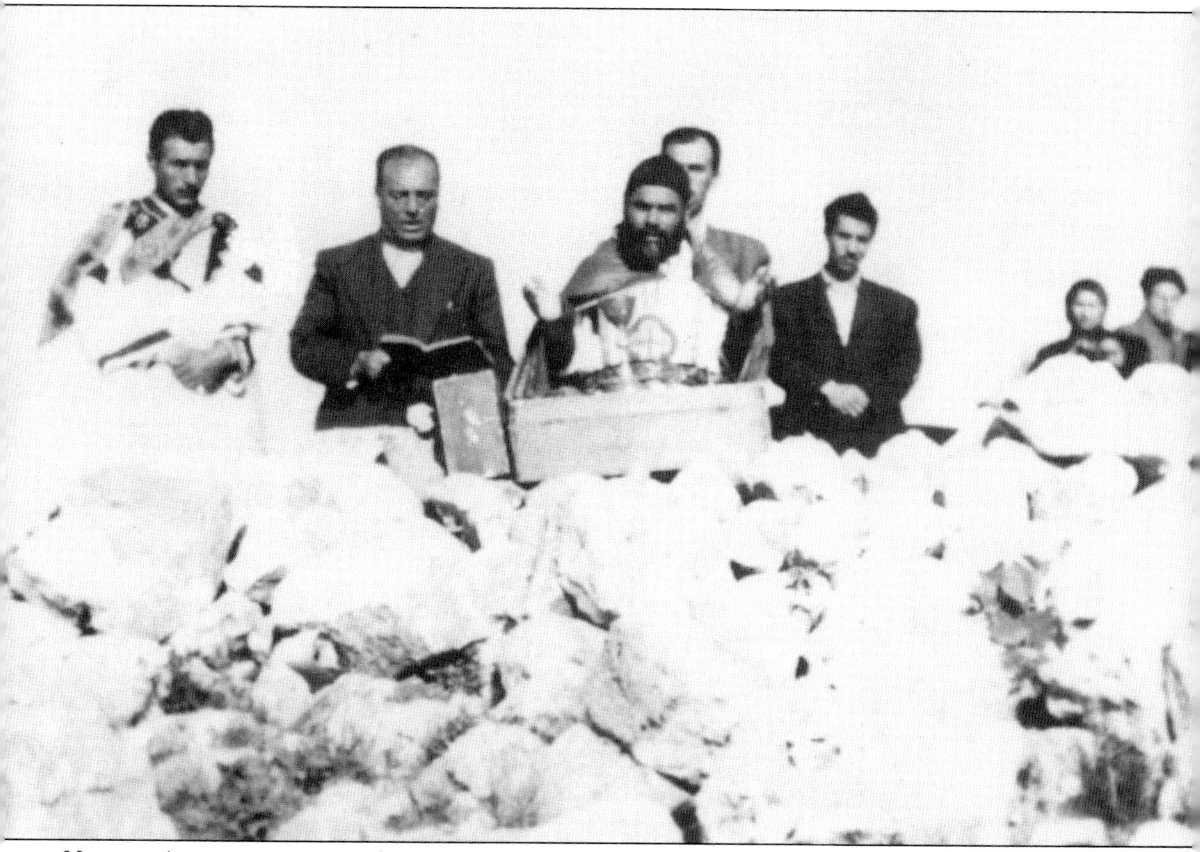

Here an Assyrian priest conducts mass at a sacred ruins around 1920. Many Assyrian churches were destroyed during the Assyrian Genocide, but the Assyrian faithful who survived attempted to continue their daily rituals, despite the ruination of much of their ancient and Christian heritage. Very few churches survived the purge instigated by the Ottomans and Kurds.

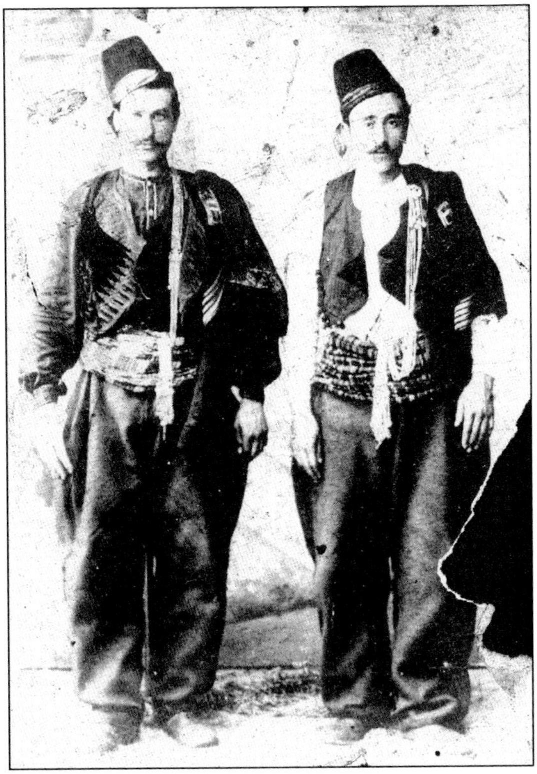

Assyrians pose in Ottoman dress in the late 1890s. While some Assyrian towns and villages retained their ethnic dress, larger towns like Harput, Mardin, and Diarbekir found Ottoman attire as the norm. This adaptation was as much for fashion sake as it was for the sake of safety while traveling throughout the Ottoman provinces during times of unrest.

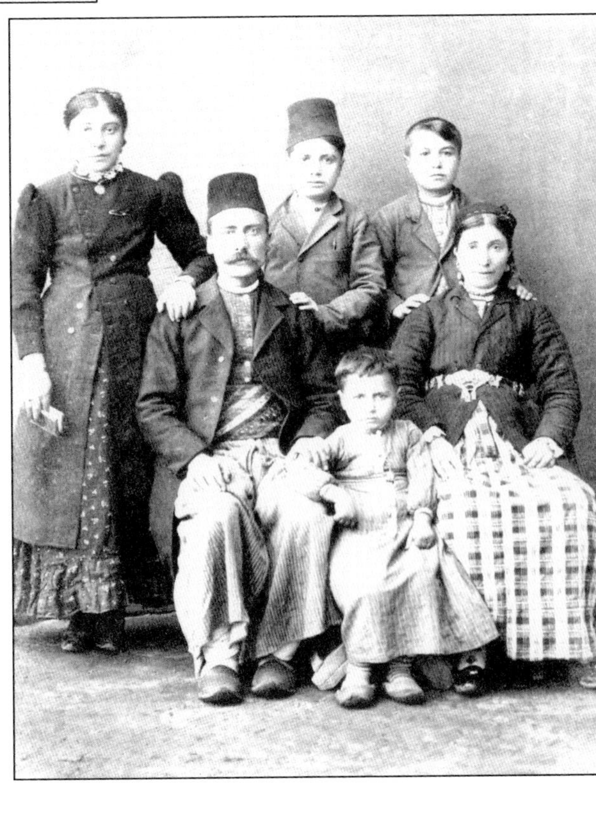

The late 1890s saw many Assyrians begin their journey away from the hand of various oppressive regimes in the Middle East. The above family took this particular photograph in 1898 just prior to leaving Constantinople (present day Istanbul) for the shores of the United States. Assyrians found the trip from their rural homes to Western Anatolia was long and difficult. Many who survived persecution sometimes found their graves on the long trip west.

This patriotic poem written in Ottoman Turkish language using Assyrian script was featured in the December 15, 1918, issue of *The New Assyria* periodical. The poem was recited and sung by Assyrians throughout the Ottoman Empire during the period of World War I. Notice the phrase *Aturiler Kardashler* roughly translated as "Assyrian Brothers."

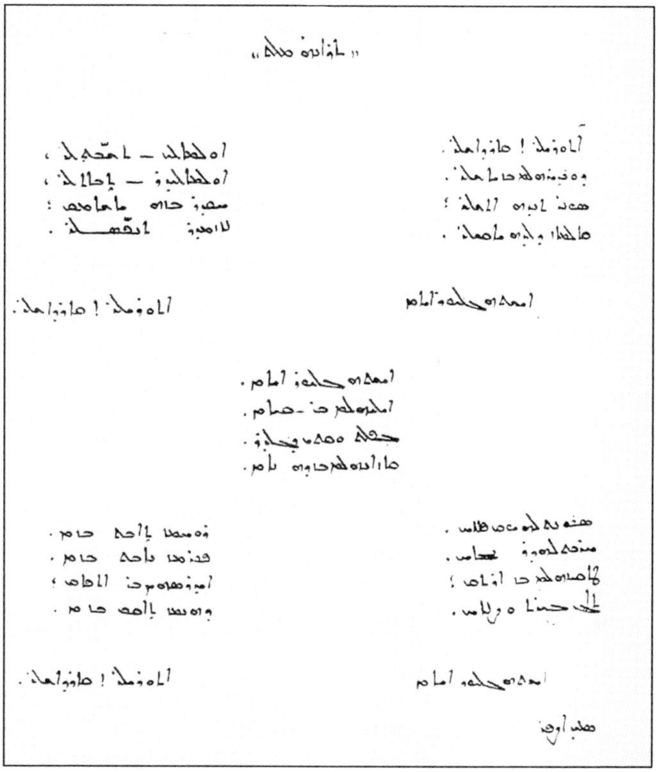

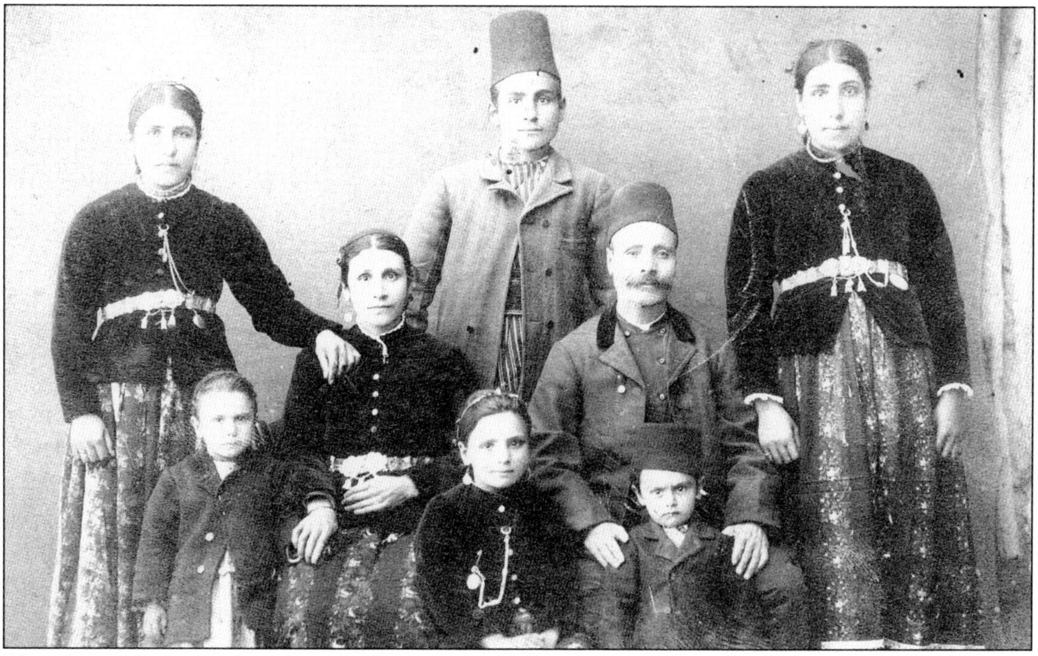

The above photograph, taken in the late 1890s, shows Assyrians in traditional Ottoman dress. The Atlas family was one of many who were known for their merchant's trade. Many Assyrians went as far as France and Russia for trade purposes. Dyeing, silk trade, and shoe making were some of the forms of employment of Assyrians in the Ottoman Empire.

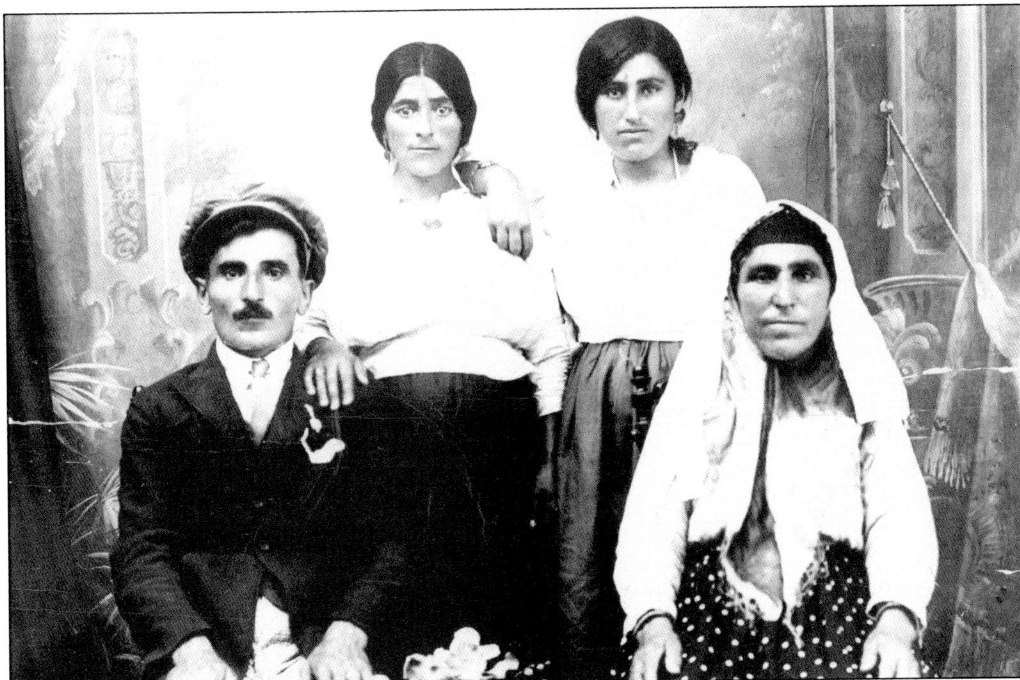

Not all Assyrians came from Anatolia. Many also came from the Assyrian homeland within the Persian frontier. Here, from left to right, Yoel Pera is seen with wife Munne Yadger Pera, sister-in-law Jerusha Yadger, and mother-in-law Jerun Yadger in Urmia, Assyria, during the early 1900s.

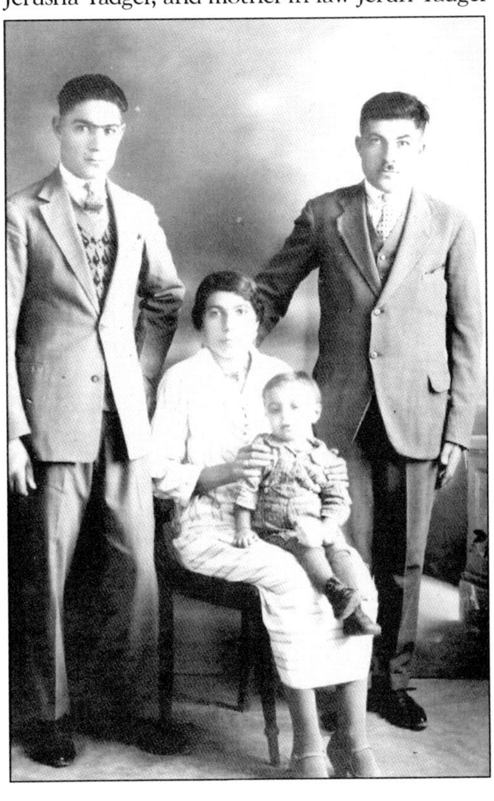

Esho Youkhana (left) is seen here with brother Odisho Youkhana (Resgala) with sister Khanno and her first child Shimson Orahem Babella, seated. Many Assyrians who were not killed during the massacres in Urmia fled to Baquba in Iraq, and were settled in refugee camps. For a personal account of the Assyrian Genocide (specifically in Urmia), please refer to Rosie Malek-Yonan's *The Crimson Field*.

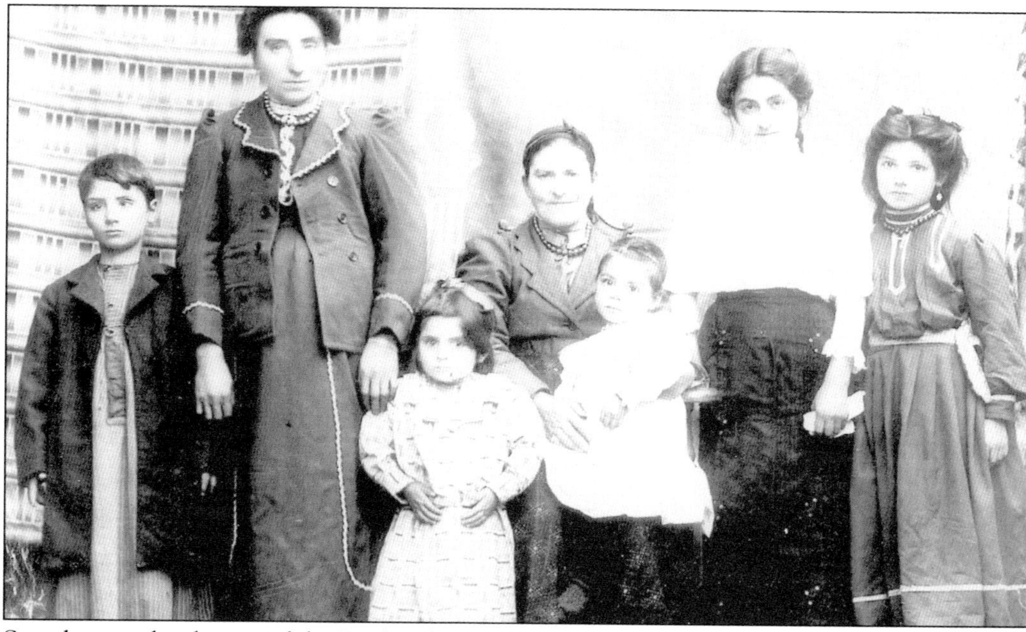

Seen here with relatives of the Dasho clan, the Kazar's traveled from Harput to Constantinople prior to leaving for New York. Patriarch Youhanna (Ohan) Donabed had already traveled to the United States, working to bring his wife and children just before 1915. Harput had already begun the deconstruction process by this time, and many Assyrians who survived the Great War began fleeing to Elazig and farther west to Constantinople to await passage abroad.

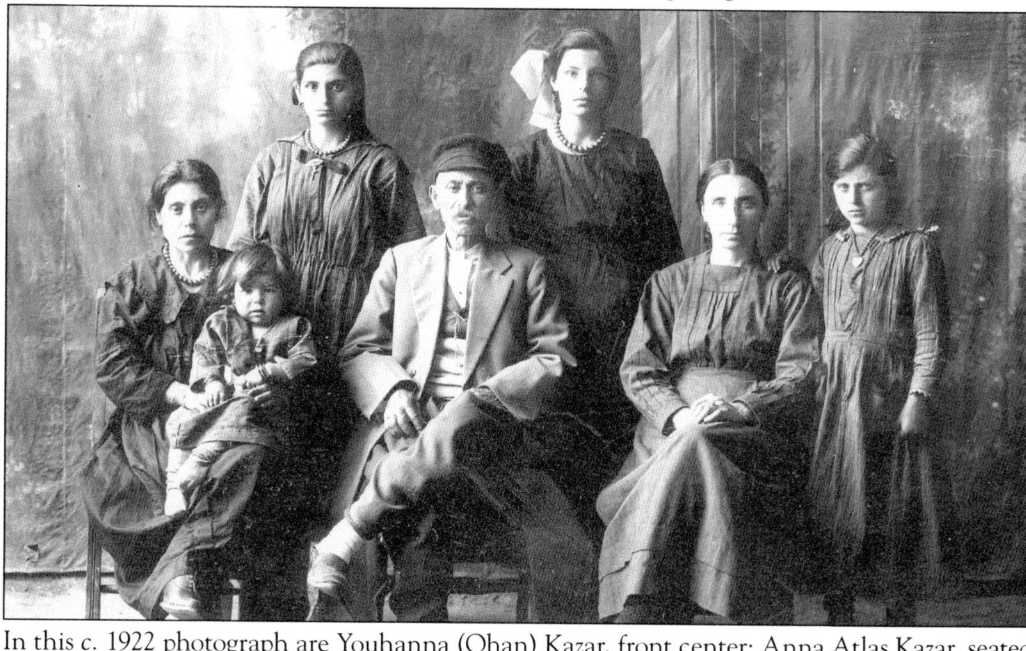

In this c. 1922 photograph are Youhanna (Ohan) Kazar, front center; Anna Atlas Kazar, seated to his right; and daughters Margaret, second row left, and Roumel, second row right. The Kazar family survived the Assyrian Genocide and managed to immigrate to the United States through Ellis Island. Assyrians like Youhanna left their families and worked until they could return with enough money to bring their relatives to the United States.

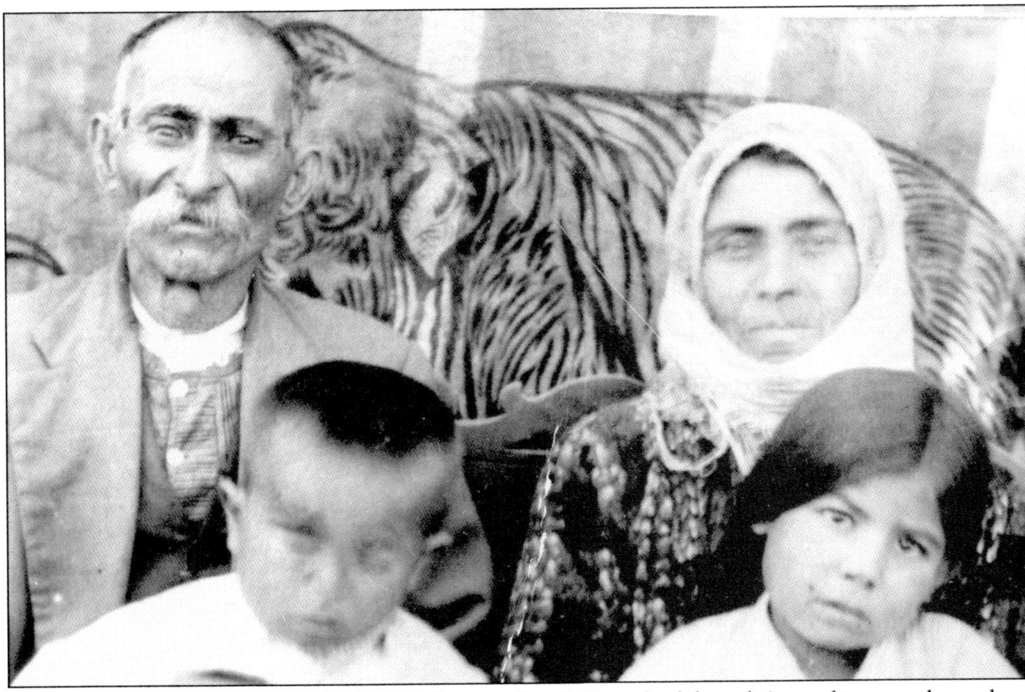

Assyrians like Behnam Donabed and Maryam Perch Donabed found Anatolia a perilous place, especially after World War I. With oldest son Bishara already in Massachusetts, they decided during the height of the Assyrian persecution that it was time to flee towards a "better life."

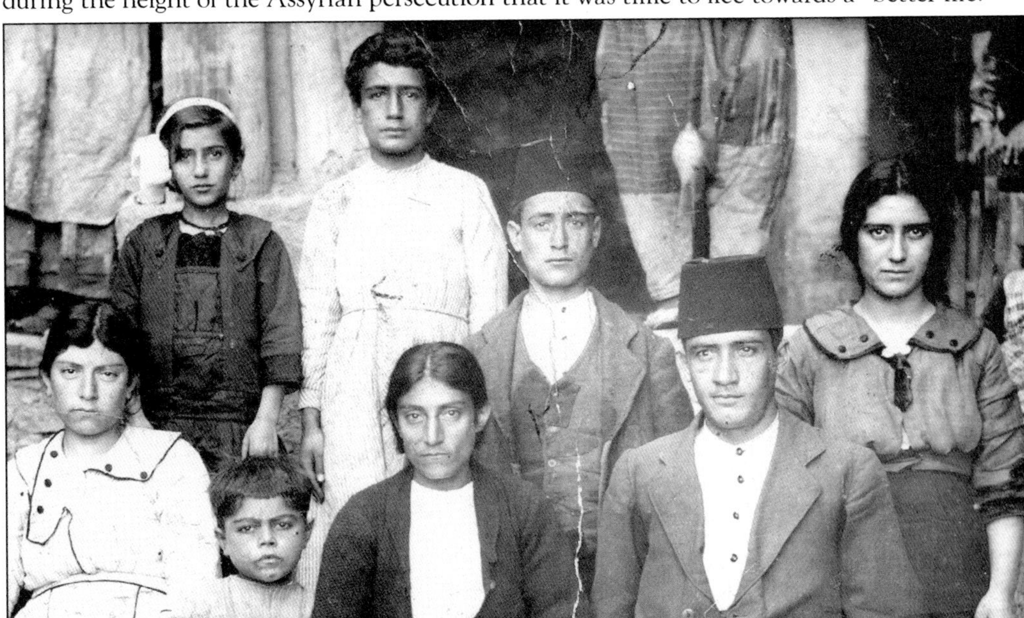

The Donabed clan is shown here in Anatolia around 1915, minus Behnam, Maryam, and eldest sibling Bishara. Seen here are Lucy (far right) and George (front right with fez), Youhanna (second row center), Sadie (top left), and Elia (top right). Like other settlers to the United States, those with larger families partially immigrated due to monetary restraints. Some remained behind until additional funds were raised.

Two

TRAVEL STAGES AND THE EARLY YEARS

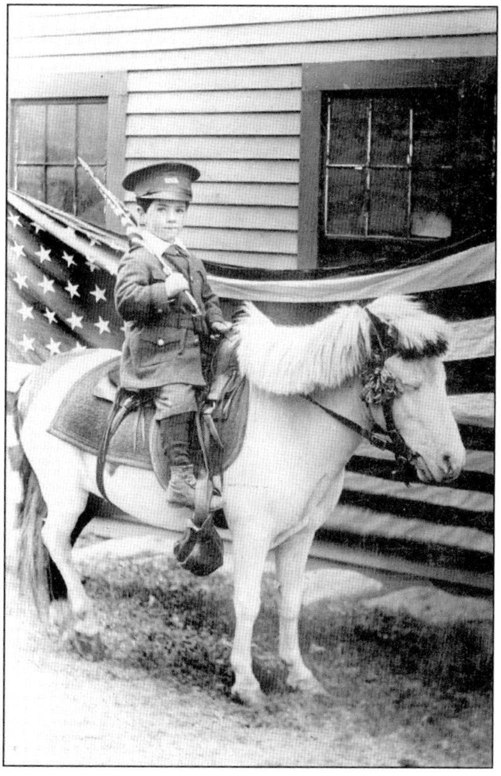

This photograph, dated May 20, 1918, is of a boy, dressed in soldier's uniform, on a pony with an American flag. Assyrians adapted quickly to their new home and embraced its laws and culture fully. As with other communities, many first generation immigrants attempted to assimilate fully into American society making survival a touch easier.

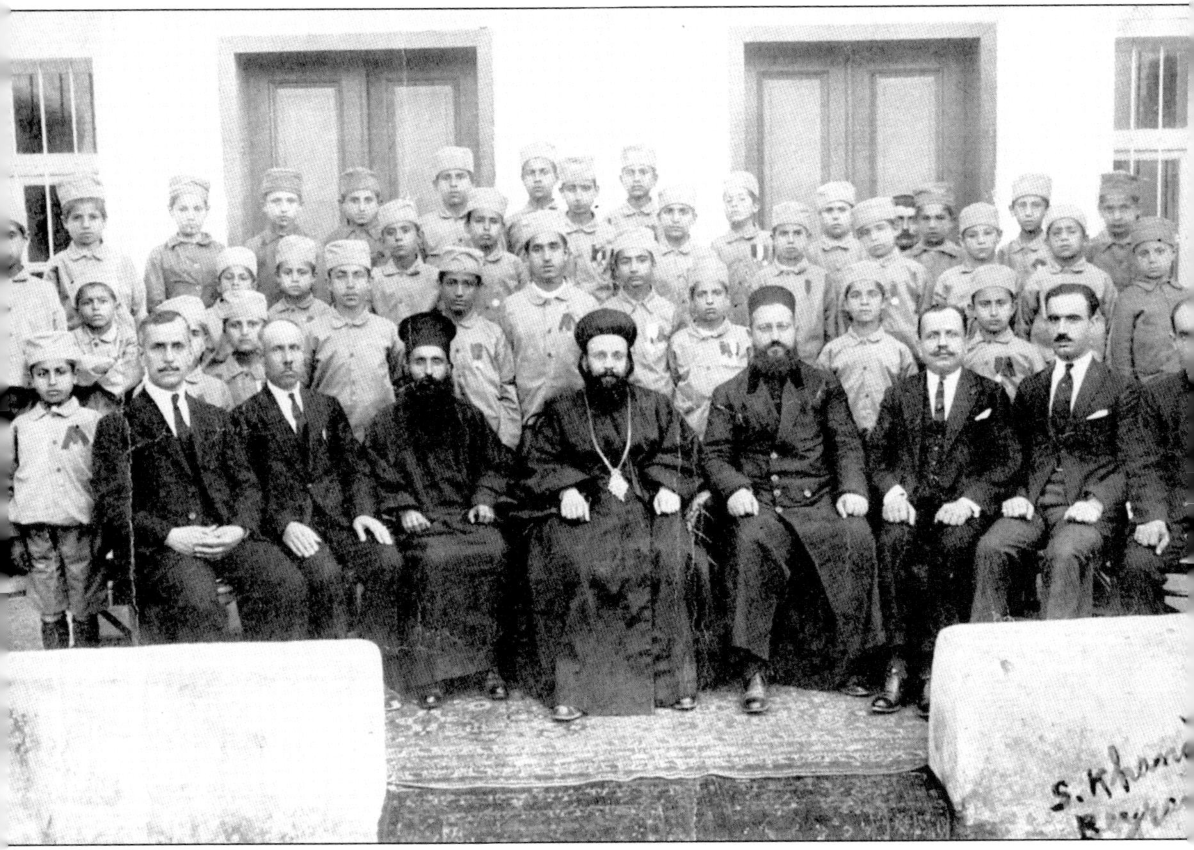

Shown here is the Assyrian School and Orphanage (*Taw Meem Simkath*) in Beirut. Harput Assyrian Fawlos Gabriel, who was orphaned and raised in the Assyrian Orphanage initiated in Adana, Turkey, in 1899, later taught in Beirut. Pictured above are the boys of the school in uniform during a visit from *Mor* Severius Afrem Barsum, seated in the center. The school is still in existence today.

The above paper illustrates Malcom G. Donabed's petition for citizenship in 1903. The document is from Worcester County and was found at the National Archives and Records Center in Waltham. Malcom Donabed was one of many Assyrians whose Naturalization papers were found at the archives along with those of the famous Dr. Abraham K. Yousef.

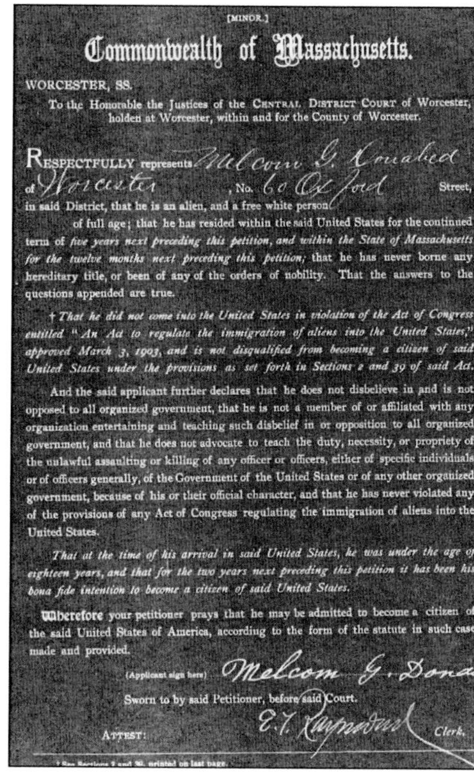

[MINOR.]

Commonwealth of Massachusetts.

WORCESTER, SS.

To the Honorable the Justices of the CENTRAL DISTRICT COURT of Worcester, holden at Worcester, within and for the County of Worcester.

RESPECTFULLY represents Melcom G. Donabed of Worcester, No. 60 Oxford Street, in said District, that he is an alien, and a free white person of full age; that he has resided within the said United States for the continued term of *five years next preceding this petition, and within the State of Massachusetts for the twelve months next preceding this petition;* that he has never borne any hereditary title, or been of any of the orders of nobility. That the answers to the questions appended are true.

† *That he did not come into the United States in violation of the Act of Congress entitled "An Act to regulate the immigration of aliens into the United States," approved March 3, 1903, and is not disqualified from becoming a citizen of said United States under the provisions as set forth in Sections 2 and 39 of said Act.*

And the said applicant further declares that he does not disbelieve in and is not opposed to all organized government, that he is not a member of or affiliated with any organization entertaining and teaching such disbelief in or opposition to all organized government, and that he does not advocate to teach the duty, necessity, or propriety of the unlawful assaulting or killing of any officer or officers, either of specific individuals or of officers generally, of the Government of the United States or of any other organized government, because of his or their official character, and that he has never violated any of the provisions of any Act of Congress regulating the immigration of aliens into the United States.

That at the time of his arrival in said United States, he was under the age of eighteen years, and that for the two years next preceding this petition it has been his bona fide intention to become a citizen of said United States.

Wherefore your petitioner prays that he may be admitted to become a citizen of the said United States of America, according to the form of the statute in such case made and provided.

(Applicant sign here) Melcom G. Dona[bed]

Sworn to by said Petitioner, before said Court.

ATTEST: E. T. Raymond Clerk.

† See Sections 2 and 39, printed on last page.

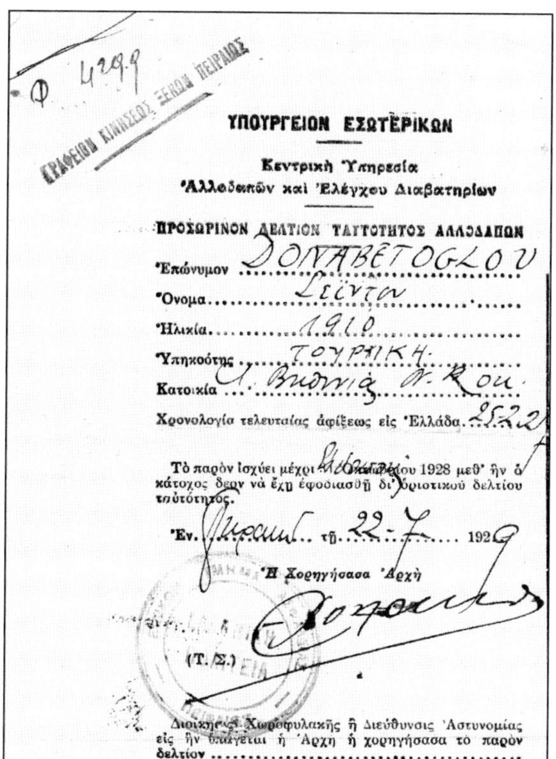

Φ 4299

ΓΡΑΦΕΙΟΝ ΚΙΝΗΣΕΩΣ ΞΕΝΩΝ ΠΕΙΡΑΙΩΣ

ΥΠΟΥΡΓΕΙΟΝ ΕΣΩΤΕΡΙΚΩΝ

Κεντρικὴ Ὑπηρεσία

Ἀλλοδαπῶν καὶ Ἐλέγχου Διαβατηρίων

ΠΡΟΣΩΡΙΝΟΝ ΔΕΛΤΙΟΝ ΤΑΥΤΟΤΗΤΟΣ ΑΛΛΟΔΑΠΩΝ

Ἐπώνυμον DONABETOGLOU

Ὄνομα Λεϊντον

Ἡλικία 1910

Ὑπηκοότης ΤΟΥΡΚΙΚΗ

Κατοικία [illegible]

Χρονολογία τελευταίας ἀφίξεως εἰς Ἑλλάδα 25.2.2[illegible]

Τὸ παρὸν ἰσχύει μέχρι [illegible] 1928 μεθ' ἣν ὁ κάτοχος δέον νὰ ἔχῃ ἐφοδιασθῇ δι' ὁριστικοῦ δελτίου ταυτότητος.

Ἐν [illegible] τῇ 22-7 192[illegible]

Ἡ Χορηγήσασα Ἀρχὴ

(Τ. Σ.)

Διοίκησις Χωροφυλακῆς ἢ Διεύθυνσις Ἀστυνομίας εἰς ἣν ὑπάγεται ἡ Ἀρχὴ ἡ χορηγήσασα τὸ παρὸν δελτίον ....

Some members of the Donabed clan who remained in Anatolia after the expulsion of most of its Assyrian inhabitants attempted to make their way to join their families in the United States. Some took passage to Greece and spent some years there, while awaiting permission to travel to North America.

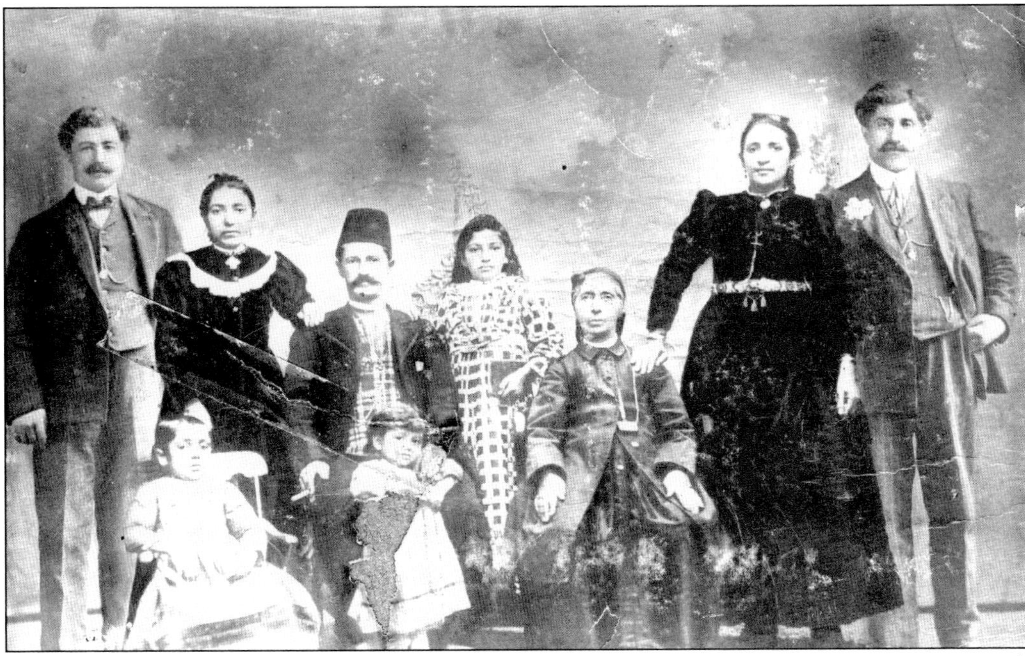

A 1905 photograph of Assyrians shows the contrast between the old Ottoman clothing style and western influences. It was common for many Assyrian patriarchs who spent most of their lives under Ottoman rule to find the new western style both extraordinary and outlandish. Most were unable to let go of their traditional dress in favor of American clothing.

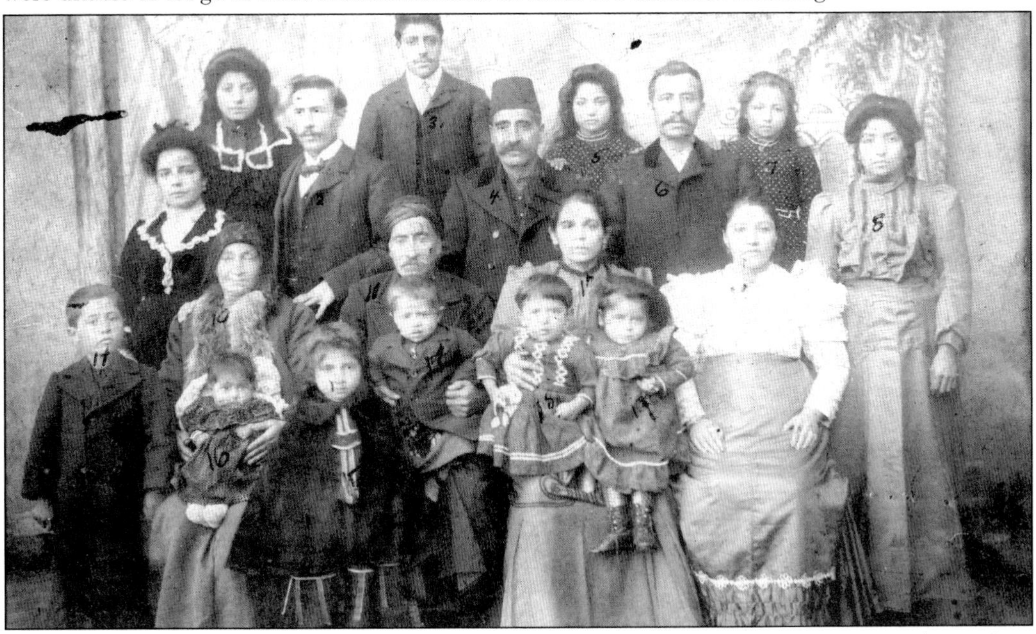

Assyrians prepare for their travel from Anatolia. Identified here are Rebecca Perch, Nishan Barsam (Selims father), Simon Barsam, Hanovah Barsam, Rahael Dasho, Haratune Barsam, Rose Barsam, Lucia Barsam (Nishan's Wife), Sara Barsam (Haratune's mother), Agiak Barsam (Haratune's father), Hanoush's wife, Yegsa Barsam (Rebecca's mother and Haratune's wife), and Ramahen Barsam.

For those of the southeastern provinces, the first major difficulty was getting to the west coast. Since Assyrians had relatives in the capital, many made the long and arduous journey to Constantinople via donkey and foot. The Dasho family was among those who traveled for business, thus giving them better contacts when reaching larger cities.

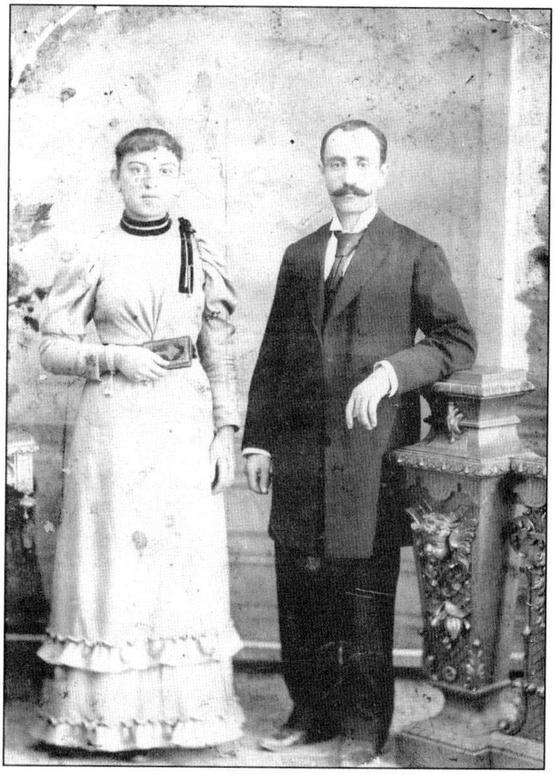

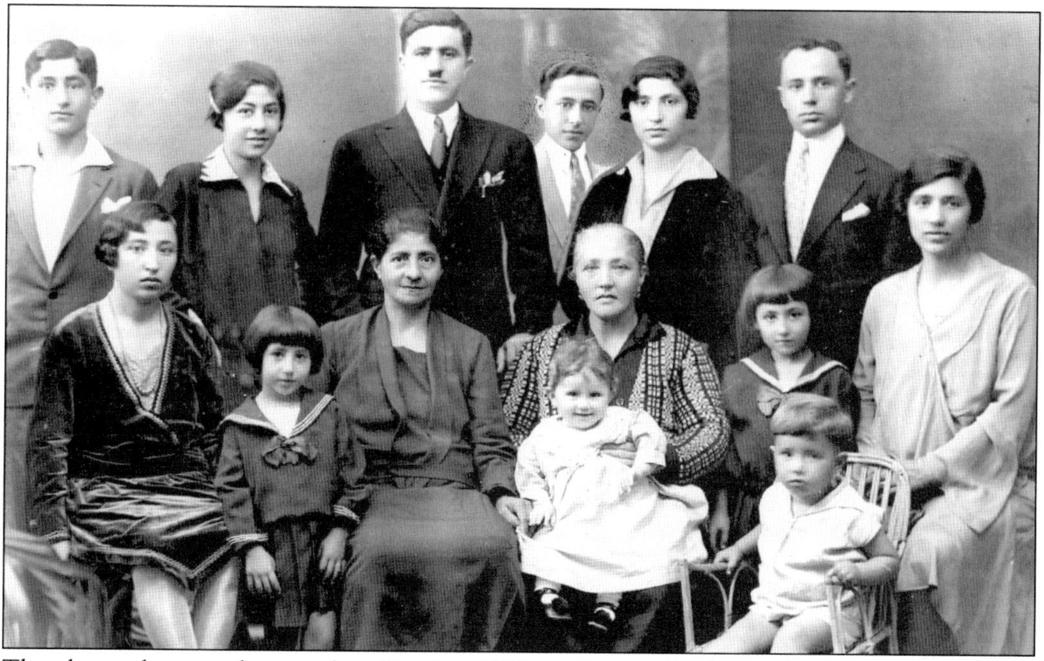

The above photograph was taken October 1928, in Beirut. Of those who fled Anatolia, many settled for a time in Syria, including the territories that later became Lebanon and Palestine. Assyrians still have sizeable communities in Beirut, Jerusalem, and Bethlehem. For the majority, however, Beirut was but a port city on the way to the West.

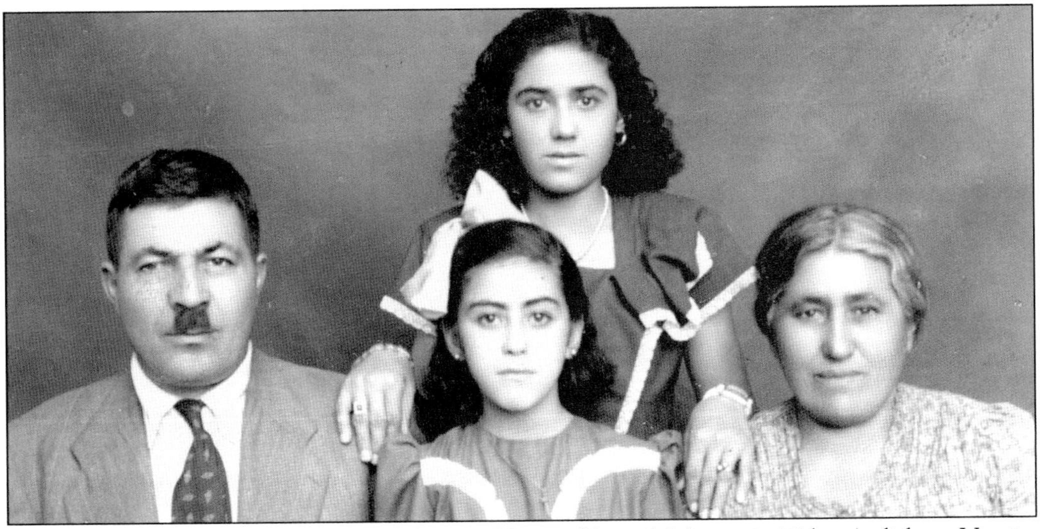

This *c.* 1940 photograph shows Odisho Youkhana (Resgala) born in Taka Ardishay, Urmia, Assyria, with wife Jerusha of *Geotapa/Soralan* and daughters Daisy (rear) and Alice (Elsie) in Baghdad, Iraq. Some displaced Assyrians were resettled in large cities with the promise of one day returning to their northern mountains and valleys. For most, they remained as second class citizens in a country whose first military expedition massacred thousands of Assyrians in the mass murder at Simele and Deirabon.

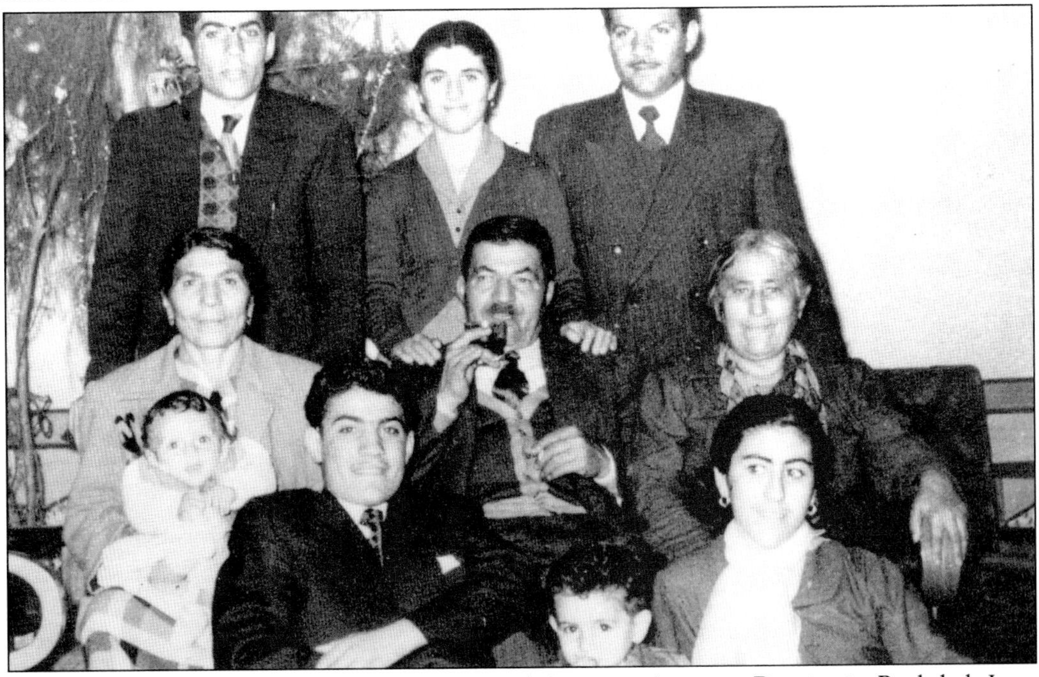

This *c.* 1950 photograph was taken in Campad Atoraya, Assyrian District in Baghdad, Iraq. Many members of this family settled in Massachusetts in transition from Iraq due to deteriorating socioeconomic conditions suffered by the indigenous Assyrians. From left to right, (first row) Johnson Babella, Dexen Babella, and Elisie Odisho Youkhana; (second row) Khanno with grandson Elia (Edison), Odisho Youkhana, and Jerusha Yadger Youkhana; (third row) Wilson Babella, Youlia Khnanisho Babella, and Shimshon Babella can be seen in the image.

New immigrants enjoyed the chance to take and send photographs to family abroad. Assyrians in Lowell used Lothrop and Cunningham Studio, located at 112 Merrimack Street. This particular photograph was taken in 1893, and pictures Peter Benjamin Baptist (Toorvanda's husband), seated in the middle.

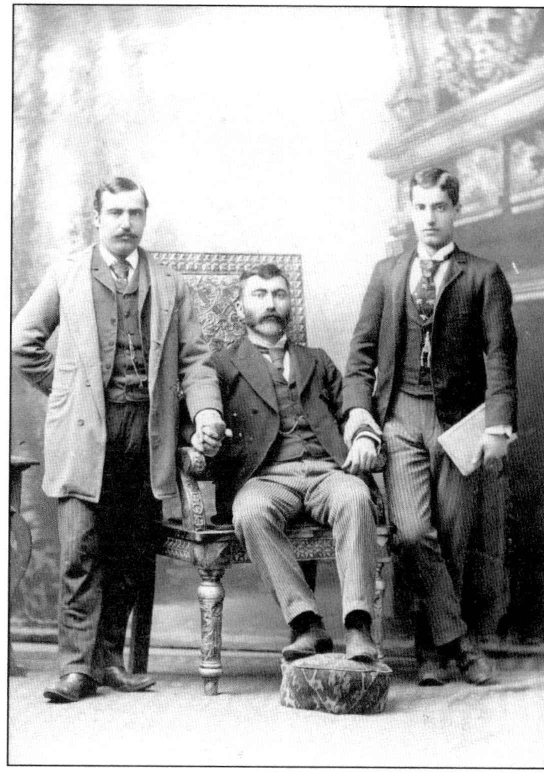

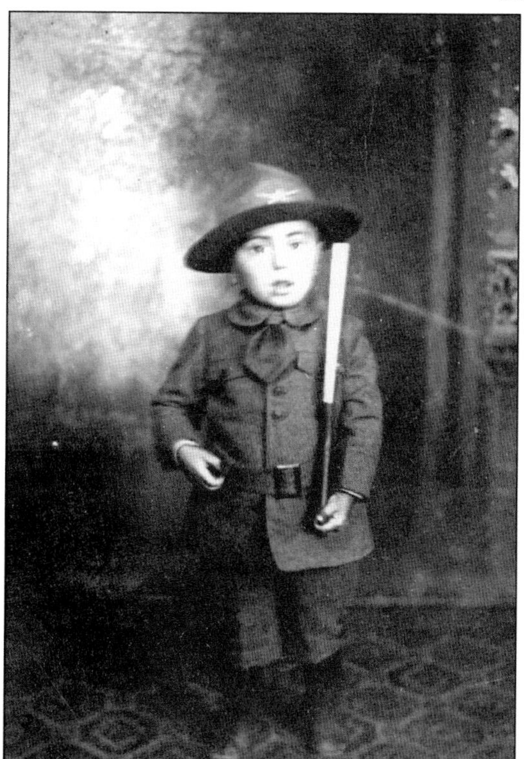

A small Assyrian child is seen here in a military uniform, holding a miniature rifle. Pictures like this were commonplace for new immigrants to the United States who tried to show their loyalty and love for their adopted country.

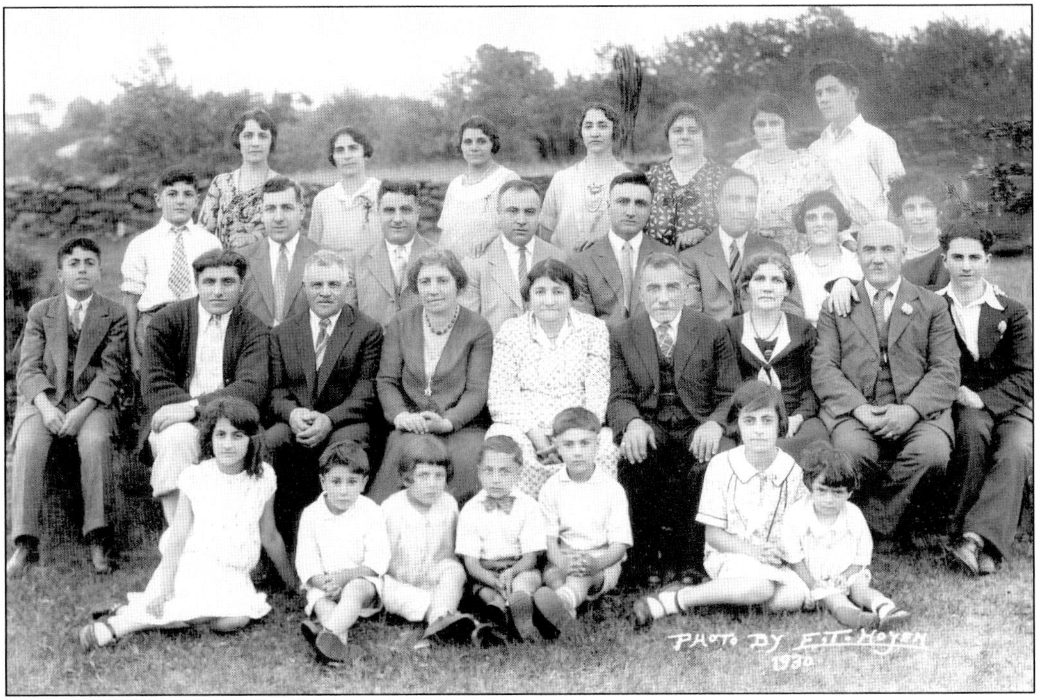

The Perch family is seen here with patriarch Bishara Perch on the family farm in the early 1900s. The photograph was taken by the local Assyrian photographer and writer, Emmanuel Hoyen.

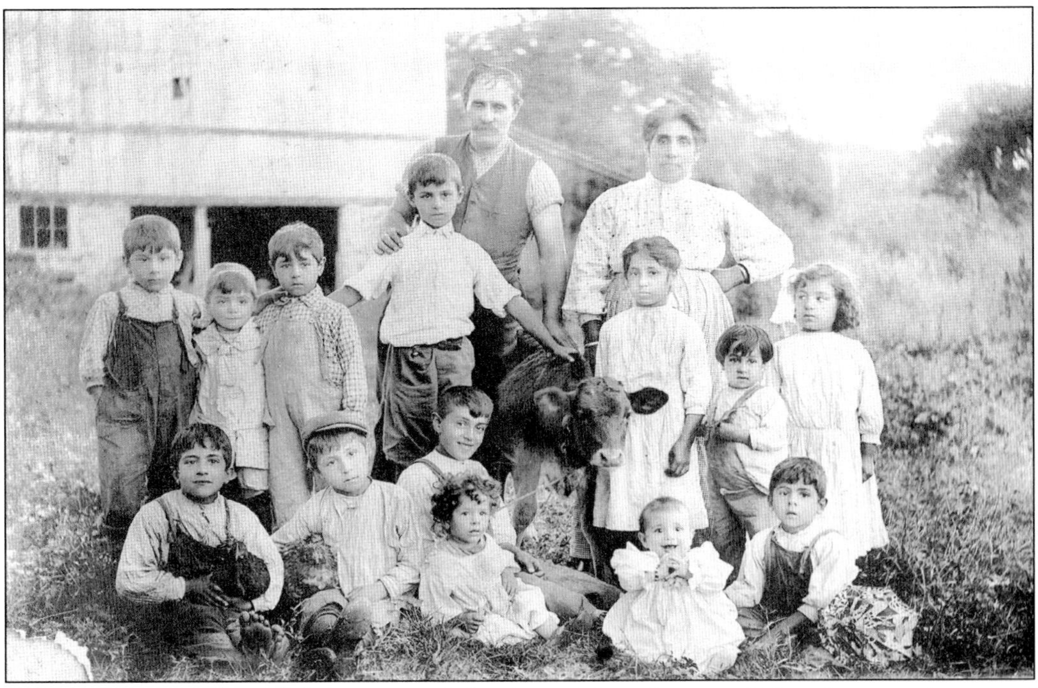

Some Assyrians continued their agrarian lifestyles in Massachusetts. Although some also moved to Fresno, California, to farm alfalfa and wheat, those who remained in Massachusetts usually tried their hand at pig, dairy, and even tobacco farming. The family cow is seen here amidst the children.

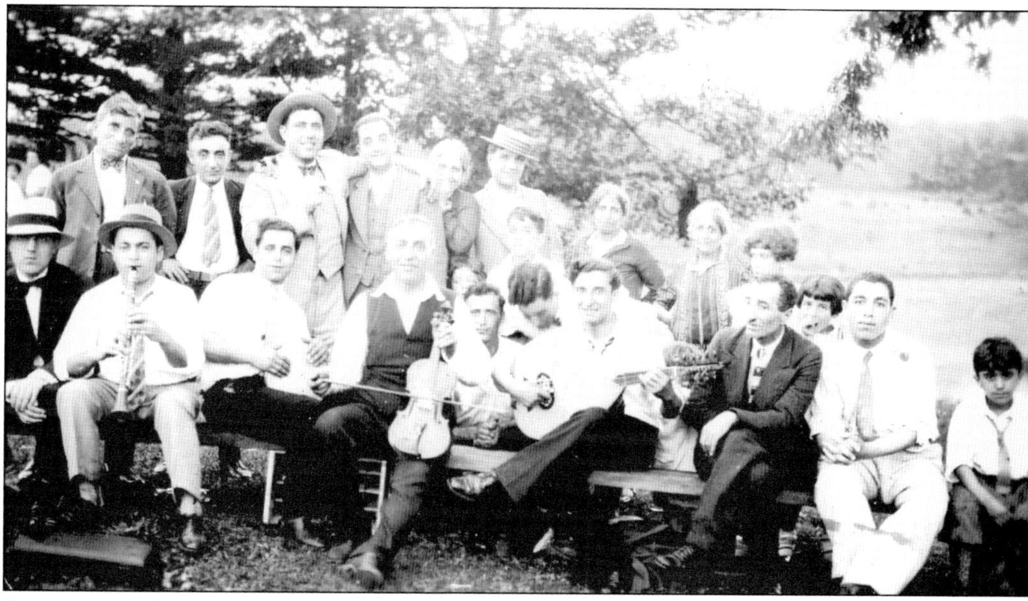

Picnics were frequent and widespread during the early Assyrian settlement in New England. Most picnics were held on private farms, or later at Camp Nineveh (Nineveh was the capital of ancient Assyria) in Shrewsbury. Seen here are Sam Samuel (son of Rev. Favlos Samuel), second from right; Peter Hoyen; and others with traditional Assyrian instruments.

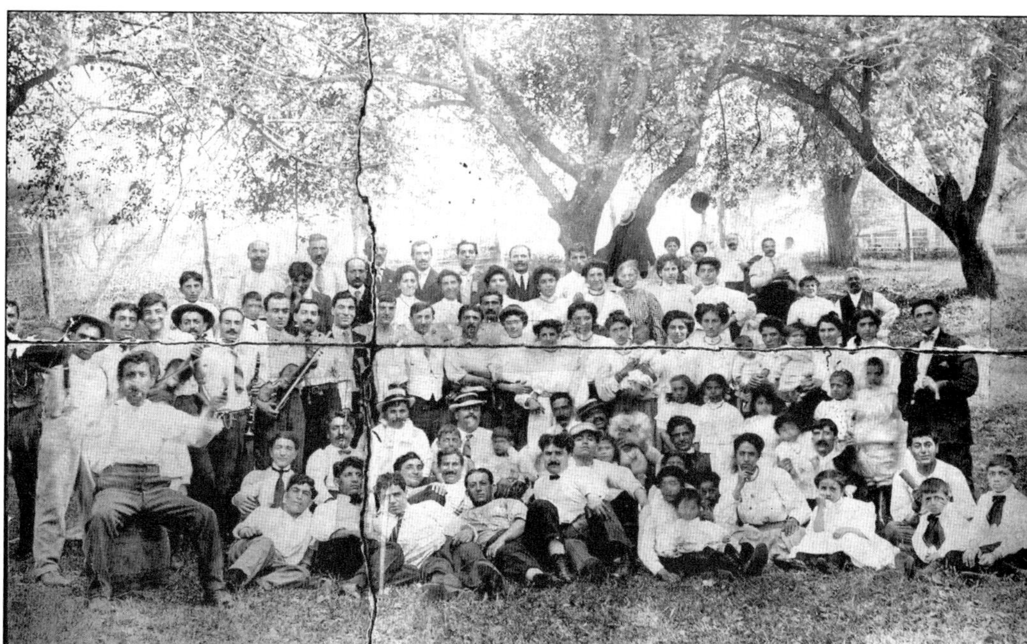

Here is another Assyrian picnic photograph taken in the early 1900s. Seen are Assyrians of Massachusetts, Rhode Island, and Connecticut gathering in Rhode Island for drinks and music. Indeed, Assyrians of the three states mingled occasionally for church, family functions, and feast days.

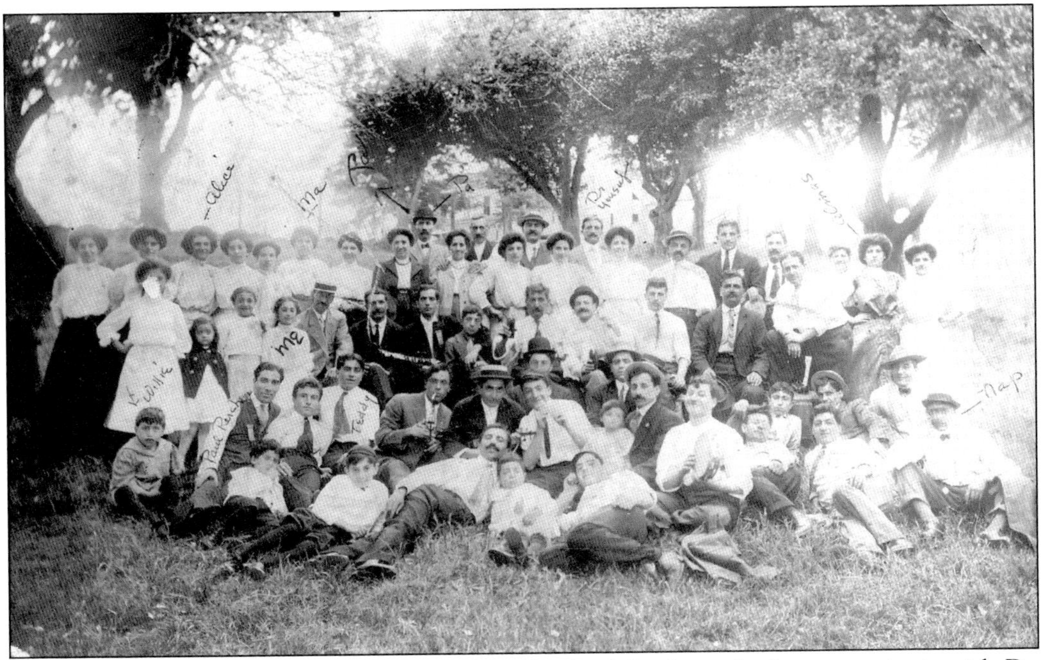

In the above picture stands Phyllis (Arslen) Saffer, Paul Perch, and others at a picnic with Dr. Abraham K. Yousef standing to the rear. Notice here, as with many other photographs, someone has written in names of some of the individuals. "Nap," who is located on the far right, is surely a nickname.

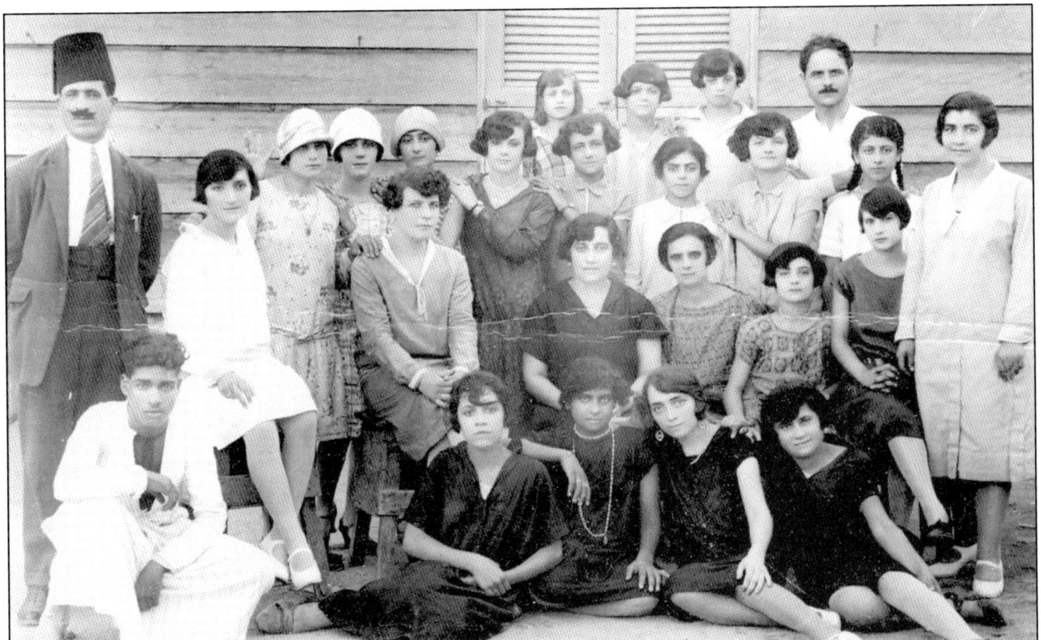

The above picture is again typical of Assyrians in transition from the Middle East to the United States. As is illustrated, men were still quite comfortable in the old style fez hat with a rather bushy mustache. The contrast between the newcomer male and the obviously western dressed females is quite dramatic.

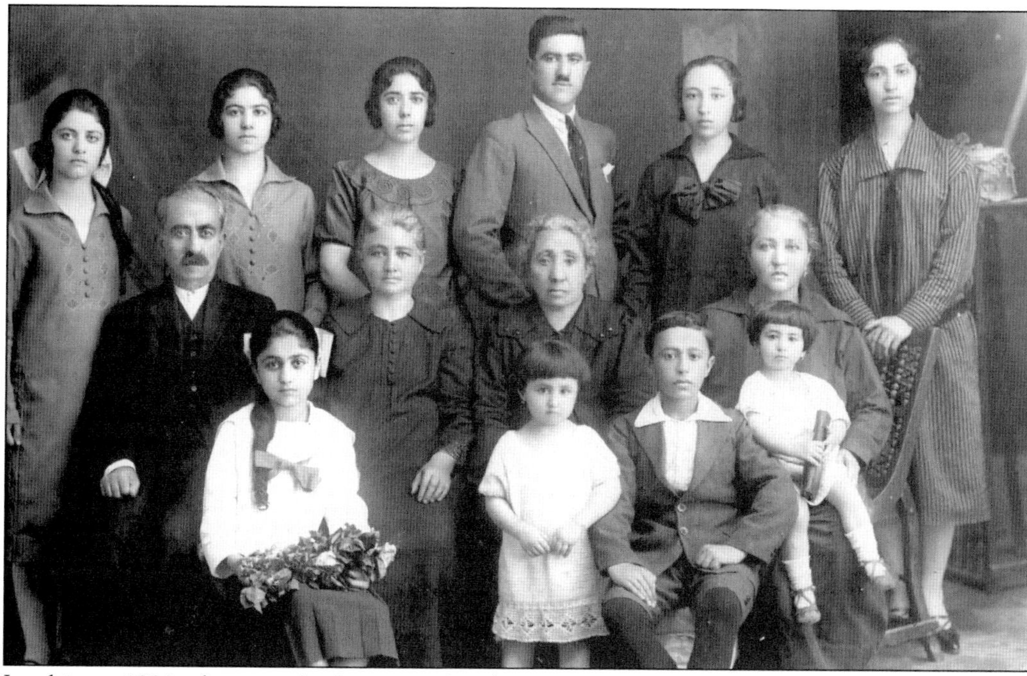

In this c. 1920 photograph the same family is seen two years later in the United States, demonstrating the adjustment that was made in a relatively short time span. The same Assyrian man is pictured above, though minus his fez, and with a different, more western, pair of trousers. This is the Barsam family of Beirut, Lebanon. Present in the image are Juliet Safer Donabed, Peruz Barsam, Marty Barsam, David Dasho, Ryal Dasho, Rose Barsam, and Yelsa Malick. The Barsam family immigrated to the United States in response to deteriorating conditions for the Assyrians of Turkey.

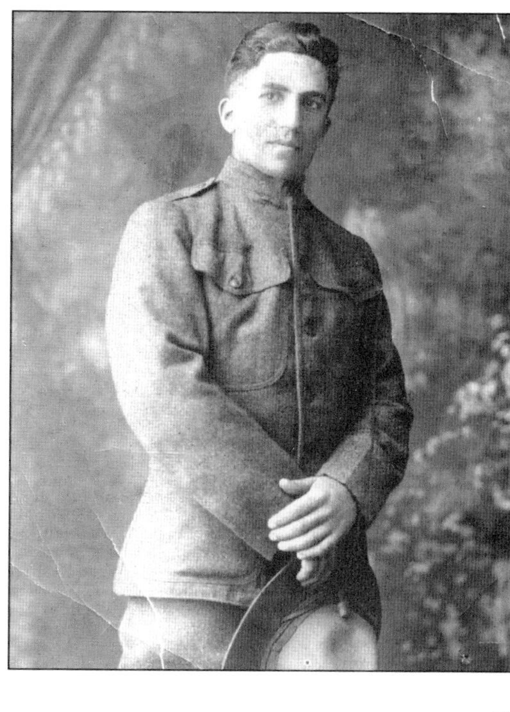

Of the various photographs encountered in the homes of elderly Assyrians, this one of "Yeron's brother-in-law" was labeled just that. Unfortunately, since most of the first generation Assyrians of the 20th century have passed on, the man's name is also lost in obscurity.

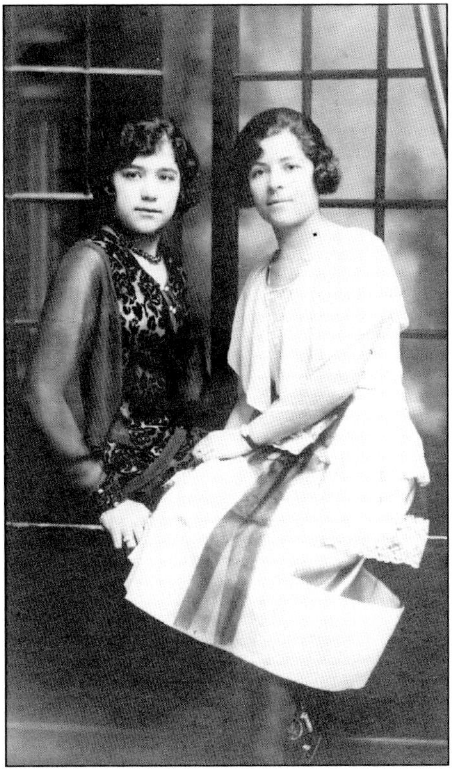

Two young Assyrian women pose in the photograph on the left. This photograph was found in the basement of Sam and Sadie Samuel in Watertown.

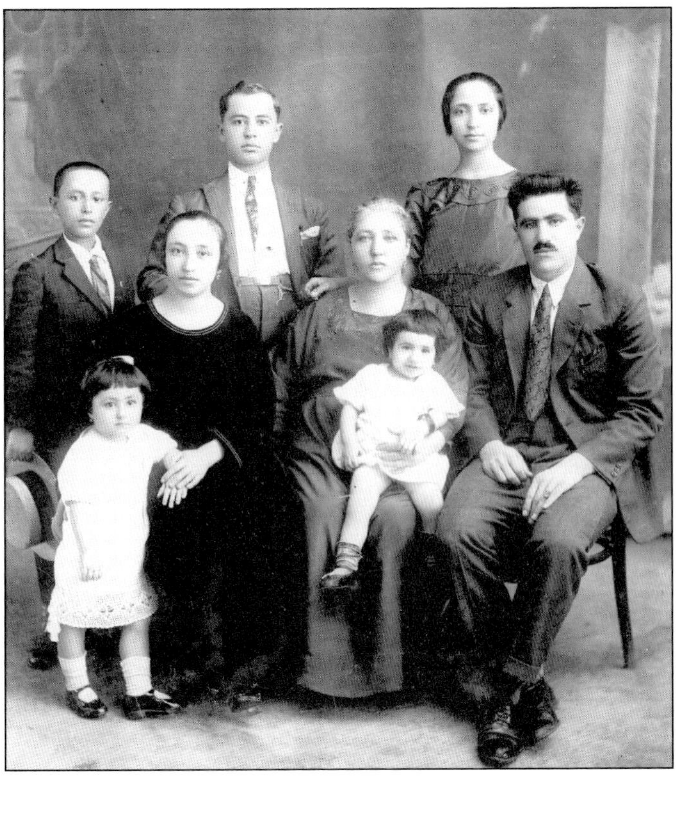

An Assyrian family poses after their first few years in the United States. Notice the dress of both men and women, with special attention to the young boy holding a hat. Assyrians, even the youth, eagerly attempted to acclimatize themselves to the New England fashion of the 1920s.

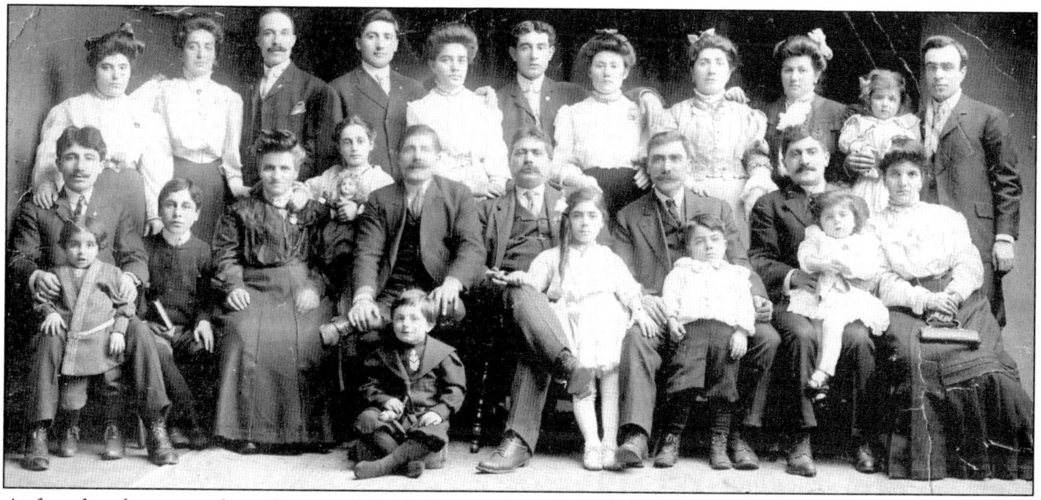

A family photograph, taken in 1905, shows the size of the extended family; not exclusive to Assyrians alone, but also with most immigrants to the United States in the late 19th and early 20th centuries. The older men and women are seen sitting while the younger couples stand good-naturedly to the rear.

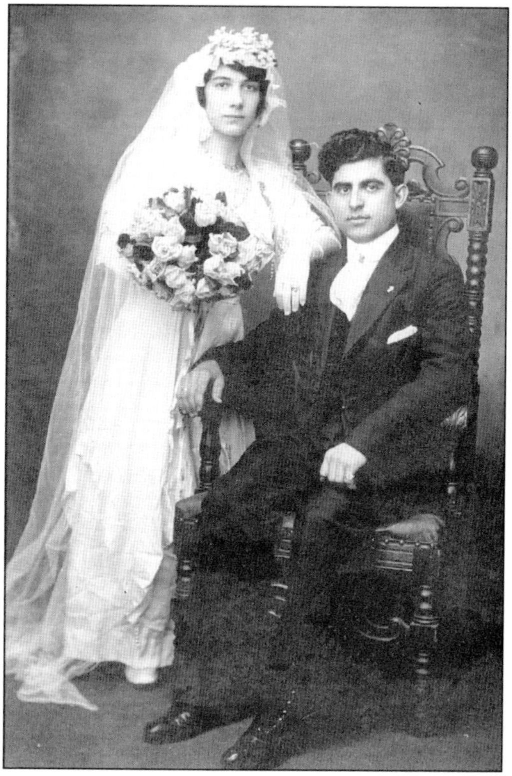

This photograph of Samuel Sahag and his bride Alice Sahag, H. Dasho's mother's sister, was taken by Empire Studio located at 12a Tremont Row in Boston. They were blessed with three daughters, Margaret, Elizabeth (Betty), and Lillian, and resided in Hyde Park for many years. The photograph was inscribed on the reverse saying, "from S. Sahag to Kasper and Phyllis Saffer."

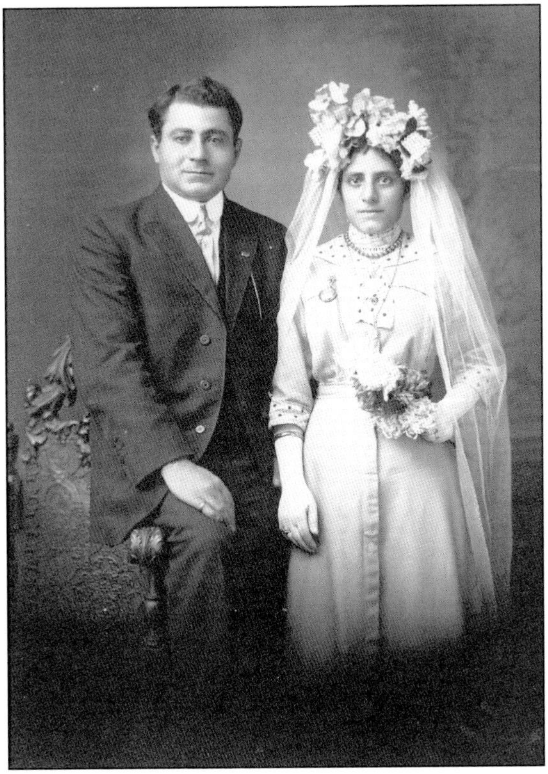

Paul Perch, cousin of Teddy Arslen, is pictured in 1913. Perch and his wife were married in the Bay State, and both of their parents were Assyrians from Harput.

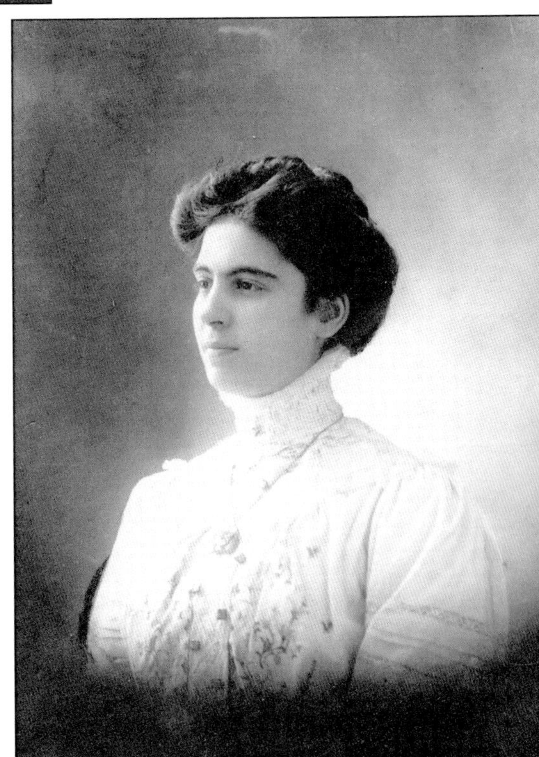

This is the portrait of Lucy Vabel of Springfield, cousin of Sophie Atlas, taken at Sumbul and Sons photography studio at 19 Main Street, Charlestown.

Three

Building a New Assyria

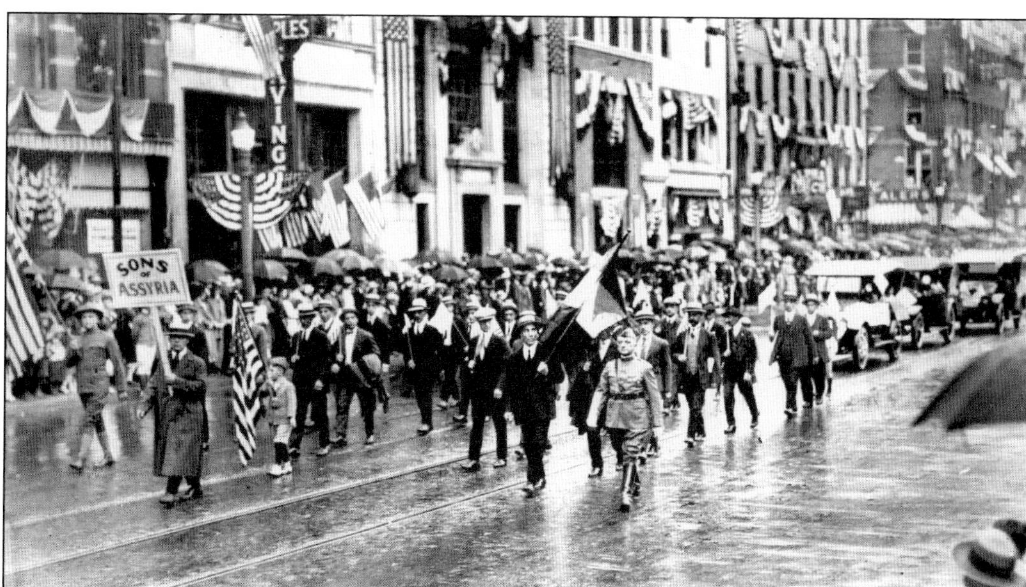

The July 4, 1922, Independence Day celebration on Main Street in Worcester was attended by the Sons of Assyria. The presence of such patriots as Capt. Dr. Abraham K. Yousef (center in military attire) invigorated the Assyrian immigrants to display their heritage and march on such a hallowed occasion as new Assyrian Americans. Many had newly immigrated, and stood proudly for their heritage during the jubilee. The Assyrians of Worcester would continue to participate in such parades throughout the early years of settlement.

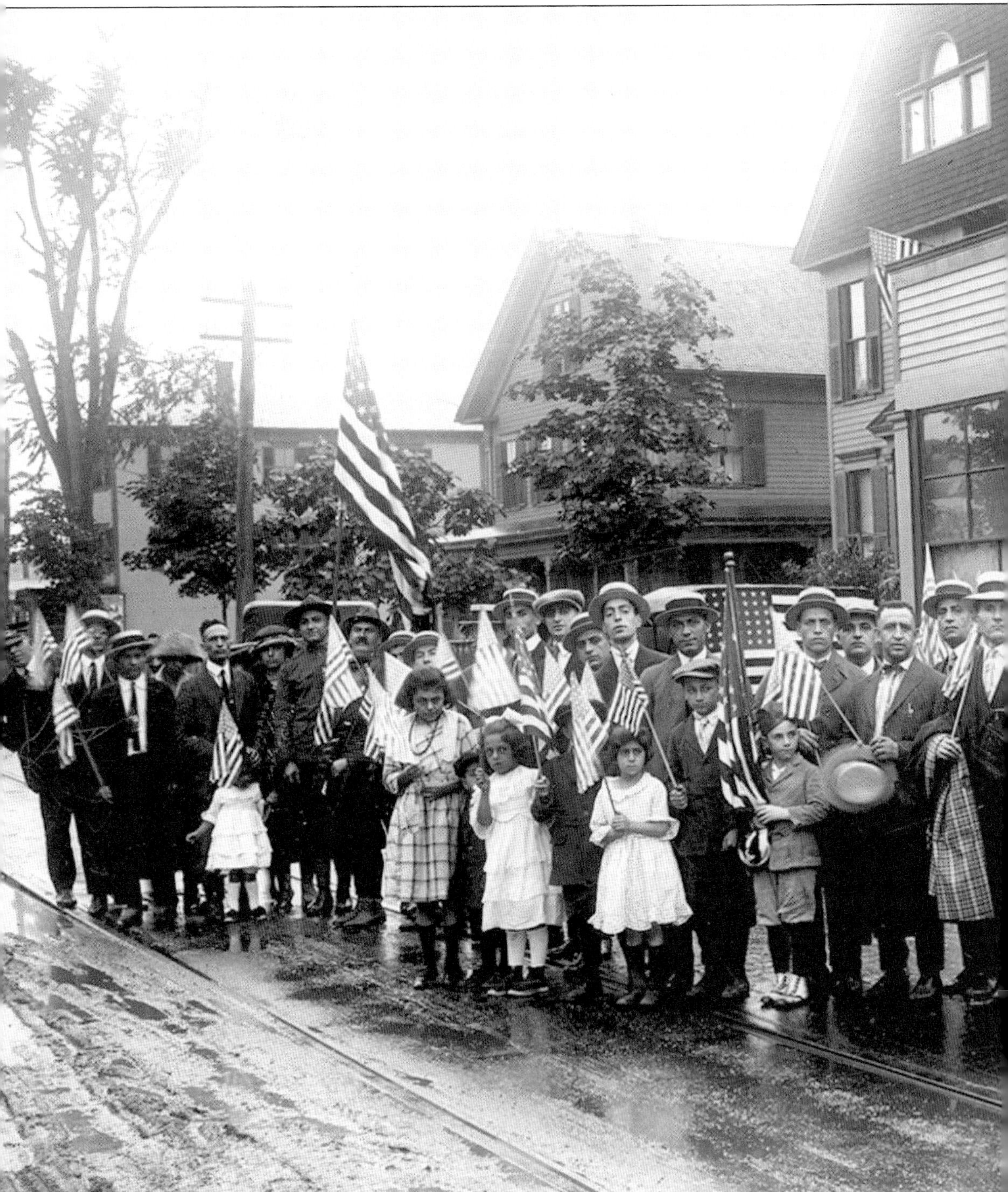

Waving the Assyrian and American flags, Captain Yousef and Assyrian veterans march on Main Street in Worcester on July 4, 1922. Following their disastrous expulsion by their Muslim neighbors, the Harput Assyrians in New England integrated enthusiastically into American society and struggled to retain their ethnic roots. Yousef himself was seen as the early leader

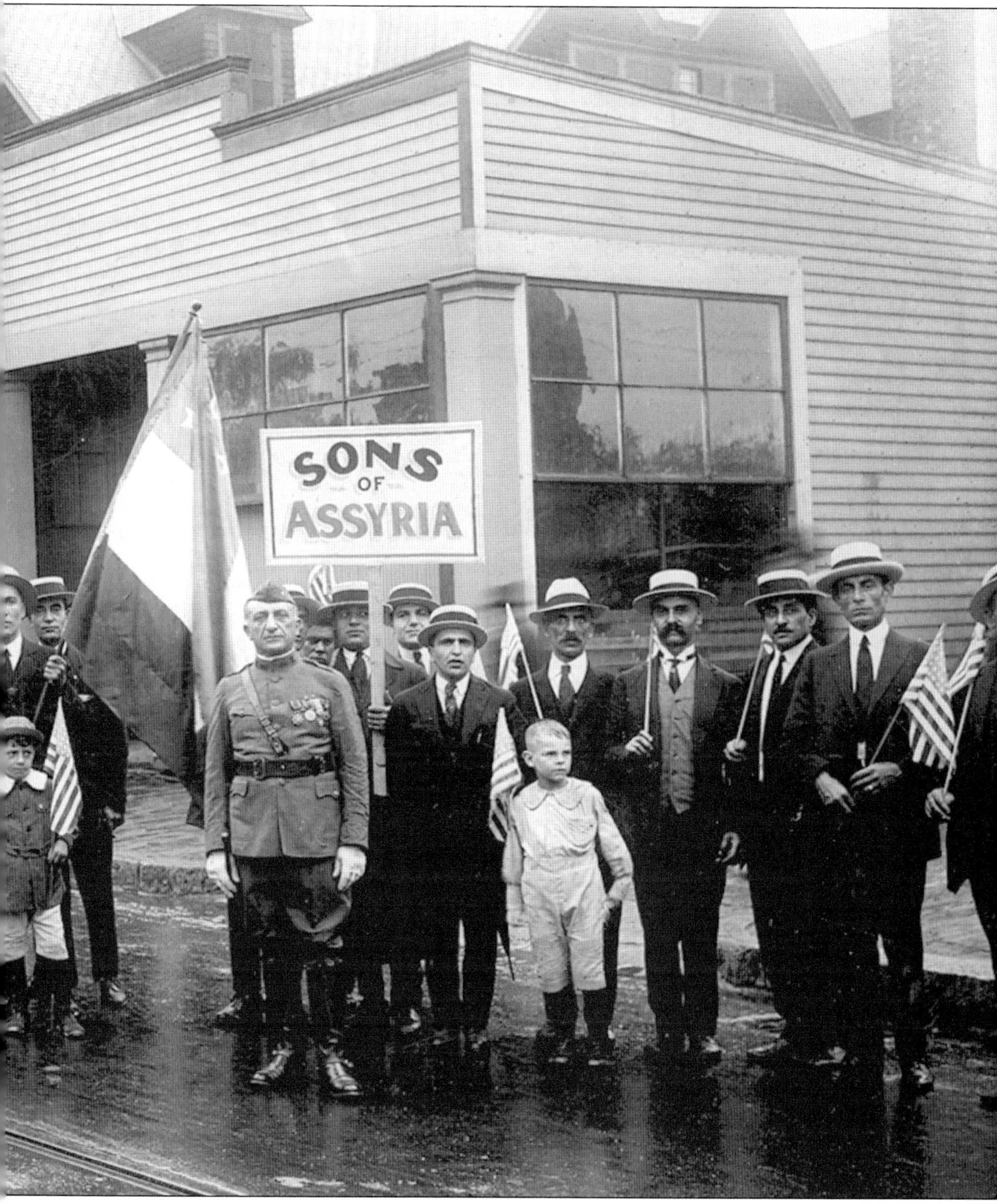

of Assyrians in New England who had immigrated from Harput, Mardin, Diarbekir, and other areas of Assyria that fell among the Ottoman provinces. Charles Perch can also been seen in the above photograph to the far left holding the American flag. (Photograph by Arthur S. Adams, photographer, of 421 Main Street in Worcester, Massachusetts.)

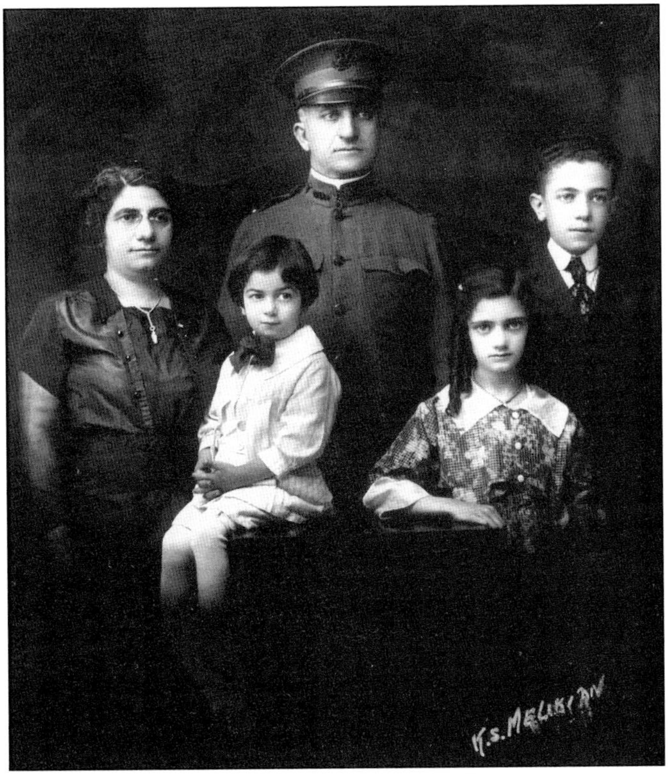

Abraham K. Yousef, who was born in Harput and graduated from Central Turkey College and Baltimore Medical College (pictured here with his sister and her children), served as a U.S. Army medic in World War I. He wrote extensively in *The New Assyria* and *Assyrian Progress* (Los Angeles, California), and initiated the Assyrian Benevolent Association in 1897 in Worcester. Shortly before his untimely death in 1924, he became a member of the Assyrian delegation to the Paris Peace Conference (1919) which put forward the demand for an Assyrian homeland.

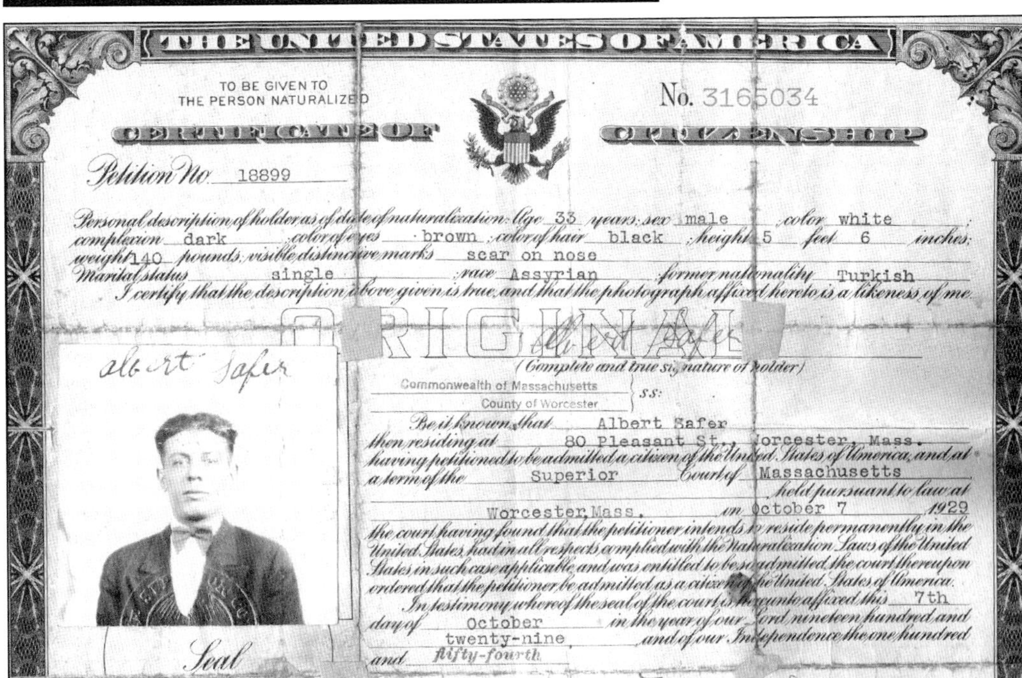

THE UNITED STATES OF AMERICA

TO BE GIVEN TO THE PERSON NATURALIZED

No. 3165034

CERTIFICATE OF CITIZENSHIP

Petition No. 18899

Personal description of holder as of date of naturalization: Age 33 years; sex male; color white; complexion dark; color of eyes brown; color of hair black; height 5 feet 6 inches; weight 140 pounds; visible distinctive marks scar on nose

Marital status single; race Assyrian; former nationality Turkish

I certify that the description above given is true, and that the photograph affixed hereto is a likeness of me.

ORIGINAL

Albert Safer
(Complete and true signature of holder)

albert Safer

Commonwealth of Massachusetts
County of Worcester } ss:

Be it known that Albert Safer then residing at 80 Pleasant St., Worcester, Mass. having petitioned to be admitted a citizen of the United States of America, and at a term of the Superior Court of Massachusetts held pursuant to law at Worcester, Mass. on October 7 1929 the court having found that the petitioner intends to reside permanently in the United States, had in all respects complied with the Naturalization Laws of the United States in such case applicable, and was entitled to be so admitted, the court thereupon ordered that the petitioner be admitted as a citizen of the United States of America.

In testimony whereof the seal of the court is hereunto affixed this 7th day of October in the year of our Lord nineteen hundred and twenty-nine and of our Independence the one hundred and fifty-fourth.

Seal

Seen here is Abdenoor (Albert) Safer's Certificate of Naturalization to the United States of America on October 7, 1929. Another native of Harput, Assyria, Abdenoor worked in factories for much of his life. He also tried his hand as a shoemaker with his cousin Youhanna Donabed.

In the early 1900s, most Assyrians in Massachusetts were married by the first priest Favlos Samuel, and upon his retirement, Rev. Peter Barsoum. Seen here are the wedding papers of Abdenoor (Albert) Safer and Margaret Kazar, dated September 1, 1945.

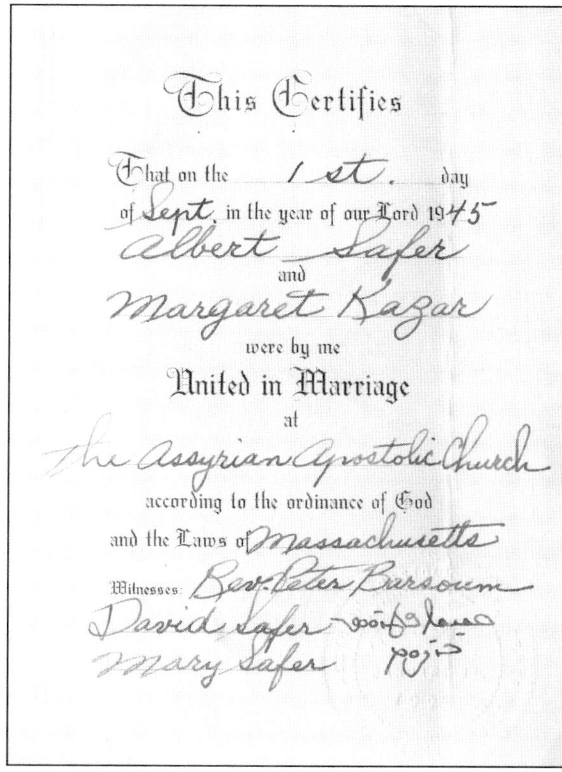

This Certifies

That on the 1st. day

of Sept. in the year of our Lord 1945

Albert Safer

and

Margaret Kazar

were by me

United in Marriage

at

The Assyrian Apostolic Church

according to the ordinance of God

and the Laws of Massachusetts

Witnesses: Rev. Peter Barsoum

David Safer

Mary Safer

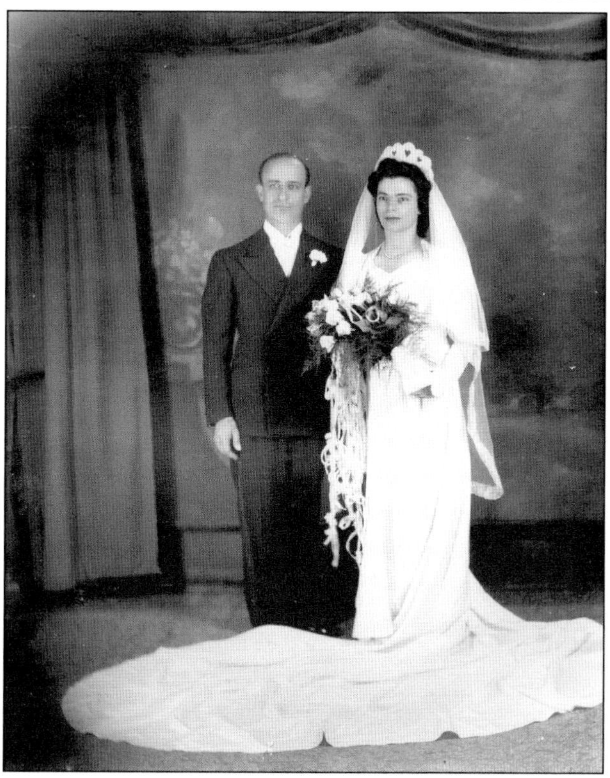

A shoemaker and factory worker, Youhanna Behnam Donabed married Roumel Kazar in Massachusetts where they lived until their passings in 1984 and 1996 respectively. They were married on September 30, 1945.

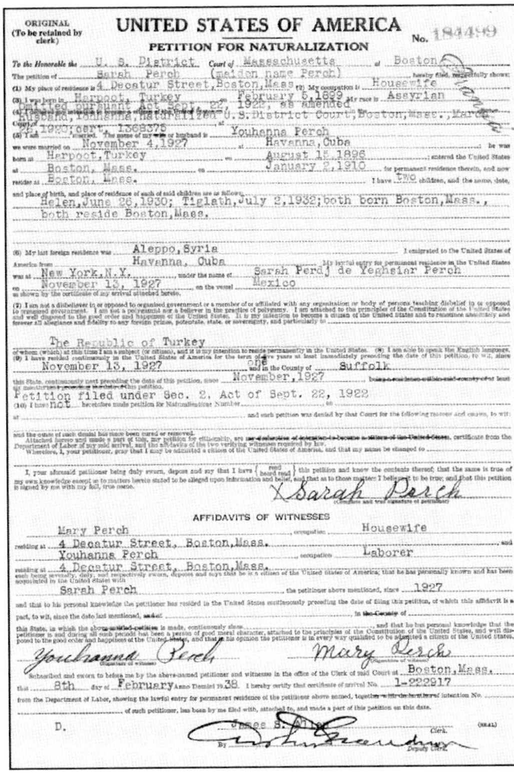

ORIGINAL (To be retained by clerk)

UNITED STATES OF AMERICA

PETITION FOR NATURALIZATION

No. 184489

To the Honorable the U. S. District Court of Massachusetts at Boston

The petition of Sarah Perch (maiden name Perch) hereby filed, respectfully shows:

(1) My place of residence is 4 Decatur Street, Boston, Mass. (2) My occupation is Housewife

(3) I was born in Harpoot, Turkey on February 5, 1899 My race is Assyrian

(4) Omitted pursuant Act Sept. 22, 1922, as amended Husband, Youhanna, naturalized U. S. District Court, Boston, Mass., March 26, 1930; cert. 1368375

(5) I am married. The name of my husband is Youhanna Perch we were married on November 4, 1927 at Havanna, Cuba he was born at Harpoot, Turkey on August 15, 1896 entered the United States at Boston, Mass. on January 2, 1910 for permanent residence therein, and now resides at Boston, Mass. I have two children, and the name, date, and place of birth, and place of residence of each of said children are as follows: Helen, June 26, 1930; Tiglath, July 2, 1932; both born Boston, Mass., both reside Boston, Mass.

(6) My last foreign residence was Aleppo, Syria I emigrated to the United States of America from Havanna, Cuba My lawful entry for permanent residence in the United States was at New York, N.Y., under the name of Sarah Perdj de Yeghsiar Perch on November 13, 1927 on the vessel Mexico as shown by the certificate of my arrival attached hereto.

(7) ... particularly to The Republic of Turkey of whom (which) at this time I am a subject (or citizen), and it is my intention to reside permanently in the United States. (8) I am able to speak the English language. (9) I have resided continuously in the United States of America for the term of one years at least immediately preceding the date of this petition, to wit, since November 13, 1927 and in the County of Suffolk this State, continuously next preceding the date of this petition, since November, 1927

Petition filed under Sec. 2, Act of Sept. 22, 1922

(10) I have not heretofore made petition for Naturalization ...

X Sarah Perch

AFFIDAVITS OF WITNESSES

Mary Perch, occupation Housewife, residing at 4 Decatur Street, Boston, Mass., and Youhanna Perch, occupation Laborer, residing at 4 Decatur Street, Boston, Mass. ... acquainted in the United States with Sarah Perch the petitioner above mentioned, since 1927 ...

Youhanna Perch Mary Perch

Subscribed and sworn to before me by the above-named petitioner and witnesses in the office of the Clerk of said Court at Boston, Mass. this 8th day of February Anno Domini 1938. I hereby certify that certificate of arrival No. 1-222917 ...

D. James S. Allen, Clerk. (SEAL)

Shown here is the Petition of Naturalization by Sarah Perch, born in Harput on February 5, 1899, and wife of Youhanna Perch. Like other Assyrians, Sarah lived in Aleppo, Syria, and emigrated from Havanna, Cuba. Notice the race section where Assyrian was entered.

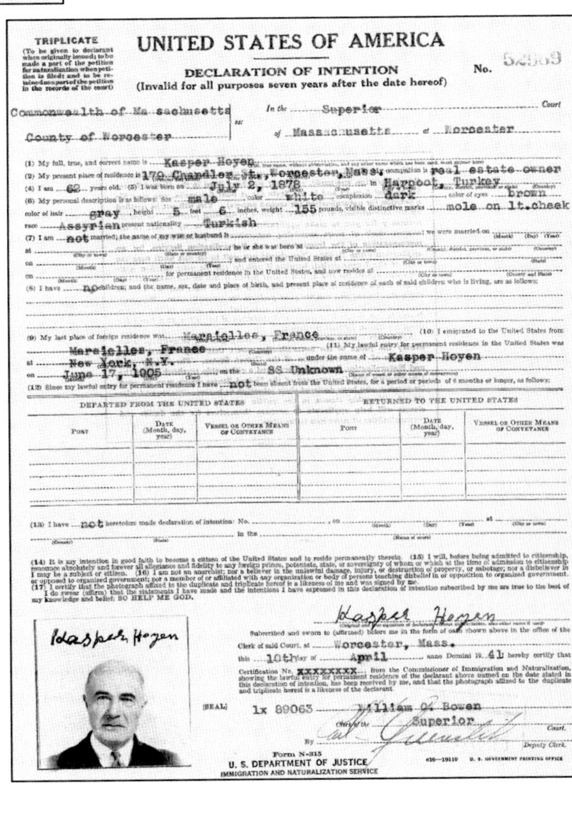

TRIPLICATE (To be given to declarant when originally issued; to be made a part of the petition for naturalization when petition is filed; and to be retained as a part of the petition in the records of the court)

UNITED STATES OF AMERICA

DECLARATION OF INTENTION

(Invalid for all purposes seven years after the date hereof)

No. 52569

Commonwealth of Massachusetts, County of Worcester, ss: In the Superior Court of Massachusetts at Worcester

(1) My full, true, and correct name is Kasper Hoyen

(2) My present place of residence is 170 Chandler St., Worcester, Mass. (3) My occupation is real estate owner

(4) I am 62 years old. (5) I was born on July 2, 1878 in Harpoot, Turkey

(6) My personal description is as follows: Sex male, color white, complexion dark, color of eyes brown, color of hair gray, height 5 feet 6 inches, weight 155 pounds, visible distinctive marks mole on lt. cheek, race Assyrian, present nationality Turkish

(7) I am not married

(8) I have no children

(9) My last place of foreign residence was Marseilles, France (10) I emigrated to the United States from Marseilles, France (11) My lawful entry for permanent residence in the United States was at New York, N.Y. under the name of Kasper Hoyen on June 17, 1905, on the SS Unknown

(12) Since my lawful entry for permanent residence I have not been absent from the United States, for a period or periods of 6 months or longer

(13) I have not heretofore made declaration of intention

Kasper Hoyen

Subscribed and sworn to (affirmed) before me in the form of oath shown above in the office of the Clerk of said Court, at Worcester, Mass. this 10th day of April anno Domini 1941 ... Certification No. xxxxxxxx ...

[SEAL] 1x 89063 William C. Bowen, Clerk of the Superior Court.

Form N-315 U. S. DEPARTMENT OF JUSTICE IMMIGRATION AND NATURALIZATION SERVICE

On the right is the Declaration of Intent of Kasper Hoyen who arrived in New York City in 1905. As is evident, travel to the United States was anything but direct. As Sarah Perch spent time in Havanna, Cuba, some Assyrians like Kasper spent some time in Marseilles, France. As in the previous image, note the entry in the race section.

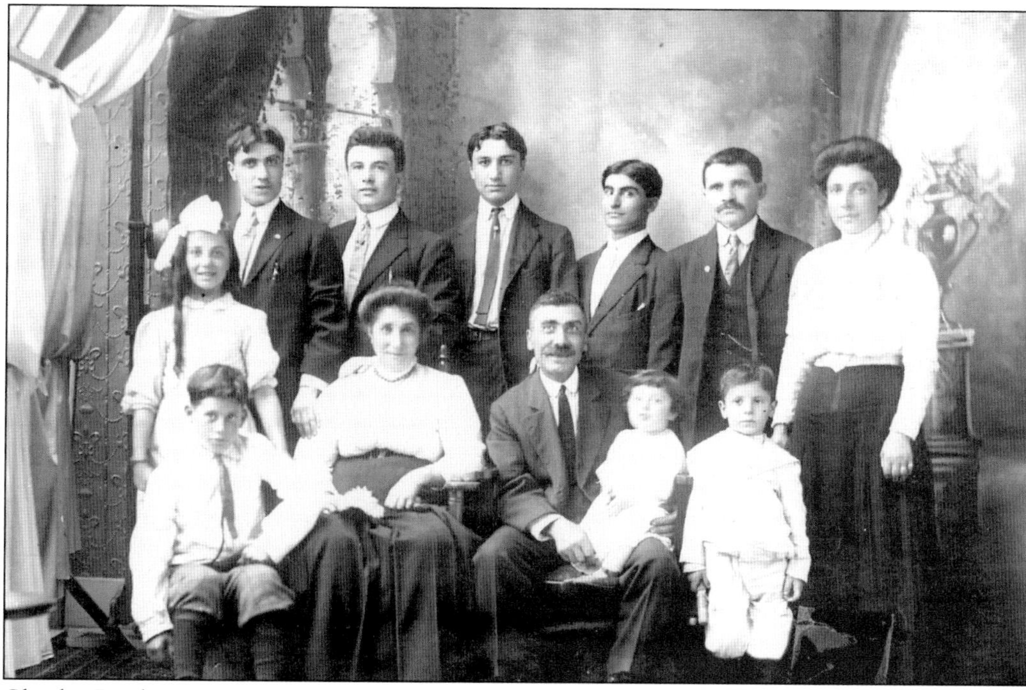

Charles Perch is seen standing in the center with the Perch clan in 1910. Many children were common among Assyrians in the Ottoman Empire. Unfortunately, due to the lack of medicines, many infants died from exposure to tuberculosis.

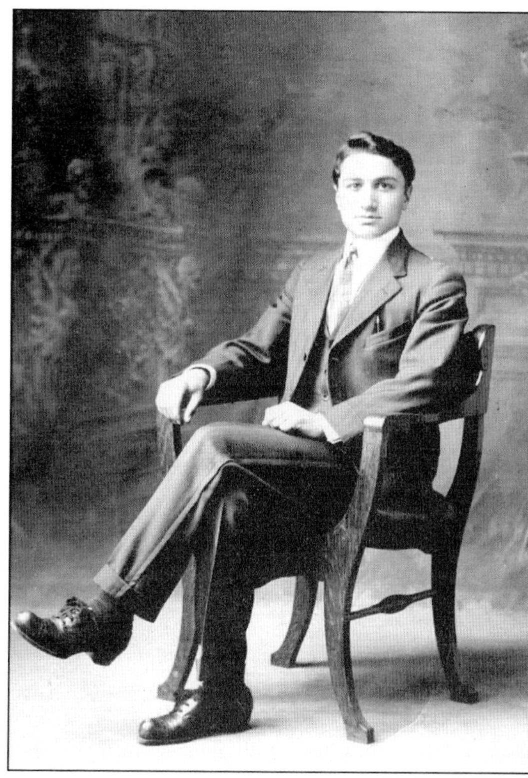

Charles Perch was born January 26, 1894, in Harput. This photograph was taken March 6, 1912. Due to its large Assyrian population, Worcester was where Perch settled and lived among his brethren for the rest of his days.

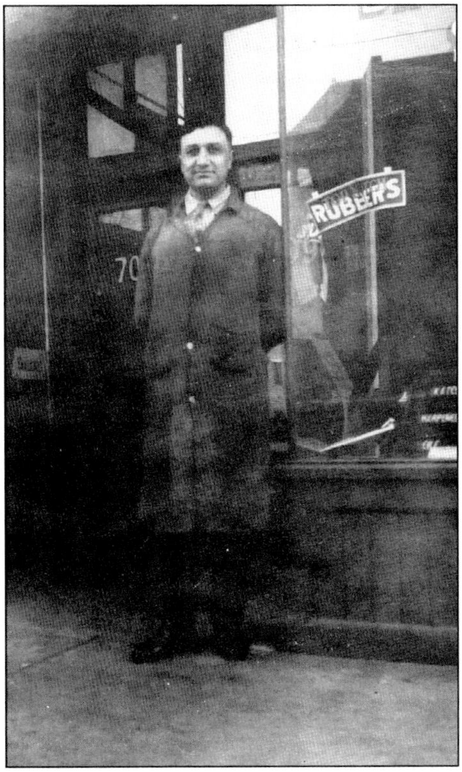

Charles Perch poses outside of his business in February 1929. After arriving at age 17 and serving time in the United States military, Perch then established his shoe working trade in Worcester as the family's main source of income.

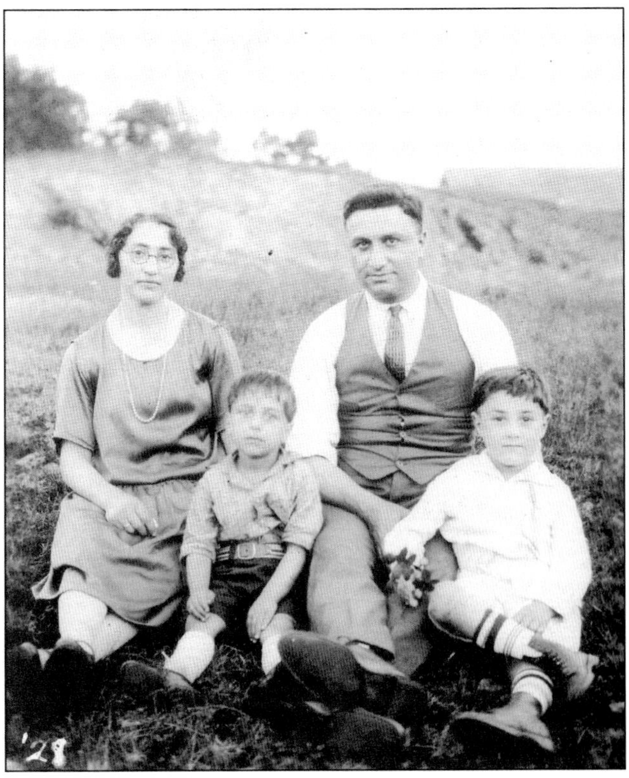

From left to right Rebecca Barsam Perch, Harold Perch, Charles Perch, and Henry Perch are seen in this 1928 photograph. The Barsam clan was well known throughout the Middle East as textile and fabric traders. They traveled as far as France for business.

Studies have shown that communities that suffer large scale massacres or genocide are predisposed to having fewer, if any, children. The Assyrians who survived the purging of their nation, were no exception. Although many families were quite large in the Ottoman Empire, those who survived the persecutions had fewer children. This is a photograph of Harold and Henry Perch, dated March 15, 1926.

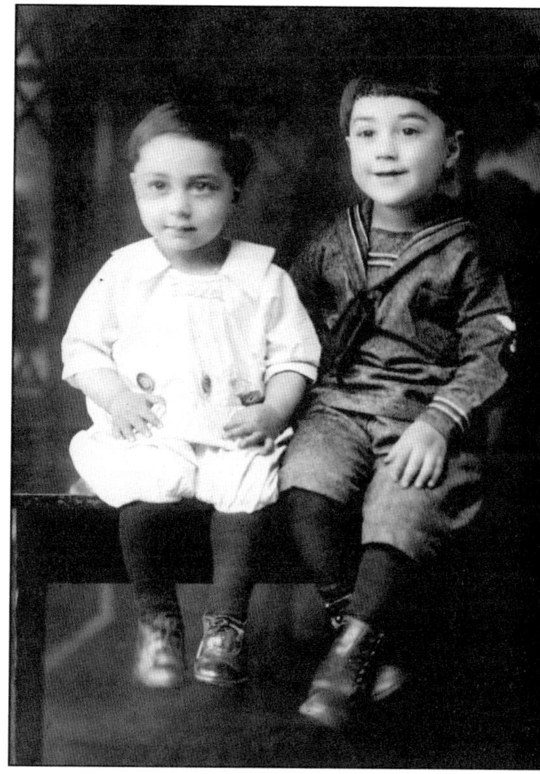

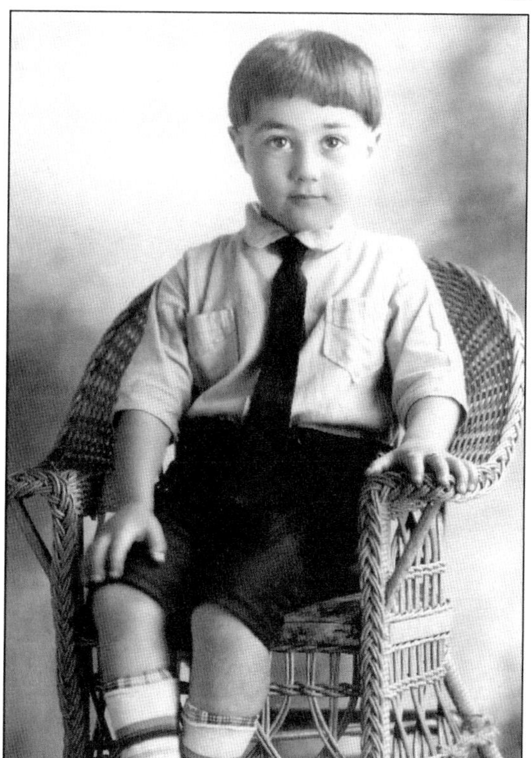

On October 11, 1927, young Henry Perch sits calmly for his portrait to be taken. Perch's future held years of military service, managing an arts and crafts store, and eventually opening his own store, Henry Perch's House of Gifts, in Worcester from 1961 to 1996.

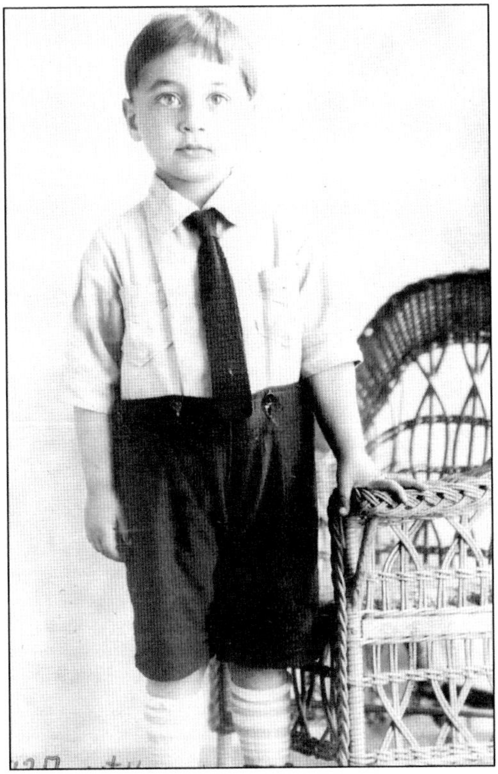

Harold Perch worked his plumbing trade for many years in Worcester. He also served as president of St. Mary's Assyrian Church in 1960, 1961, and then again in 1970.

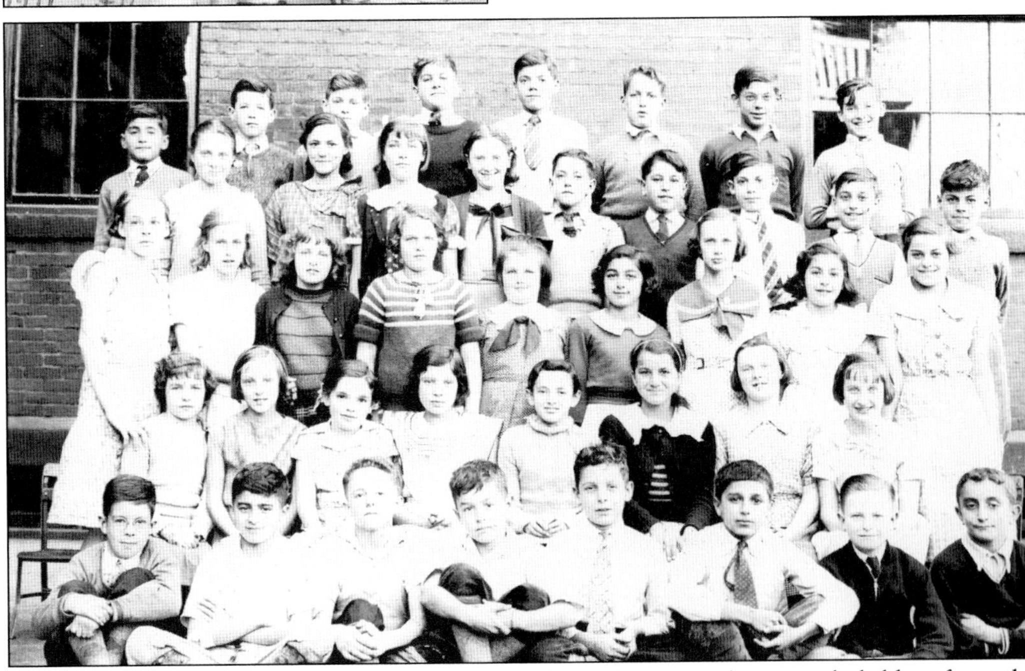

Harold Perch can be seen standing in the second row from top, the second child in from the right. The Chandler Street School in Worcester was home to his older brother Henry, who was an eighth grade student at the time. Here Harold is seen with his sixth grade classmates on October 15, 1935.

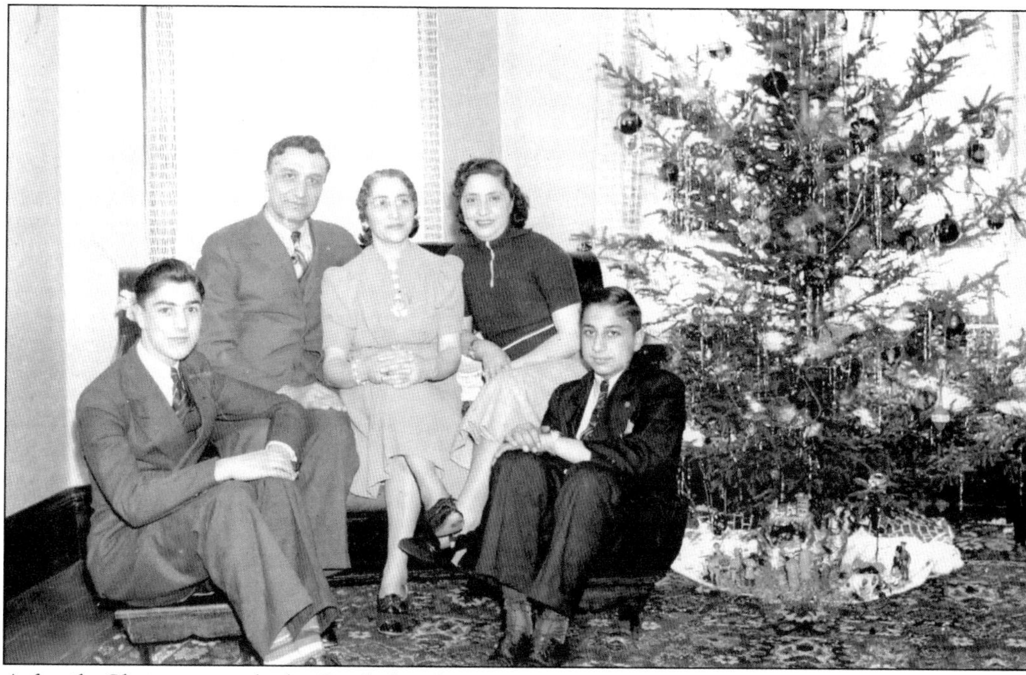

A family Christmas with the Perch family was a joyous occasion. Assyrians spent Christmas Eve with family members in preparation for the grand service at St. Mary's church on December 25.

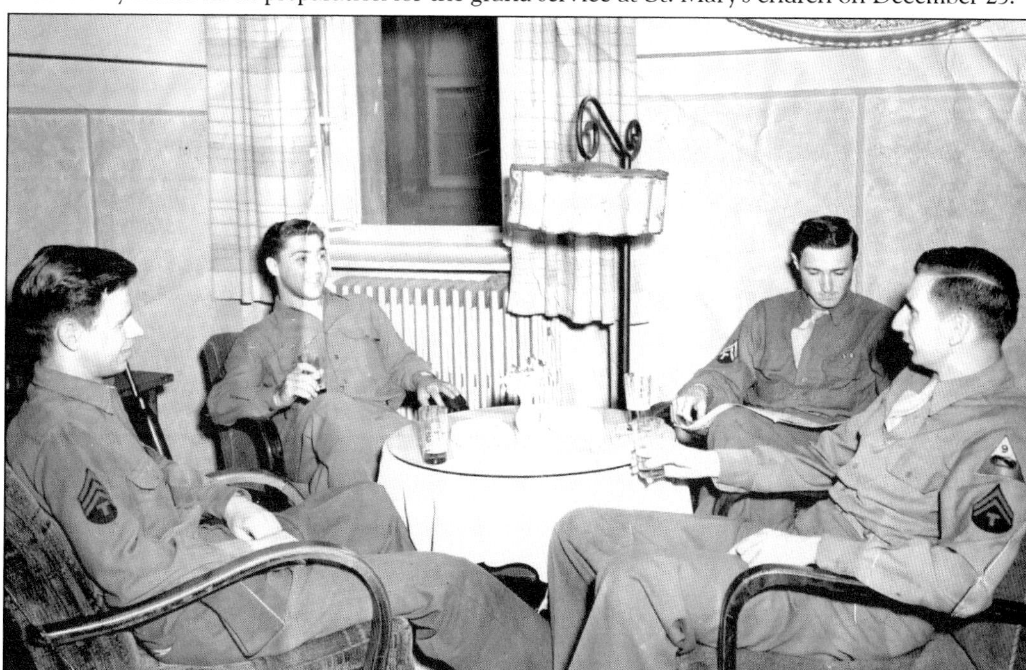

Following in the footsteps of his father, Henry Perch served both locally and abroad during his years of military service. Henry was one of numerous veteran Assyrians who served the United States proudly for many years. Interestingly, many second generation Assyrians still serve as high ranking military officials today.

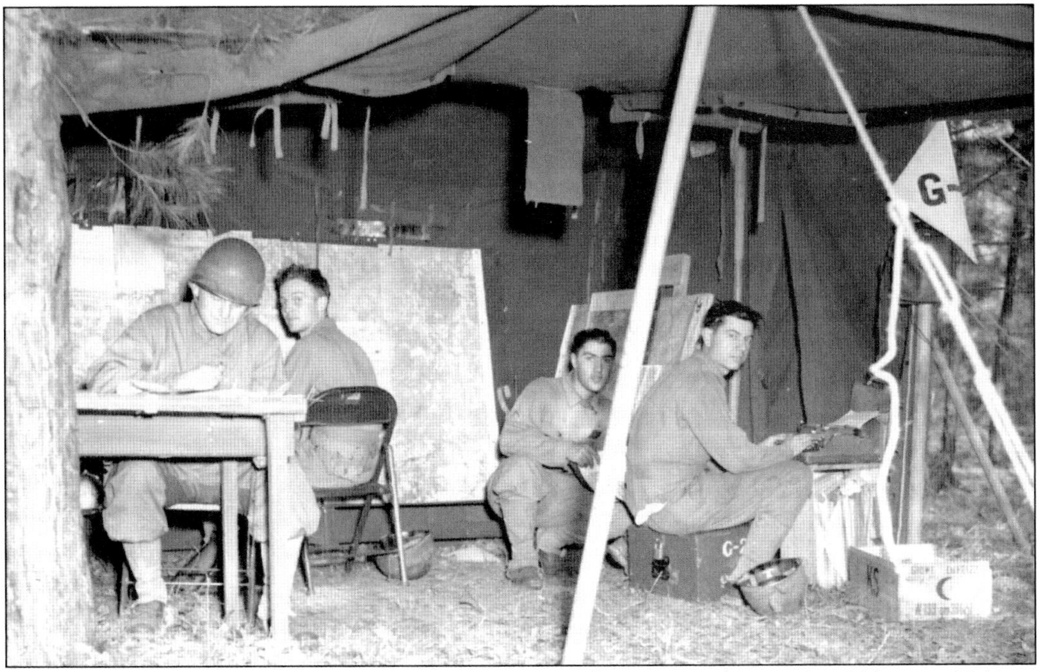

American born Assyrian Henry Perch was maneuvers from November 1943 to February 1944, as shown in this photograph. When Henry returned to Massachusetts, he spent years working at the navy yard in Chelsea prior to establishing his own business.

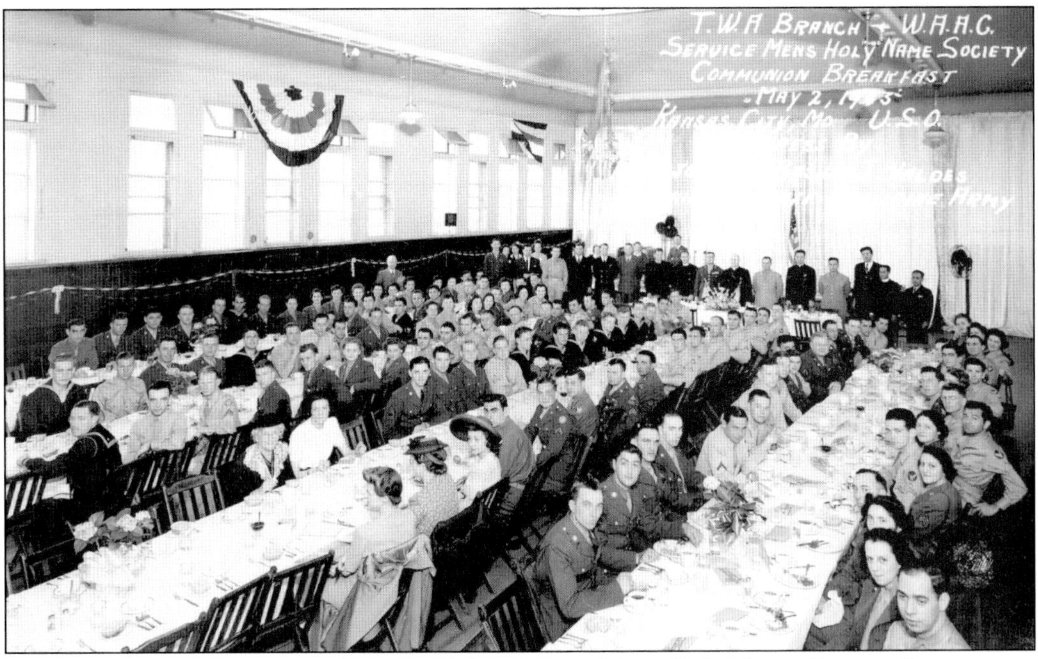

The May 2, 1945, TWA Branch and WAAC Service Mens Holy Name Society Communion Breakfast was held in Kansas City, Missouri, and featured Henry Perch as one of the attendees. The address for the day was given by Maj. Gen. Basilio J. Valdes, the chief of staff of the Philippine Army.

Many people in the photographs and portraits found among the collections of various Assyrian families were unrecognizable. This photograph is one of these that appears quite aged and therefore unidentifiable. The only information known was the discovery of the name Toros Donabed inscribed on the rear. The photograph was taken by W. J. Freeman Studio in Lowell.

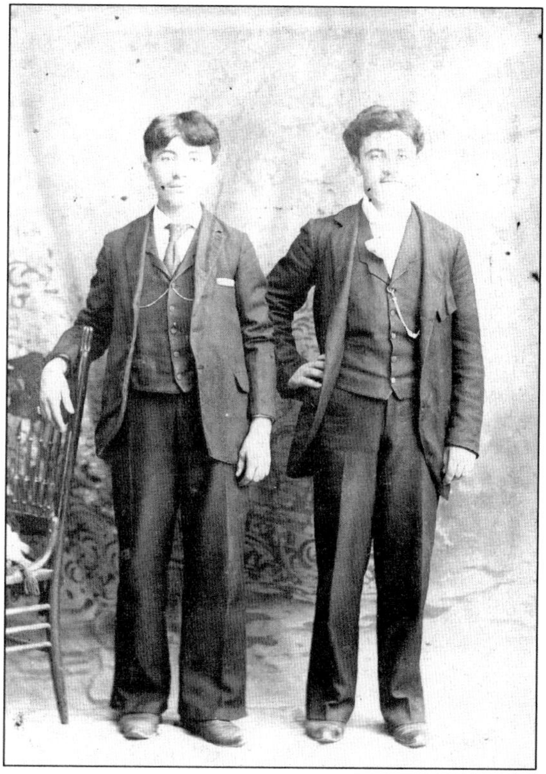

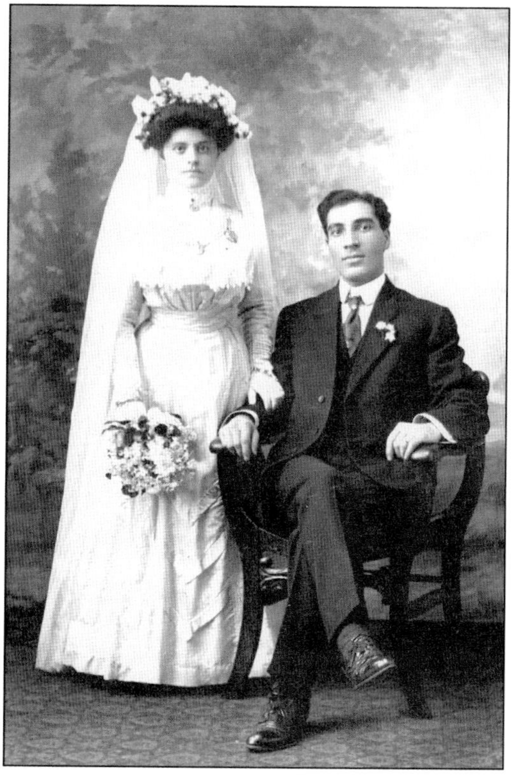

Paul Perch and Sophia were married in Worcester in the early 1920s. Paul spent most of his time coordinating Assyrian organization activities such as the gala in honor of Surma D'Beth Mar Shimun, sister to the patriarch of the Church of the East.

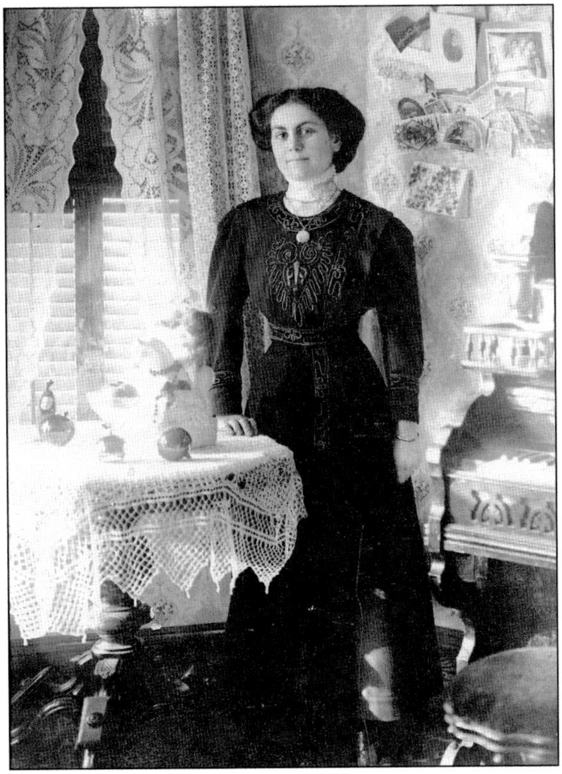

Notice the collection of early family photographs on the back wall. Few Assyrians settled in Dorchester, finding Worcester, Lowell, and Watertown as preferable locations with larger populations of their brethren.

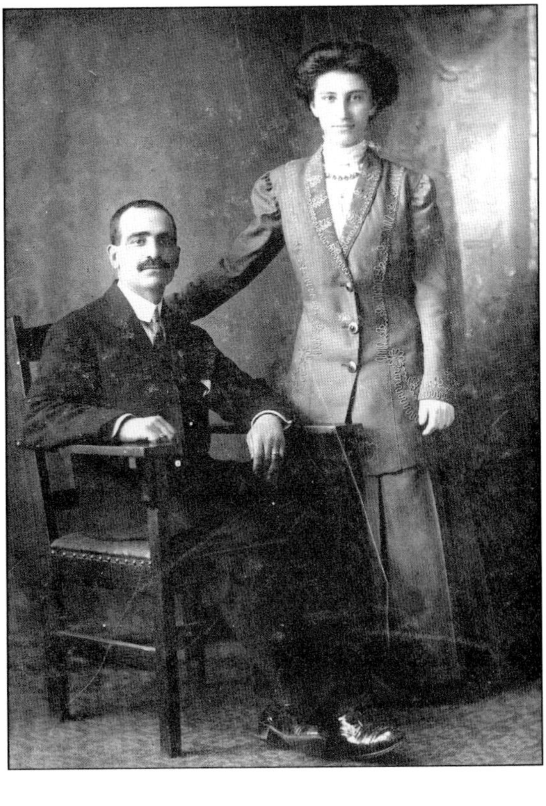

A photograph of a man and woman taken at Dudley Studio located at 217 Dudley Street in Boston is seen here. Some members of the community had variety stores in the Boston area, while others worked for Hood Rubber in the early 1900s.

In 1900 and just prior, the first Assyrians who settled in Massachusetts established a nationalist association based on the writings of Professor Ashur Yousef of Harput. The early group was named the Assyrian Five Association. This gentleman was associated with the early group.

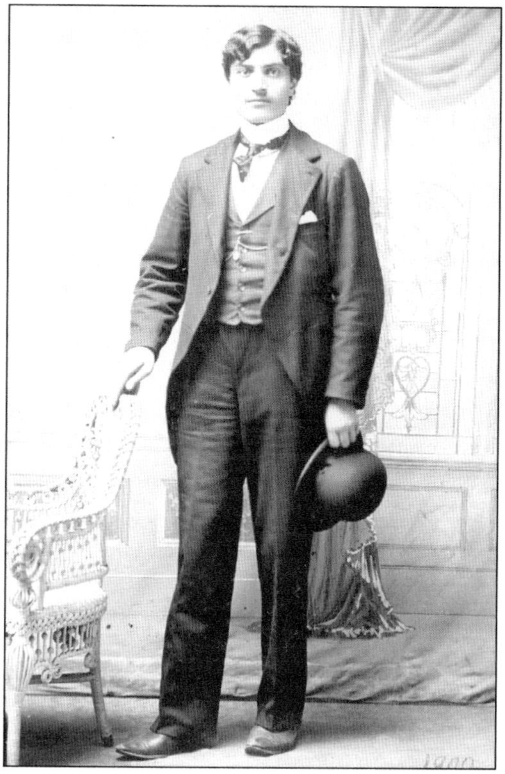

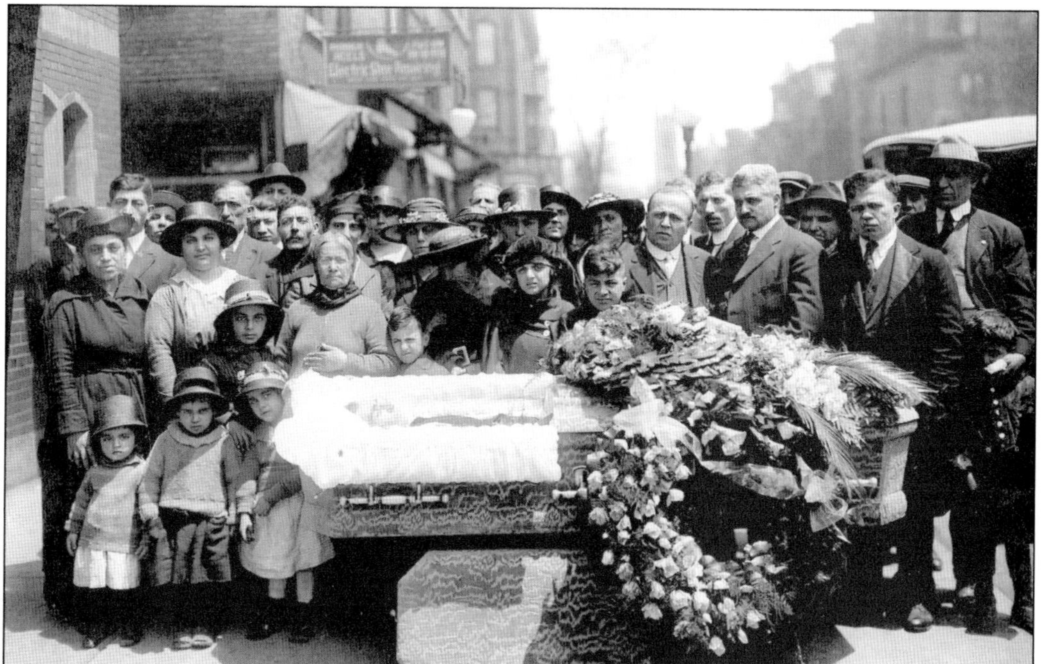

Though the identity of the deceased is a mystery, it is evident that the deceased man was noble and well admired by the public. This is the only funeral photograph of its kind from the collections of Massachusetts Assyrians.

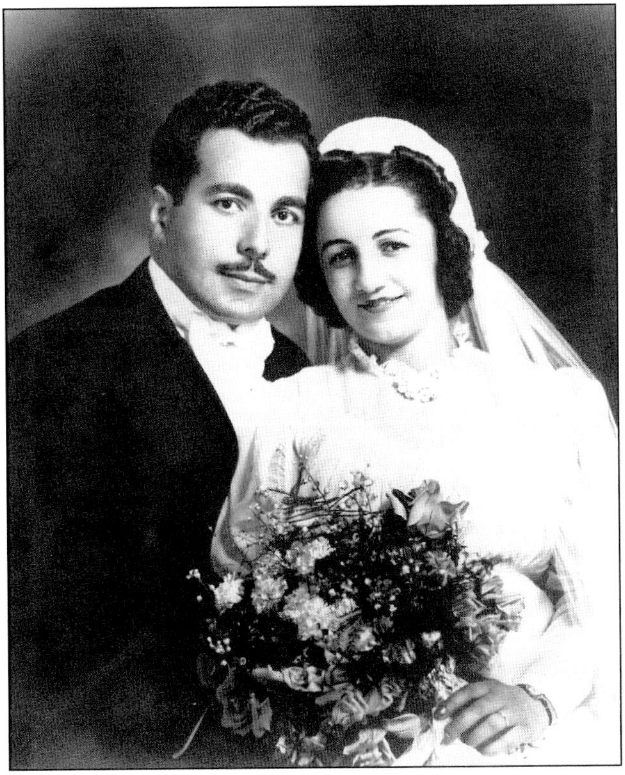

As son of the Reverend Favlos Samuel and brother to high deacon Sam Samuel, George Samuel spent many years as an active member of the church. George married young June George with whom he had two children, Albert and Alfred. They resided in Watertown for many years.

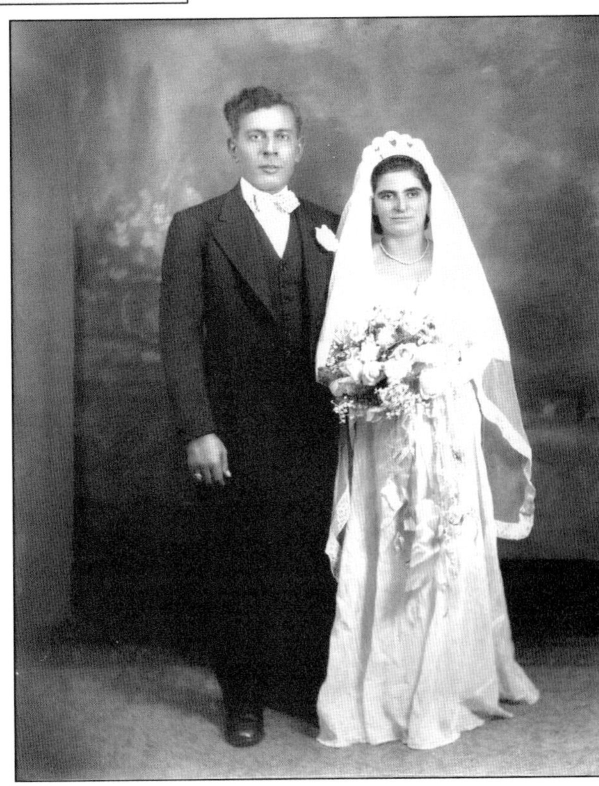

Abdenoor (Albert) Safer and Margaret Kazar Safer spent their married lives on Dudley Street in Roxbury prior to moving to 83 Deforest Street in Hyde Park. Both Roxbury and Hyde Park are sections of Boston. Abdenoor was a well known clarinet player and spent his early bachelor years traveling cross country on the railroad system. He and Margaret had no children. Their gravestone stands in Milton.

This is the wedding photograph of Peter Kazar and Helen Samuel. The Kazars later had two daughters, Janice and AnnLou. Peter Kazar and his family spent the majority of their lives in Dorchester, where he owned a variety store, suitably named Pete's Variety.

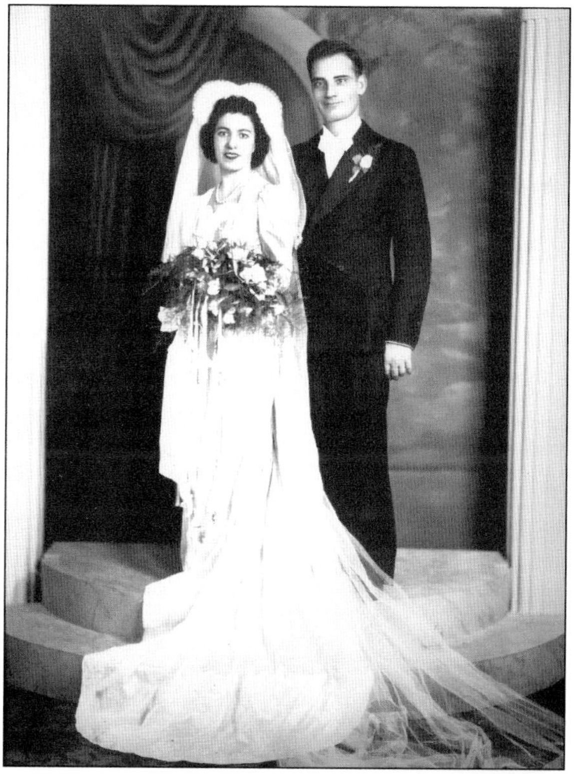

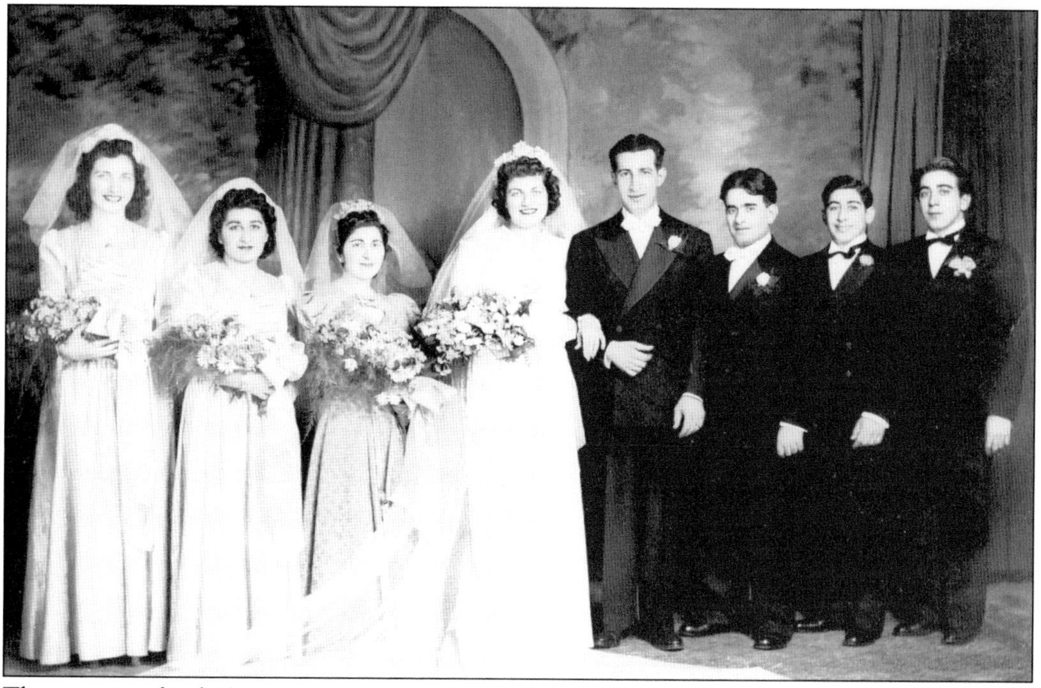

The majority of early Assyrian immigrants married other Assyrians. Some Harput Assyrians married those from Diarbekir and Mardin who settled in New Jersey. Those who settled in California were absorbed into the larger Assyrian community that immigrated from Iran and Iraq.

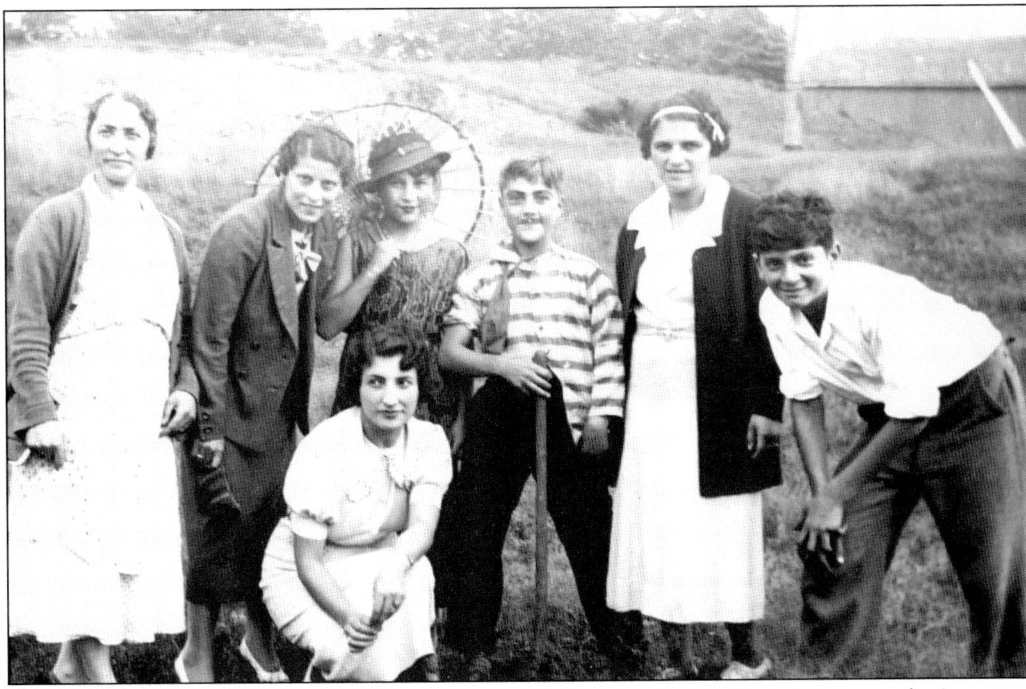

Many Halloween parties were held by Assyrians with proceeds usually going to needy Assyrians overseas. Here children stand on the Perch farm dressed in Halloween costumes. Henry Perch stands in the center with false moustache.

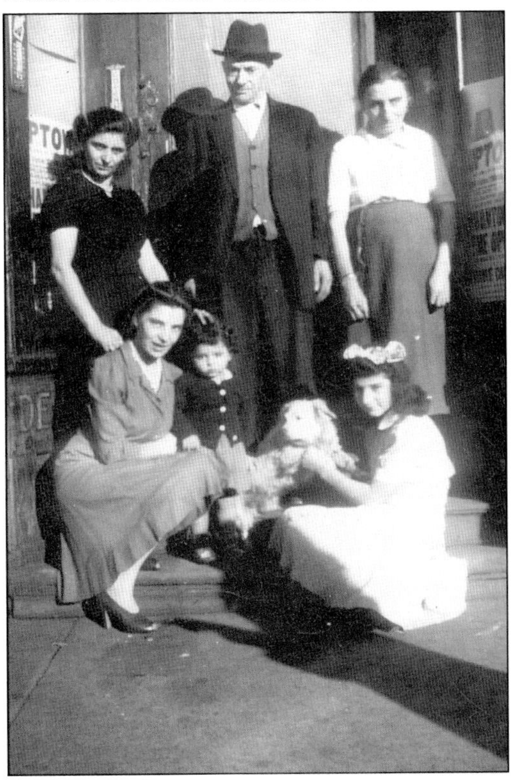

The Kazar family stands outside of their family-run variety store on Dudley Street in Roxbury. From left to right are (first row) Roumel, infant boy, Jolie the dog, and Charlotte Kashish; (second row) Margaret, Youhanna (Ohan), and Anna.

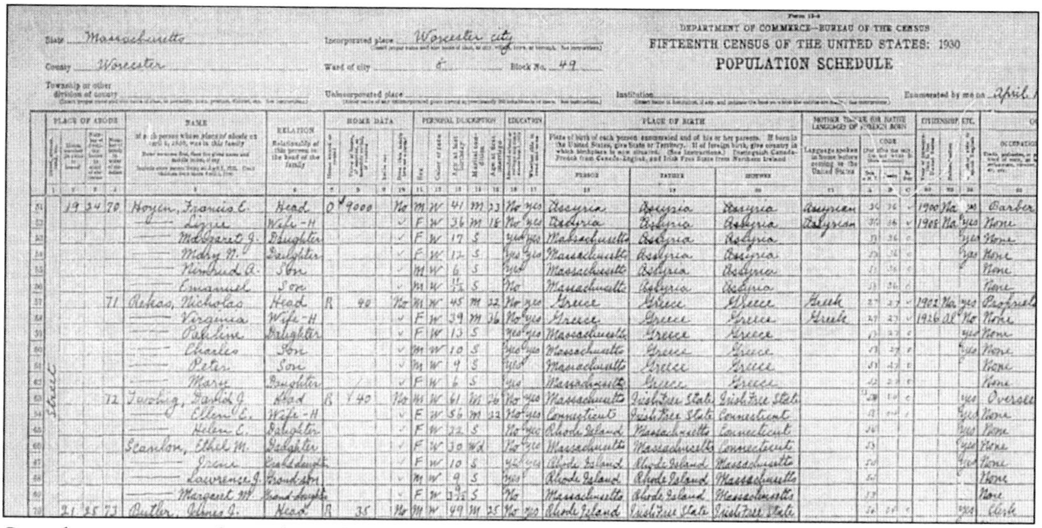

DEPARTMENT OF COMMERCE—BUREAU OF THE CENSUS
FIFTEENTH CENSUS OF THE UNITED STATES: 1930
POPULATION SCHEDULE

State: Massachusetts — County: Worcester — Incorporated place: Worcester city — Ward of city: 5 — Block No.: 49 — Enumerated by me on April

Line	Dwelling	Family	Name	Relation	Home	Value/Rent	Sex	Color	Age	Marital	Age at marriage	Birthplace (person)	Father	Mother	Language	Immigration	Occupation
51	19 34	70	Hoyen, Francis E.	Head	O	9000	M	W	41	M	23	Assyria	Assyria	Assyria	Assyrian	1900	Barber
52			—— Lizzie	Wife-H			F	W	36	M	18	Assyria	Assyria	Assyria	Assyrian	1908	None
53			—— Margaret J.	Daughter			F	W	17	S		Massachusetts	Assyria	Assyria			None
54			—— Mary M.	Daughter			F	W	12	S		Massachusetts	Assyria	Assyria			None
55			—— Nimbud A.	Son			M	W	6	S		Massachusetts	Assyria	Assyria			None
56			—— Emmanuel	Son			M	W	7/12	S		Massachusetts	Assyria	Assyria			None
57		71	Rekas, Nicholas	Head	R	40	M	W	45	M	22	Greece	Greece	Greece	Greek	1902	Proprietor
58			—— Virginia	Wife-H			F	W	39	M	36	Greece	Greece	Greece	Greek	1926	None
59			—— Pauline	Daughter			F	W	13	S		Massachusetts	Greece	Greece			None
60			—— Charles	Son			M	W	10	S		Massachusetts	Greece	Greece			None
61			—— Peter	Son			M	W	9	S		Massachusetts	Greece	Greece			None
62			—— Mary	Daughter			F	W	6	S		Massachusetts	Greece	Greece			None
63		72	Twohig, David J.	Head	R	40	M	W	61	M	26	Massachusetts	Irish Free State	Irish Free State			Overseer
64			—— Ellen E.	Wife-H			F	W	56	M	22	Connecticut	Irish Free State	Connecticut			None
65			—— Helen E.	Daughter			F	W	22	S		Rhode Island	Massachusetts	Connecticut			None
66			Scanlon, Ethel M.	Daughter			F	W	30	Wd		Massachusetts	Massachusetts	Connecticut			None
67			—— Irene	Granddaughter			F	W	10	S		Rhode Island	Rhode Island	Massachusetts			None
68			—— Lawrence J.	Grandson			M	W	9	S		Rhode Island	Rhode Island	Massachusetts			None
69			—— Margaret M.	Granddaughter			F	W	3	S		Massachusetts	Rhode Island	Massachusetts			None
70	21 35	73	Butler, Elmer J.	Head	R	35	M	W	49	M	25	Rhode Island	Irish Free State	Irish Free State			Clerk

Seen here is a page from the 1930 census of the United States, which contains the names of the Hoyen family in the initial position. Francis Emmanuel Hoyen and his wife had four children, as can be seen above. Notice the place of birth and language spoken at home is Assyria and Assyrian respectively. The Hoyen family is but one of many who made sure to have it known that Assyria was their country of origin.

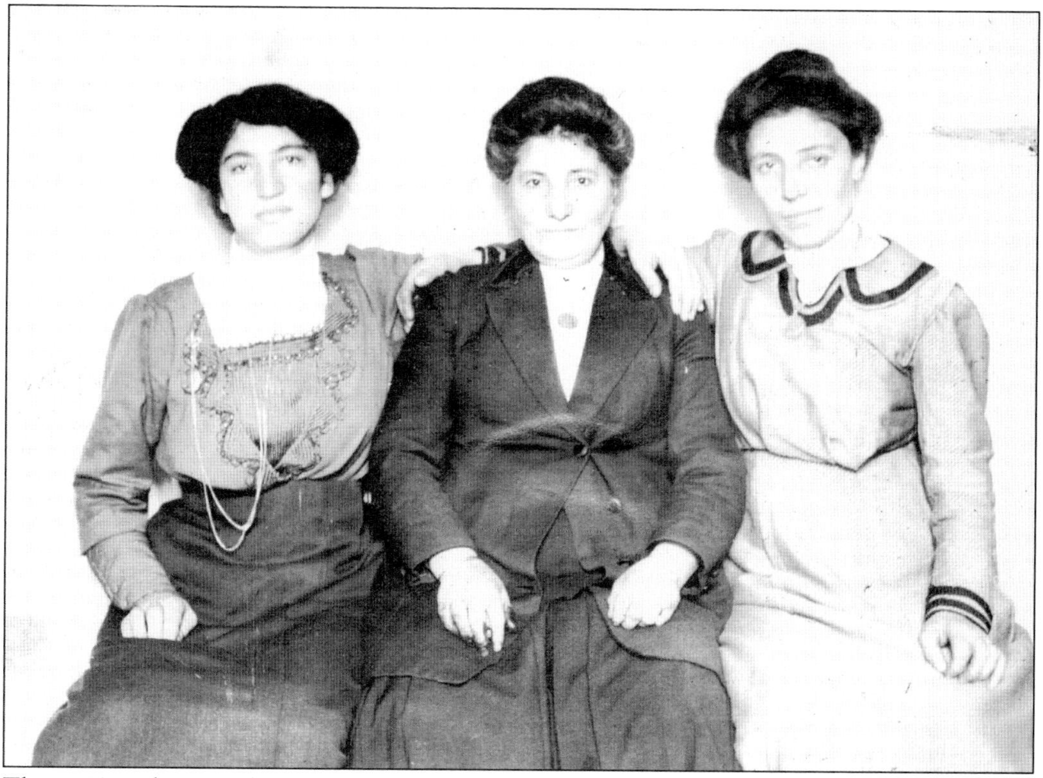

This *c.* 1910 photograph, taken in Worcester, shows, from left to right, Anagil (Anne) Chavoor, Anna Keshish Perch, and Mary Manoog. All three women were born in the town of Harput and immigrated to the United States at the beginning of the 20th century.

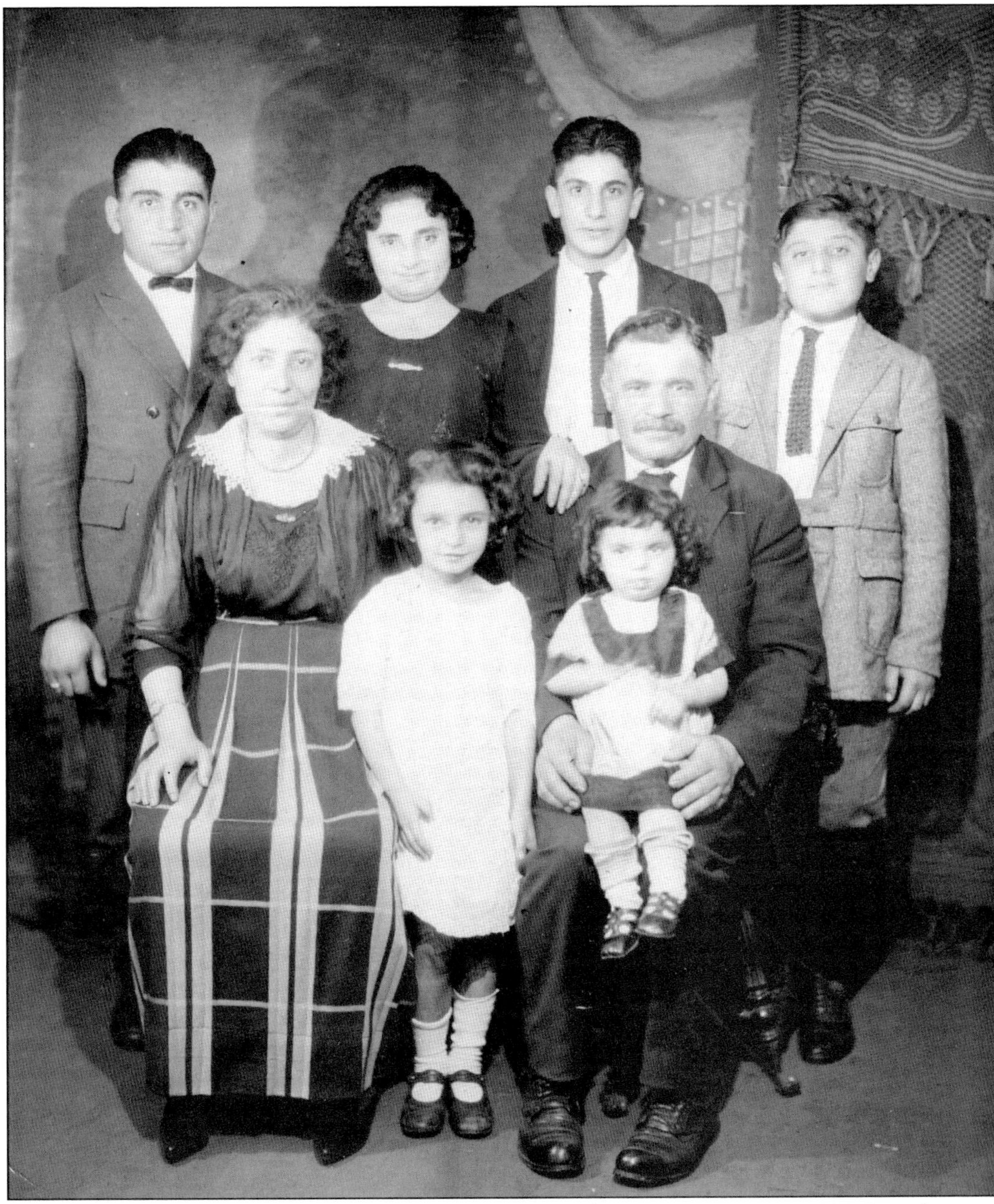

Shown here is a portrait of the Harput Manoog family taken in Worcester in 1922. Seen here are Charles Manoog Jr., John Manoog, Barsom Manoog, Mary Perch, and Charles Manoog Sr.

One of the smaller clans, the Elby family's portrait seen here was taken in 1926. Selim Elby (pictured center) was a well respected figure among the Assyrians in Massachusetts.

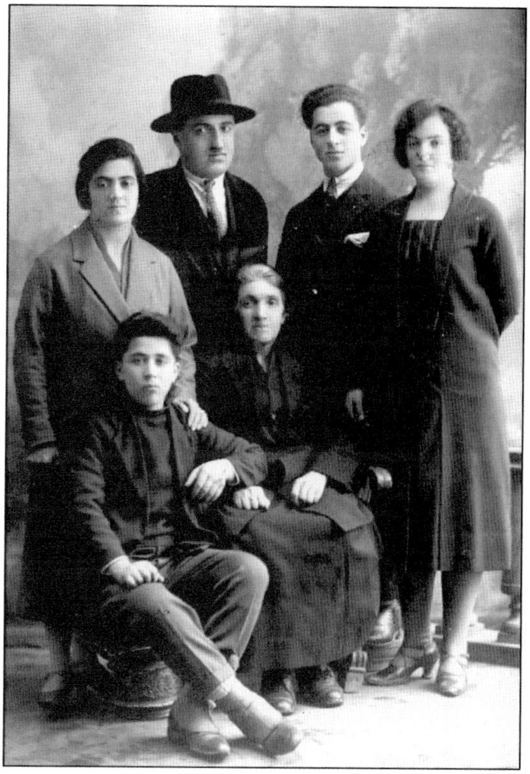

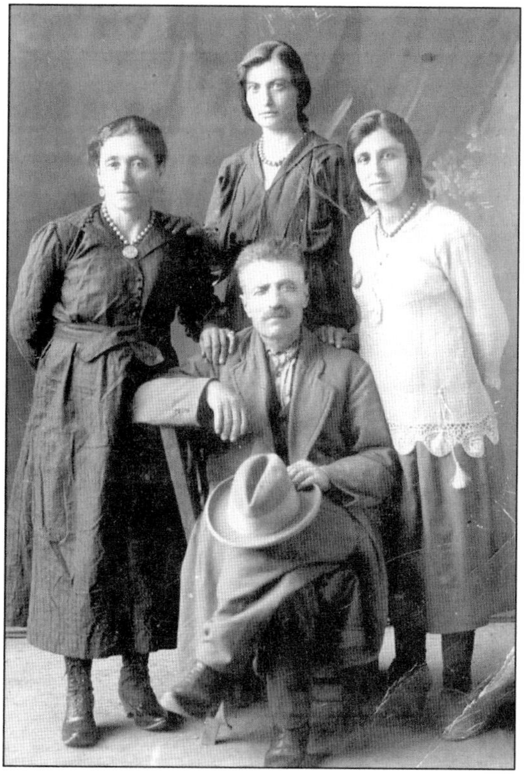

Those pictured in this 1926 photograph are also seen in the large photograph of the dignitary funeral on page 49.

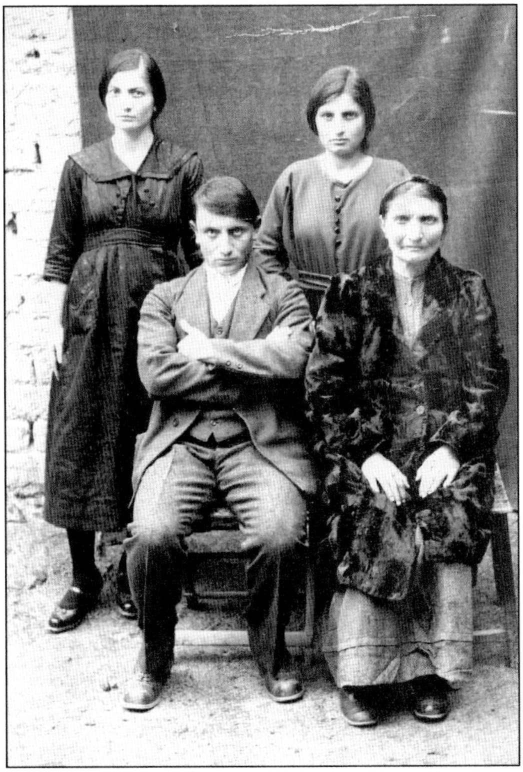

A fair amount of Assyrians passed through Ellis Island on their way to Massachusetts. As stated earlier, the majority of their journey consisted in docking at numerous ports between Turkey and the American coast.

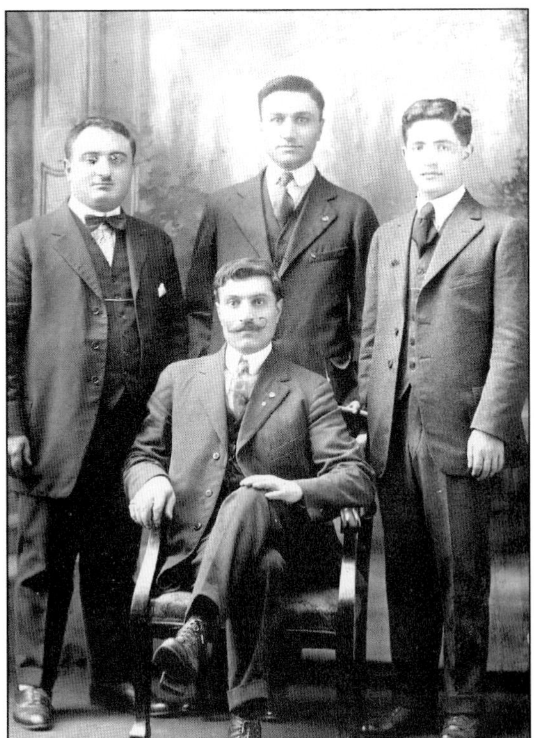

On hand here are both Charles Perch (father of Henry and Harold), top middle, and, on the right, the famous David Barsum Kashish (Perley) in 1920. Why David changed his name from Kashish to Perley is uncertain.

David Perley was known for his philosophical views on Assyrian Nationalism. "Jacobites are Jacobites only by virtue of their religious faith; they are Assyrians by virtue of their nationality. As such they resent any injustice that is directed against any part of their national composition for 'no distance breaks the tie of blood; brothers are brothers evermore.' "

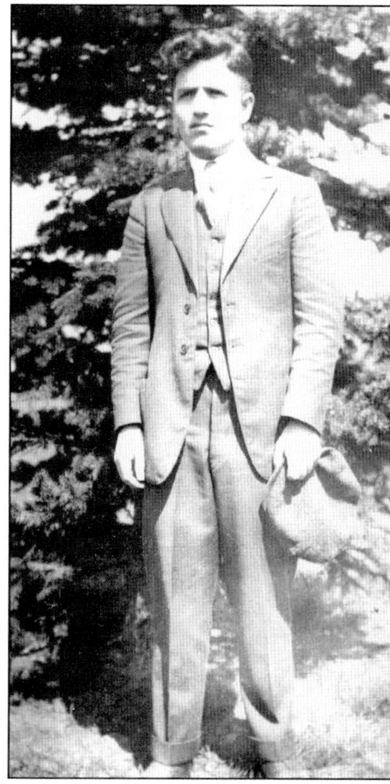

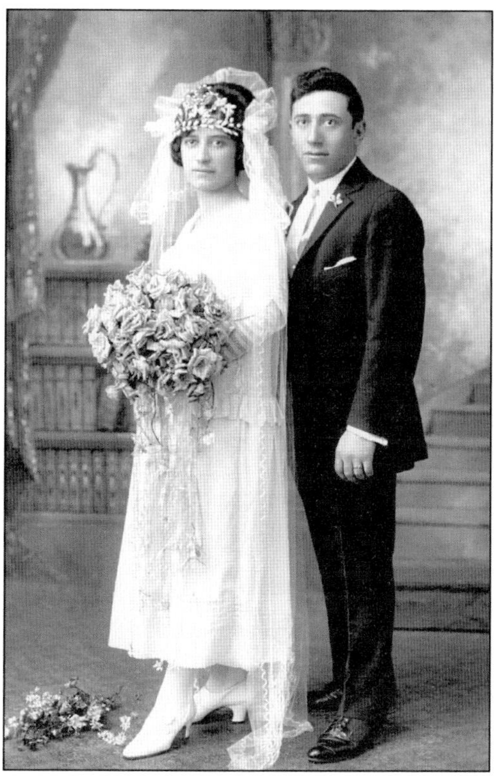

Seen here is another marriage photograph taken in Worcester during the early years of immigration for the Assyrian community to the United States in the beginning of the 20th century.

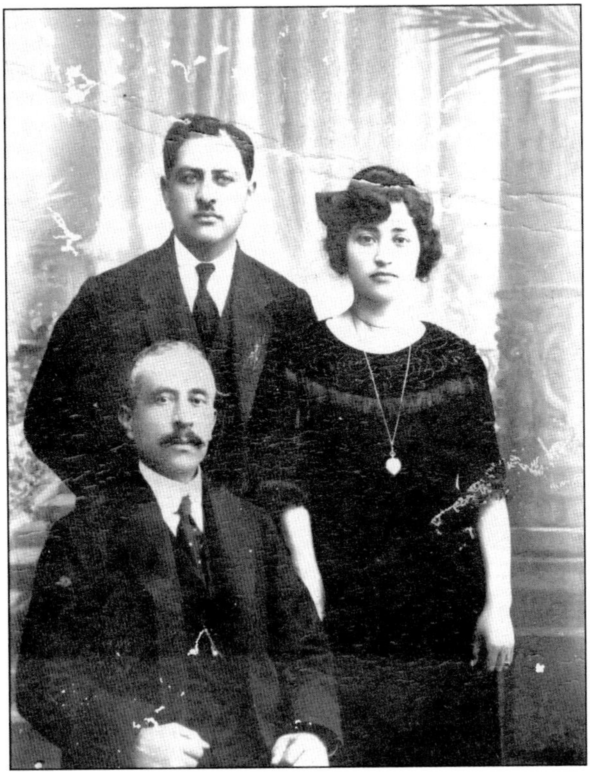

This photograph of the Barsam family, taken in Beirut, Lebanon, is seen here. Rebecca Barsam Perch and her father Artin Barsam are present in the image.

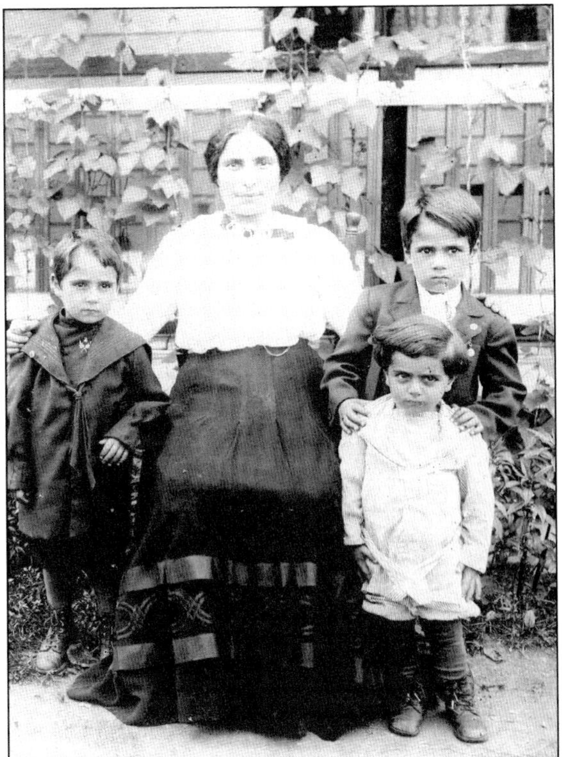

The children in this picture had numerous Assyrian role models to emulate. Of the many prominent Assyrians in Massachusetts were artist John Dasho, activists Ashur and Mack Chavoor, advocate Gabriel Namen, and philosopher and philanthropist David Barsum Perley.

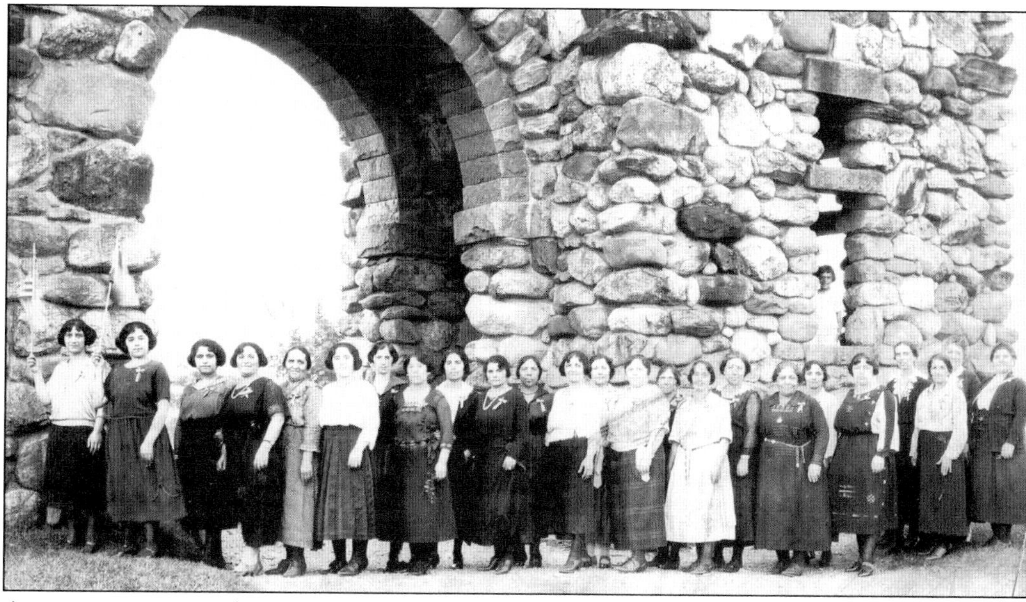

Assyrian women in the Middle East were known for being the most educated as well as most tempered though years of war and hardship. Though the surrounding peoples treated their women as second class, Assyrian women were treated with equality from ancient times to the modern era. Unfortunately, the current rule of the Middle East has aided in the subjugation of all women, and Assyrian women in particular. Assyrian women are seen here at a trip to Bancroft Tower in Worcester around 1923.

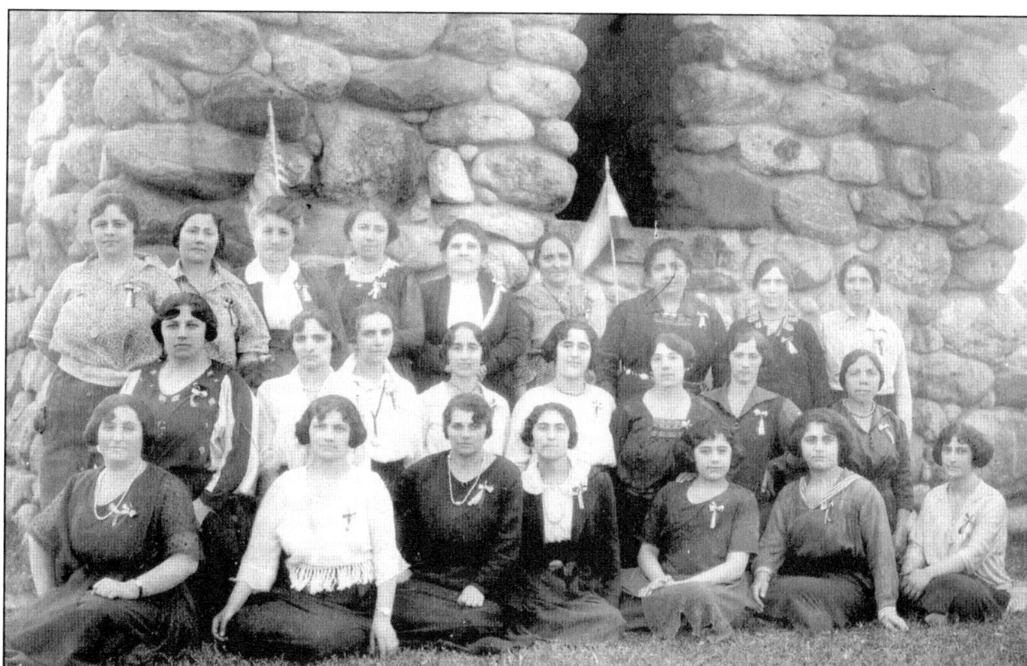

Also taken at Bancroft Tower, the (old) Assyrian and American flags can be seen in the background. Among the attendees are Mary Arslen in the first row, second from right, and Toorvanda Baptist in the third row, fifth from the left.

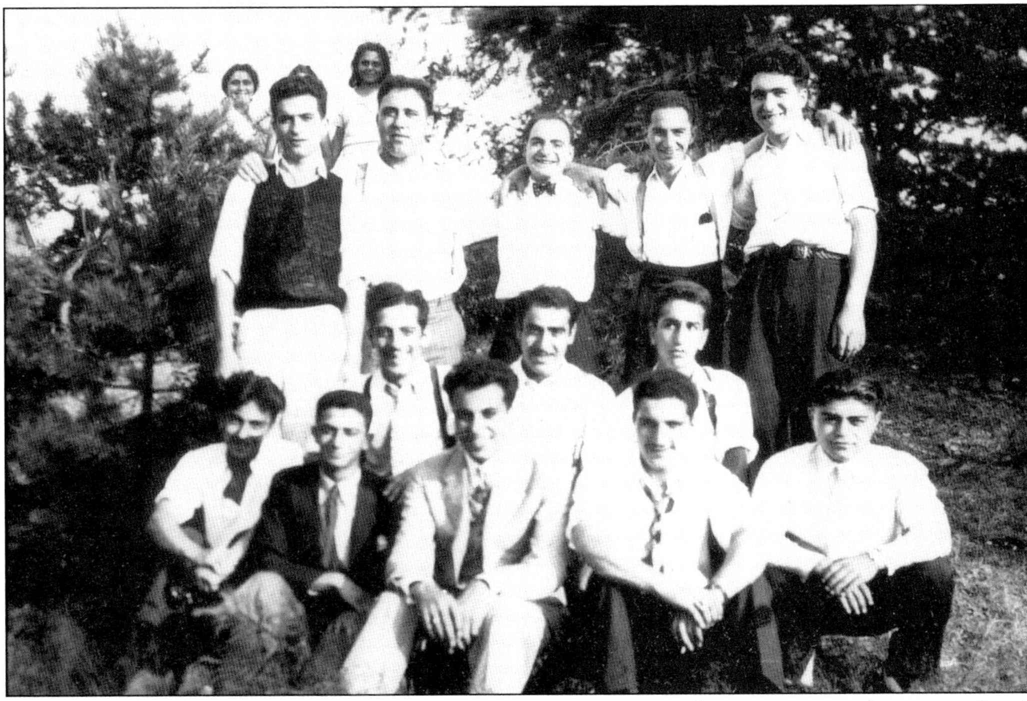

During the early decades of settlement in Massachusetts, picnics and parties occurred every weekend. Staying together was the initially concern of many newly made Americans of Assyrian background.

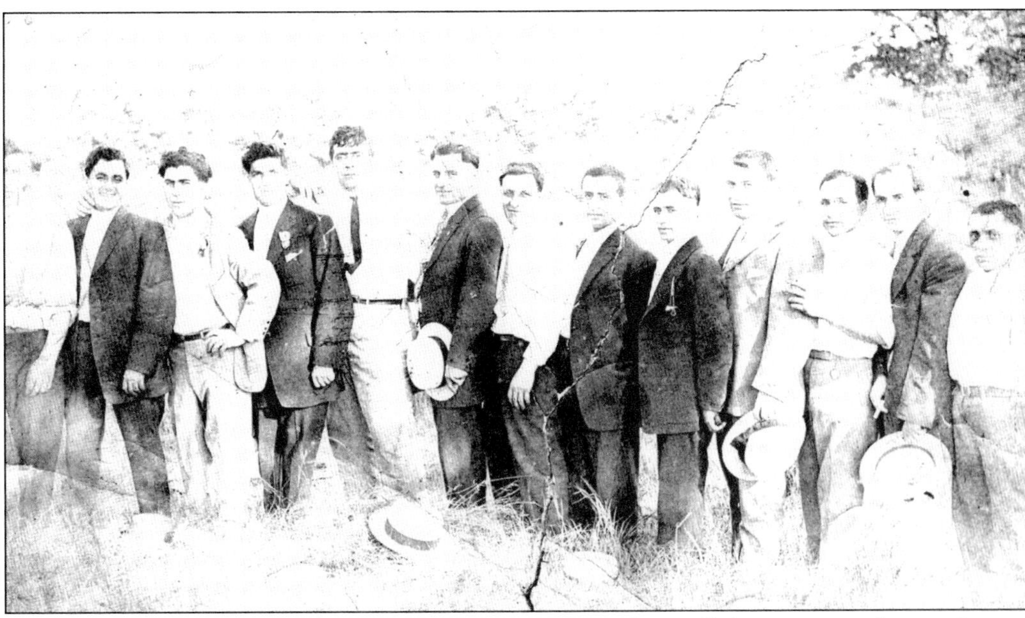

A c. 1920 photograph is seen here of Assyrian men posing for a still shot at an outdoor gathering. Early immigrants used picnics as one of the primary mechanisms of cultural survival, as it provided a common meeting place for recreational activities.

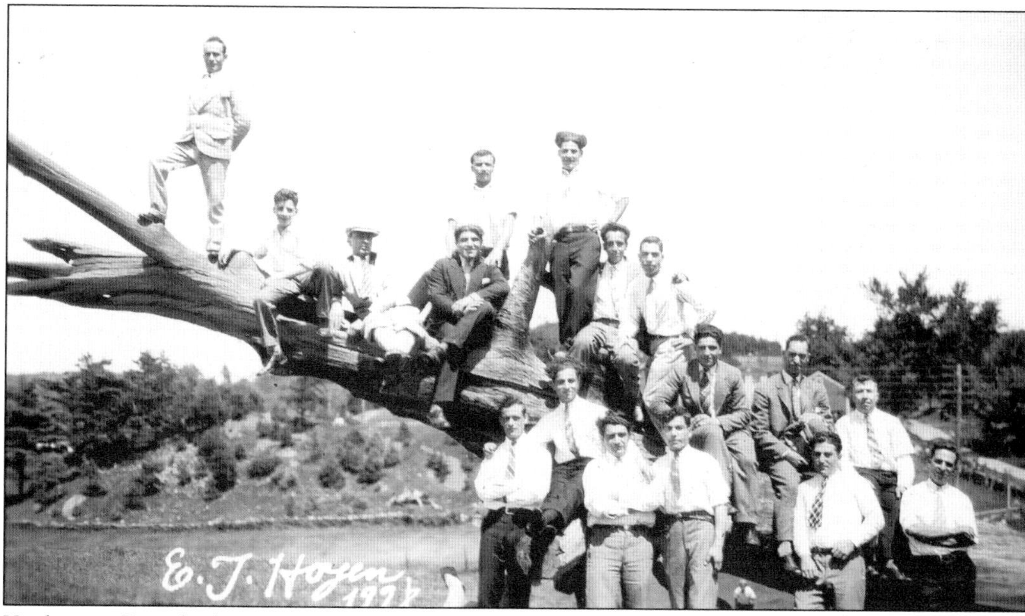

Youhanna Donabed, David Safer, Sam Samuel, and Bishara Donabed are among those posing in this photograph. The above Assyrians were seen regularly together at various events and outings. In fact, many of the young men worked together in various Assyrian cultural and educational assemblies. The photograph was taken by E. T. Hoyen in 1928.

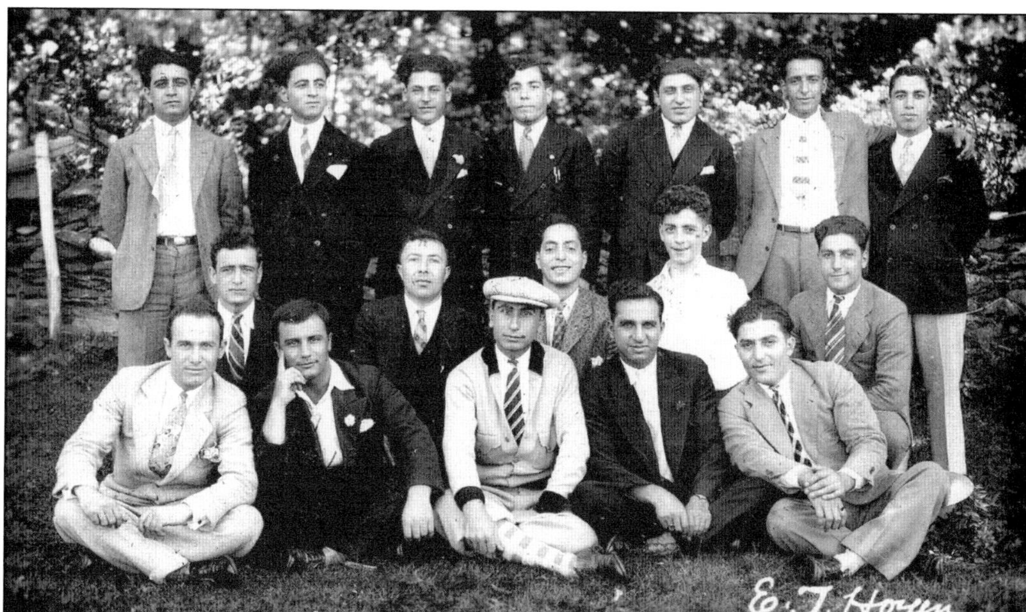

Seated in the frst row, middle is George Donabed from Rhode Island, and to his left is David Safer. Youhanna Donabed is the first man on the left in the second row. Seen in the third row from left to right are Bishara Donabed, Selim Elby, unknown, George Samuel, George Elbag, unknown, and Sam Samuel. This 1928 photograph was one of many copies that circulated the houses of the aforementioned individuals.

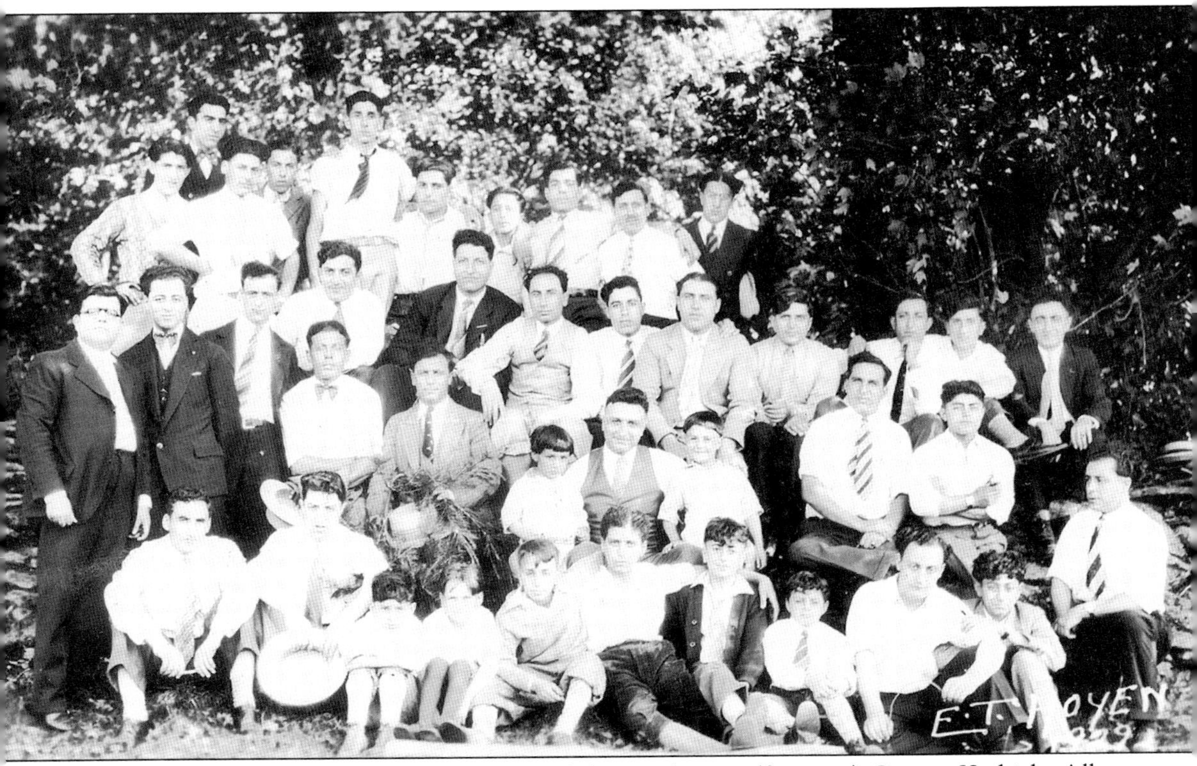

Seen here in this 1929 photograph, from left to right, are (first row) George Kashish, Albert Perch, Bell Azarian, Yousef Papas, John "Bagels" Ohan, Jake Samuel (of California), Emmanuel Perch (son of Zianna), unknown, William Perch, Peter Perch, and Albert Perch; (second row) Abdenoor (Albert) Safer, David Safer, Harold Perch, Charles Perch, Henry Perch, Abe Elbag, and Peter Hoyen; (third row) Charles Safer, Selim Elby, Youhanna Donabed, Mack Chavoor, Daniel Alexander, George Donabed (of Rhode Island), Samuel Samuel, William Baptist, Jacob Chavoor, Simon Arslen, Art Arslen, and George Hoyen; (fourth row) George Ovanes, Kasper Saffer, George Elbag, Herbert George, Kander ?, unknown, Mr. Elby, unknown, George Samuel, and Alfred George.

Four

Secular Organizations and Events

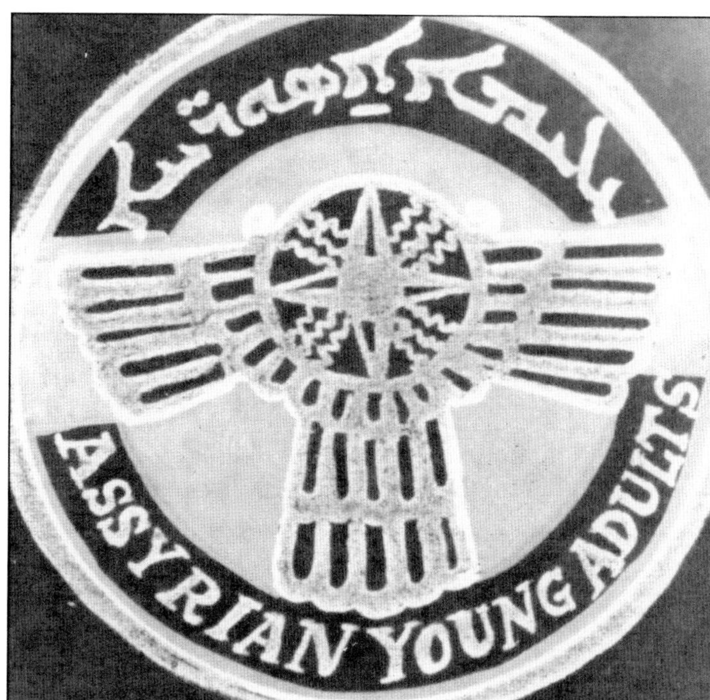

The crest of the Assyrian Young Adults Association was established on November 5, 1972, in Worcester. The aims of the Assyrian Young Adults Association were as follows: "To encourage and strengthen the relationship between Assyrian young people; to create a generation that realizes its obligation to its people, and to preserve the Assyrian heritage, dignity and American democracy." Dues were $6.

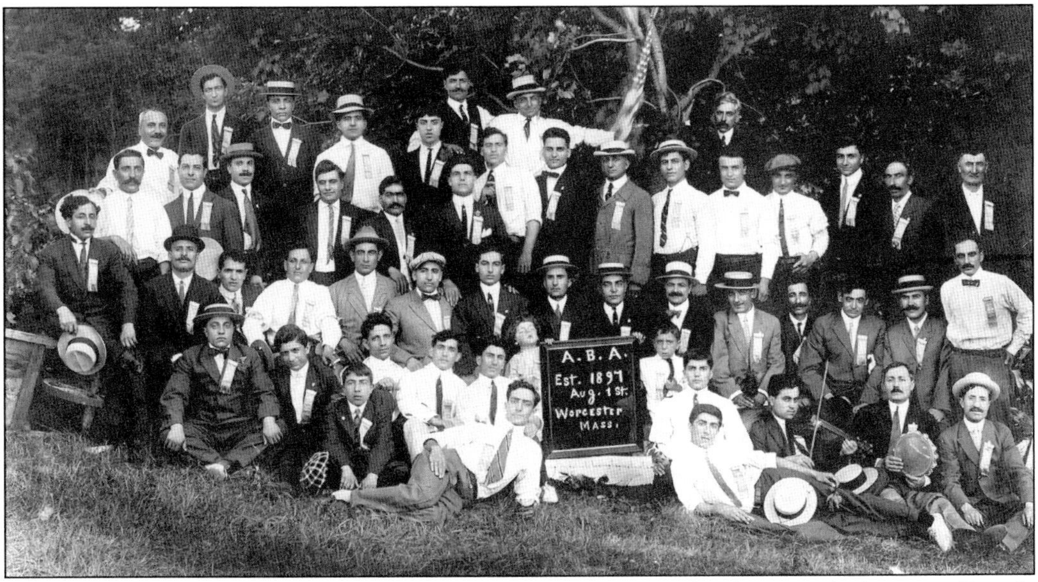

Established in 1897 and incorporated in 1911 in Worcester, the (Harpoot) Assyrian Benefit Association helped Assyrian refugees fleeing after the Ottoman massacres of 1895–1896. Seen in the 1914 photograph are Colombus, Simon Dasho, Albert Perch, Bishara (Avedis) Chavoor, Dr Abraham K. Yousef, Paul Perch, Mike Keshish Perley, Charles Perch, Simon Ohan, Yacoub Elbag, Albert Chavoor, Arakel Ohan, Charles Bedig, Simon Barsam, Peter Perch, Kasper Dasho, Arthur Chavoor, Jacob Ohan, Teddy Arslen, Nishan Ohan, and Dave Eskender.

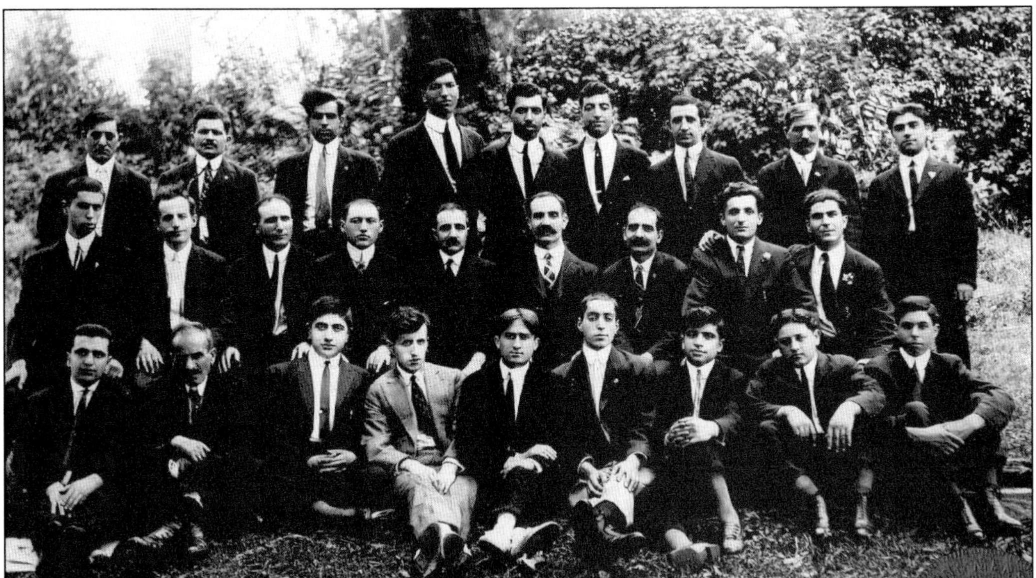

The Assyrian Young Men's Association of Boston was established on October 1, 1912. In the second generation, many such organizations disappeared with community assimilation. Other associations in New England included the Assyrian Five Association of Boston, Assyrian St. Ephrem Association of Central Falls, Rhode Island, Assyrian Mar Afrem Benevolent Society of Lowell, Harpoot Assyrian United Educational Fund, Assyrian Ladies Association of Worcester (established in 1908), and the Assyrian Benefit Association of Worcester (established in 1897).

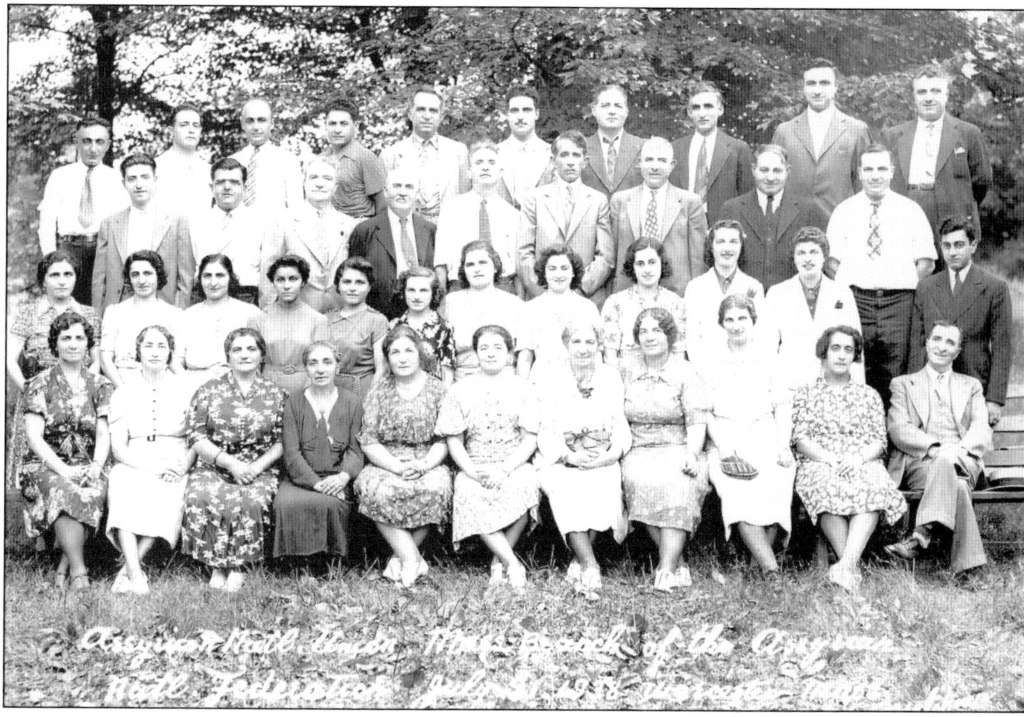

This is the membership photograph of the Assyrian National Union, an affiliate member of the Assyrian American National Federation, taken on July 31, 1938, in Worcester. Some known members in the second row are Mary Arslen, Mary Baptist, Hazel Saffer, Annie Perch, Phyllis Arslen, Annie Pappas, Stella Arslen, Dorothy Perch, and Rose Perch.

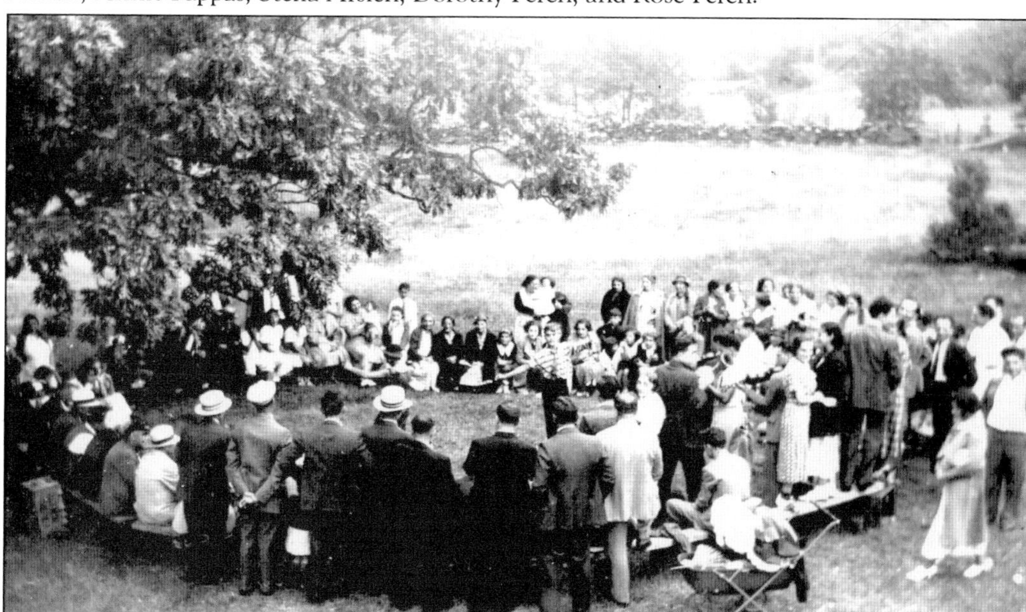

A young boy dances at the picnic of the Assyrian National Union, which took place on August 11, 1935, in Worcester. Though sponsored by the Assyrian National Union, all events were open to Assyrians and non-Assyrians alike for the purpose of reveling in the Assyrian culture.

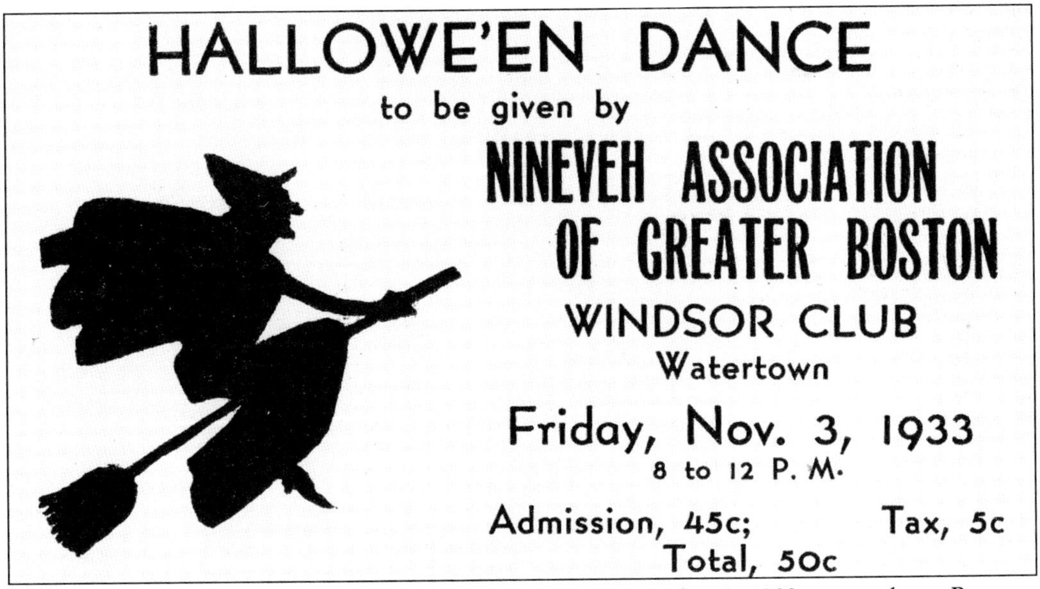

An invitation to a Halloween party in Watertown, on November 3, 1933, is seen here. Because they settled where they could find employment, especially in the textile industry, the Assyrians of Massachusetts opened a series of associations all over the Commonwealth. Then as today, such events aim to raise funds, often for cultural and educational activities in the Middle East. Since the Simele massacre in Iraq had occurred a few months before this dance, in August 1933, the organizers probably fund-raised for relief for the surviving widows and orphans.

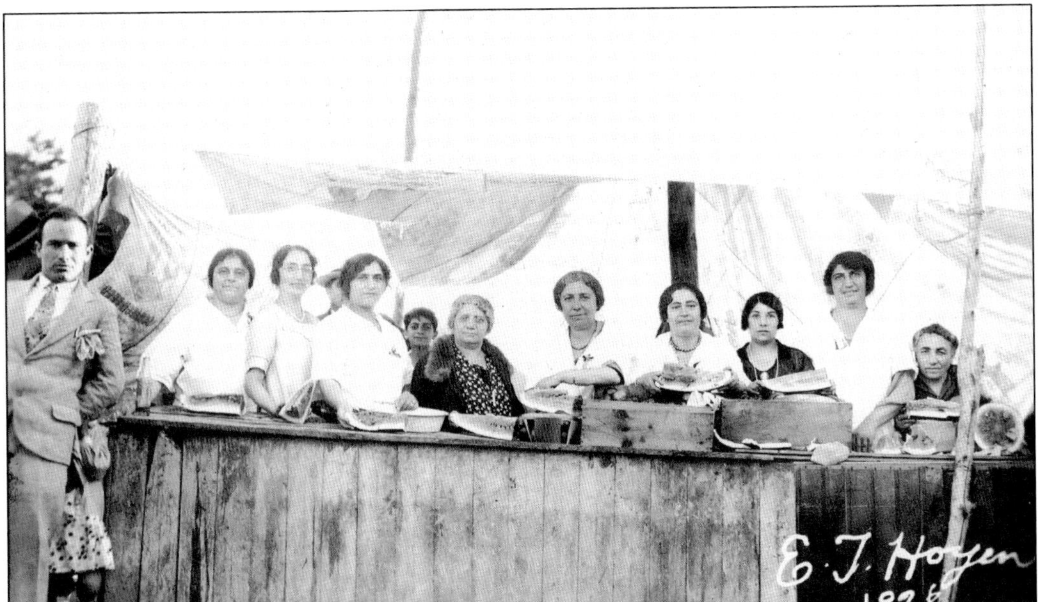

Phyllis (Arslen) Saffer (far left), at six years old, hides behind a man during a 1928 picnic. Each association held events regularly which were open to the public. On many occasions, Assyrians entertained American dignitaries with their folk music and dance, and exotic food dishes.

This is the New Year's Eve Party and Frolic flyer of the United Assyrian Association of Massachusetts, which took place on December 31, 1951, in Boston. Music for the evening was provided by David Safer, George Ohan and Company, regulars at Assyrian events. David Safer was a violinist while George Ohan played the oud, a typical Assyrian instrument.

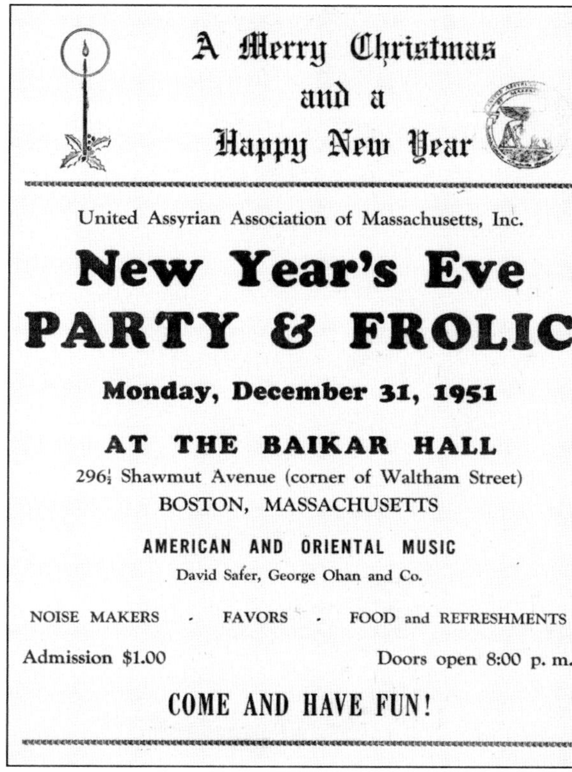

A Merry Christmas
and a
Happy New Year

United Assyrian Association of Massachusetts, Inc.

New Year's Eve
PARTY & FROLIC

Monday, December 31, 1951

AT THE BAIKAR HALL

296½ Shawmut Avenue (corner of Waltham Street)
BOSTON, MASSACHUSETTS

AMERICAN AND ORIENTAL MUSIC
David Safer, George Ohan and Co.

NOISE MAKERS - FAVORS - FOOD and REFRESHMENTS

Admission $1.00 Doors open 8:00 p. m.

COME AND HAVE FUN!

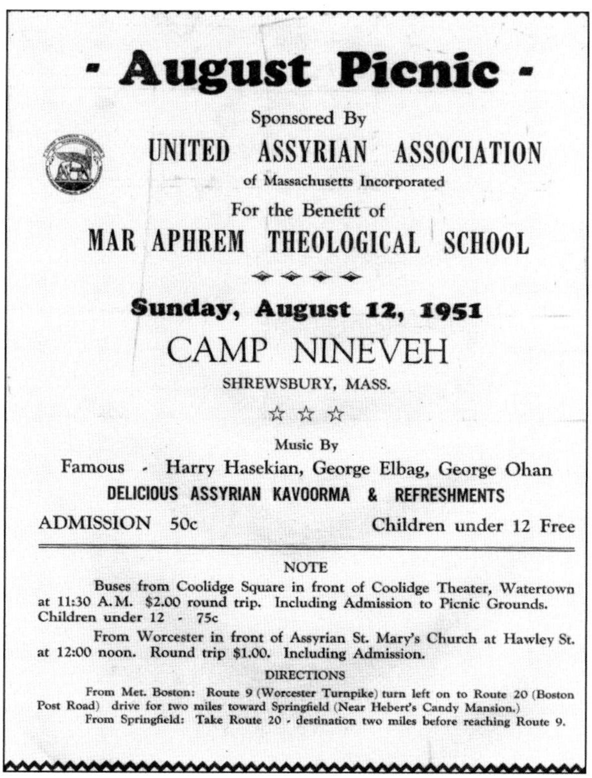

- August Picnic -

Sponsored By
UNITED ASSYRIAN ASSOCIATION
of Massachusetts Incorporated
For the Benefit of
MAR APHREM THEOLOGICAL SCHOOL

Sunday, August 12, 1951

CAMP NINEVEH
SHREWSBURY, MASS.

☆ ☆ ☆

Music By
Famous - Harry Hasekian, George Elbag, George Ohan
DELICIOUS ASSYRIAN KAVOORMA & REFRESHMENTS

ADMISSION 50c Children under 12 Free

NOTE

Buses from Coolidge Square in front of Coolidge Theater, Watertown at 11:30 A.M. $2.00 round trip. Including Admission to Picnic Grounds. Children under 12 - 75c

From Worcester in front of Assyrian St. Mary's Church at Hawley St. at 12:00 noon. Round trip $1.00. Including Admission.

DIRECTIONS

From Met. Boston: Route 9 (Worcester Turnpike) turn left on to Route 20 (Boston Post Road) drive for two miles toward Springfield (Near Hebert's Candy Mansion.)
From Springfield: Take Route 20 - destination two miles before reaching Route 9.

Shown here is the flyer for the August Picnic of the United Assyrian Association of Massachusetts (UAAM) for the benefit of the Mar Aphem Theological School, which supported Assyrian clergy. It took place on August 12, 1951, on the grounds of Camp Nineveh, which was purchased by the UAAM for the purpose of holding Assyrian gatherings (for example, picnics, parties, and barbecues). The music of the day was provided by George Ohan and Company with Assyrian singer George Elbag.

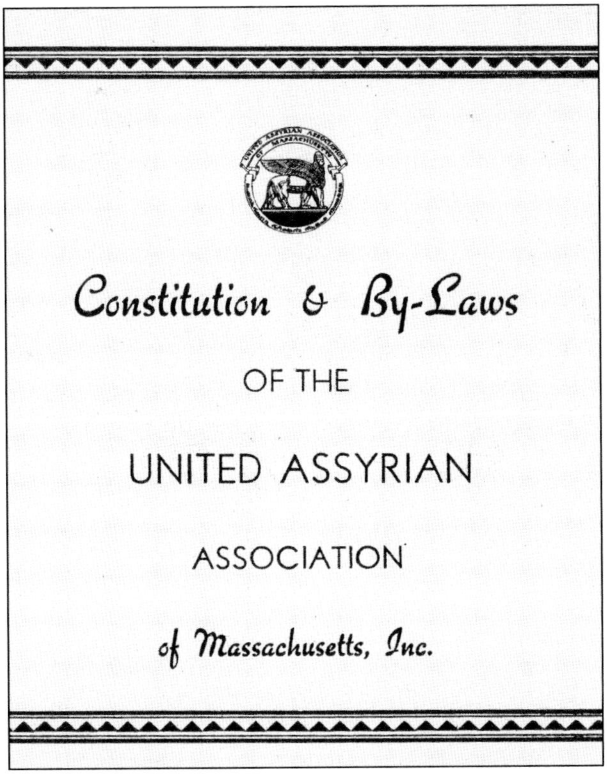

Constitution & By-Laws

OF THE

UNITED ASSYRIAN

ASSOCIATION

of Massachusetts, Inc.

The United Assyrian Association of Massachusetts was incorporated on June 9, 1949. The UAAM, which is an active organization to this day, was created through the merger of the following organizations: Assyrian Boston United Association, Harpoot United Association, Assyrian National Union, and the Assyrian American Progressive Union. The UAAM was the hosting affiliate of the Assyrian American National Federation Convention, which was held in September 2005 at the Sheraton in Boston.

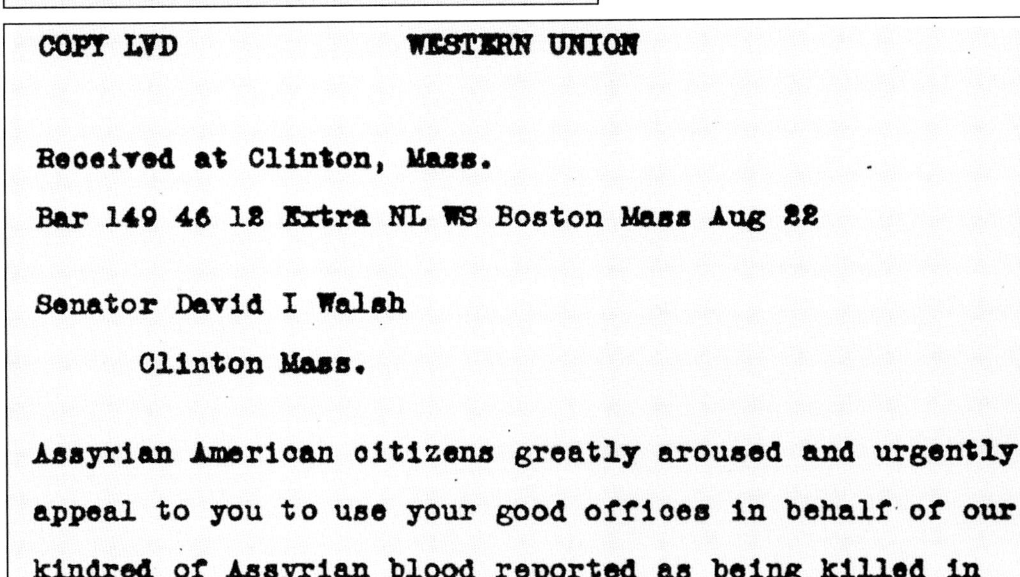

COPY LVD WESTERN UNION

Received at Clinton, Mass.

Bar 149 46 12 Extra NL WS Boston Mass Aug 22

Senator David I Walsh

Clinton Mass.

Assyrian American citizens greatly aroused and urgently appeal to you to use your good offices in behalf of our kindred of Assyrian blood reported as being killed in massacres by Kurds and Iraq forces.

Seen here is a letter sent to U.S. senator David I. Walsh from Harry G. Bedig, president of the United Assyrian Association of Boston. The date of the letter is August 22, 1933, less than two weeks after the violent massacres of thousands of unarmed Assyrian men, woman, and children in and around Simele at the hands of the Iraqi Army and Kurds.

The program of the 29th annual Assyrian American National Federation (AANF) convention, held on Labor Day weekend of 1962, in Boston, is seen here. The AANF was established in 1933 after the horrid massacres at Simele and Deirabon. Its original purpose was to enlighten the public to the atrocities faced by Assyrians worldwide, and to further the pursuit of a homeland.

The Twenty-ninth
ASSYRIAN AMERICAN
FEDERATION CONVENTION

August 30, 31, September 1, 2, 3
1962

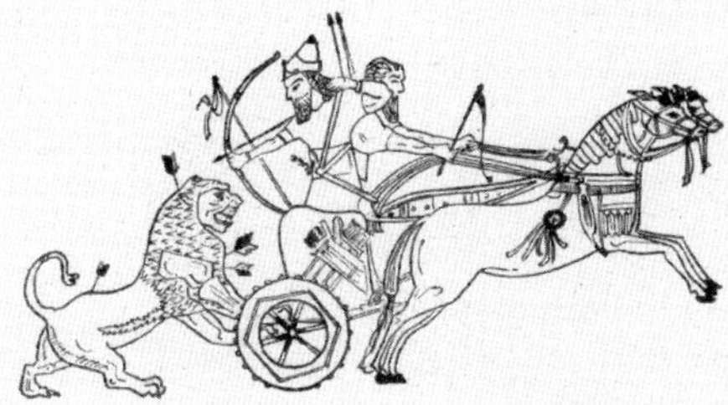

STATLER-HILTON HOTEL

Boston, Massachusetts

September 3, 1962

MONDAY

10 A.M. to ?

ANNUAL FEDERATION PICNIC

Sponsored by

UNITED ASSYRIAN ASSOCIATION
OF MASSACHUSETTS

CAMP NINEVEH

ROUTE 20—SHREWSBURY, MASSACHUSETTS
(next to Hebert Candy Mansion)

SHI-KA-BA, REFRESHMENTS
AND
MUSIC BY
ARTIE BARSAMIAN

Chairman
KASPER SAFFER

The UAAM was the hosting affiliate of the above convention. The UAAM and its chairman, Kasper Saffer, set the bar for future conventions. It was not until 2005 that the national convention returned to the Boston area.

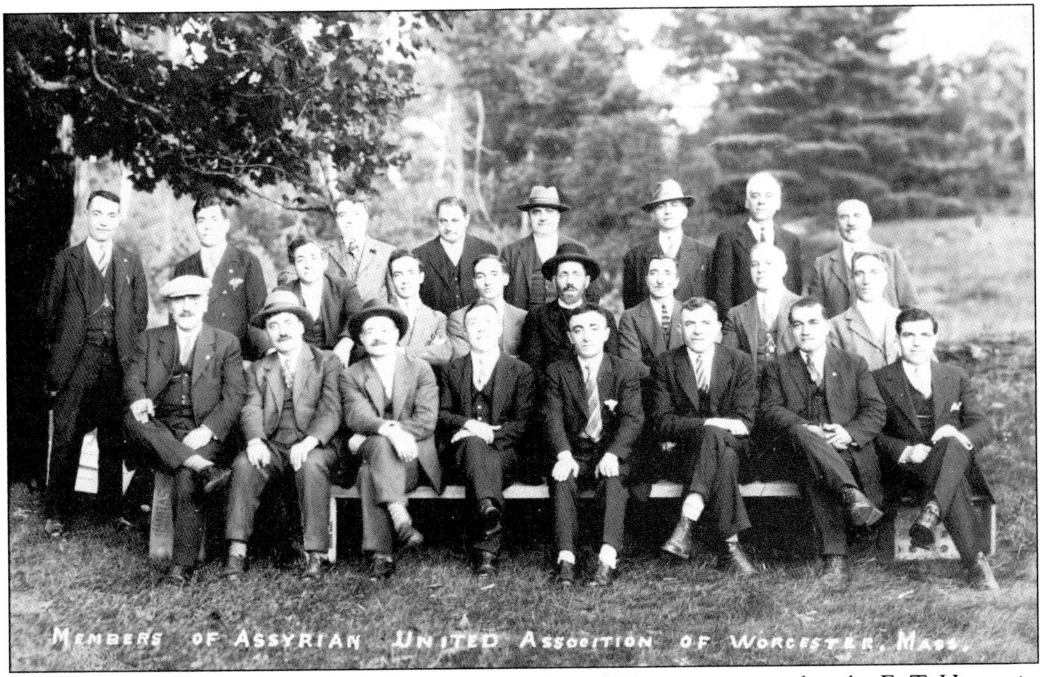

This photograph of the Assyrian United Association of Worcester, was taken by E. T. Hoyen in 1928. Pictured are George Samuel (second in from top left), George Hoyen, Paul Perch, Sahag Perch, Charles Yousef, Ilbag Ilbag, Beshara Perch, Yacoub Elbag, Nishan Ohan, Albert Chavoor, Fr. Favlos (Paul) Samuel, Peter Elbag, Anton Ohan, Paul Perch, Simon Ohan, John Ohan, Charlie Ohan, Barsam Iskender, George Hoyen, Barsam Barsam, George Hoyen, and Harry Hoyen.

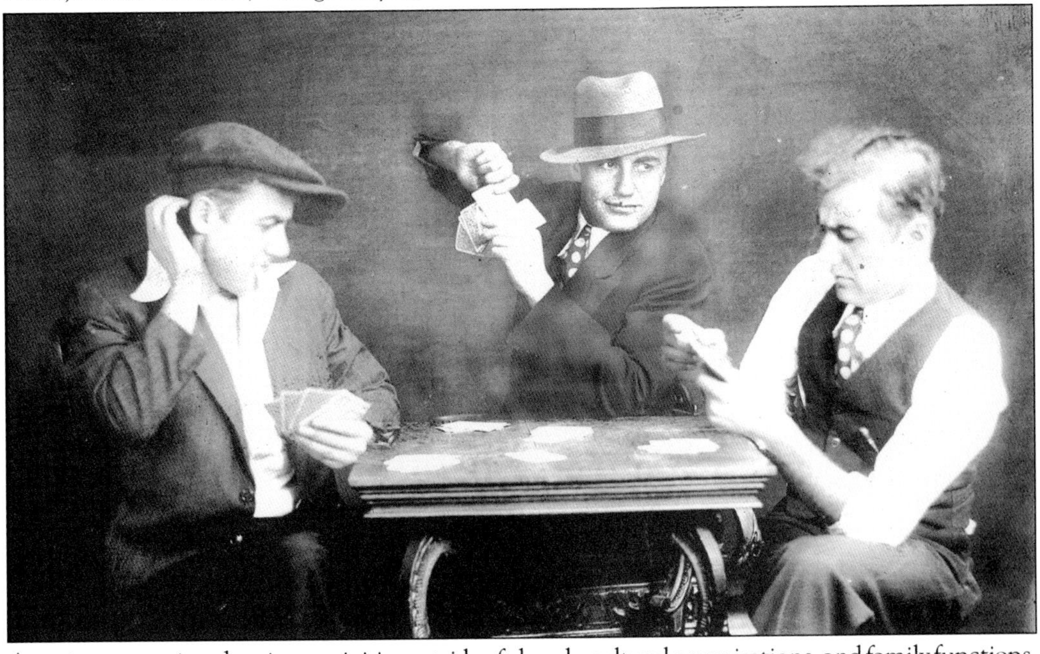

Assyrian men enjoyed various activities outside of church, cultural organizations, and family functions. Sports and card playing were favorite pastimes of the first and second generation Assyrians. Chess and Backgammon were among the favorite strategy games played on a regular basis.

A page from *The New Assyria* periodical, volume I number 10, from June 15, 1917, was a brilliant display of publishing that spoke to Assyrians of various church sects and countries of origin. Unfortunately, many of these old divisions have resurfaced through church and political leaders.

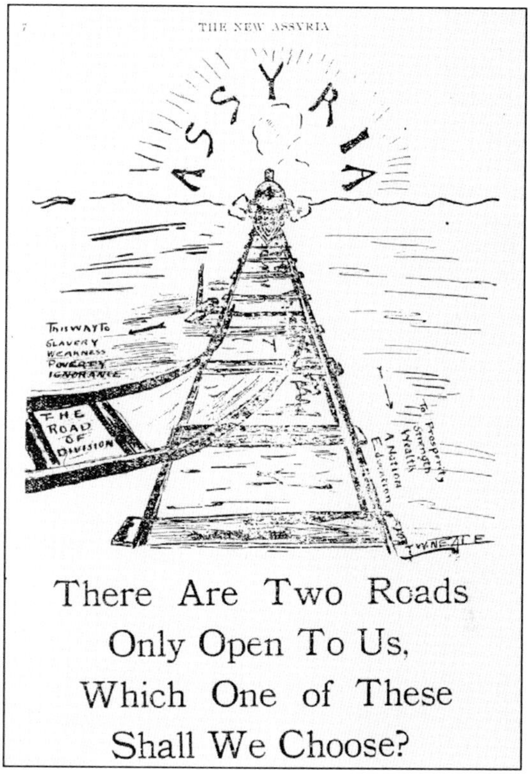

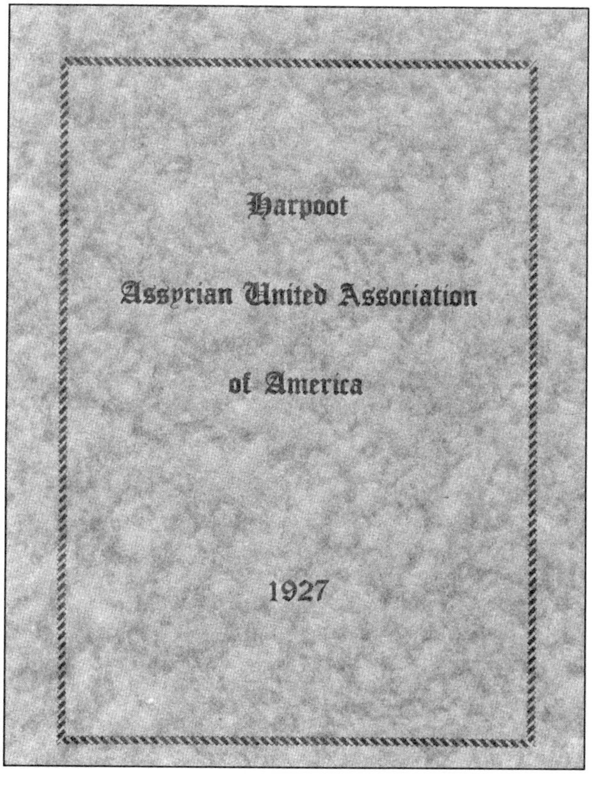

These are the bylaws of the Harpoot Assyrian United Association of America. Established in Worcester, in 1927, the organization was first only open to "Jacobite Assyrians of Harpoot" before broadening its membership base.

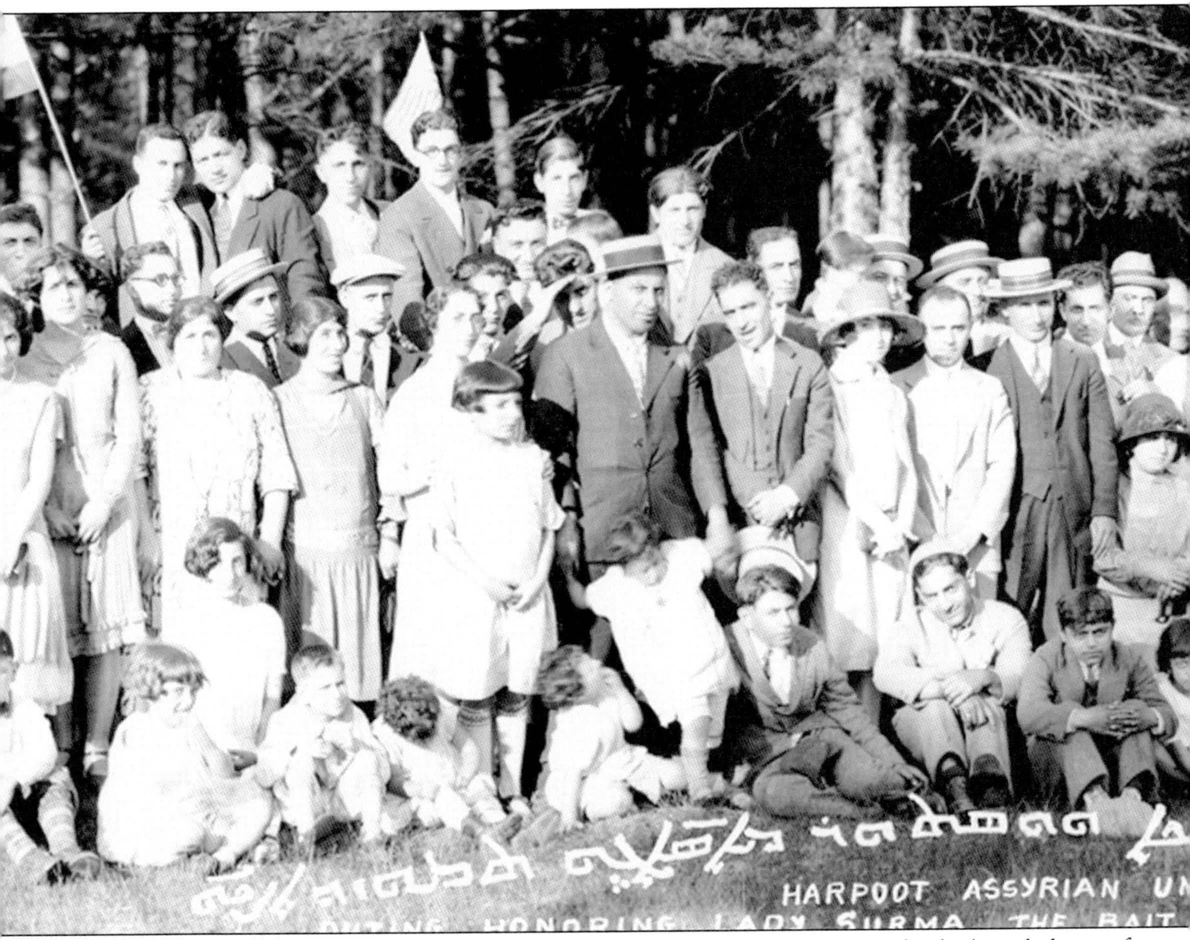

Assyrians of the Jacobite rite (today incorrectly called Syrian/Syriac Orthodox) and those of the Nestorian (Church of the East) paid no heed to ecclesiastical differences as seen here in the July 4, 1926, picnic to honor Lady Surma, sister of the Church of the East patriarch who was martyred at the hands of Kurdish insurgents. Among the over 300 people in attendance were Paul and Sophia Perch, George Donabed, Sophia Simonian, Almas Elbag Namen, George Hoyen, Farida Elbag Tashjy, Mabel Ohan, the Papaz family, Arakel Ohan, Albert Perch, Evelyn Bedig,

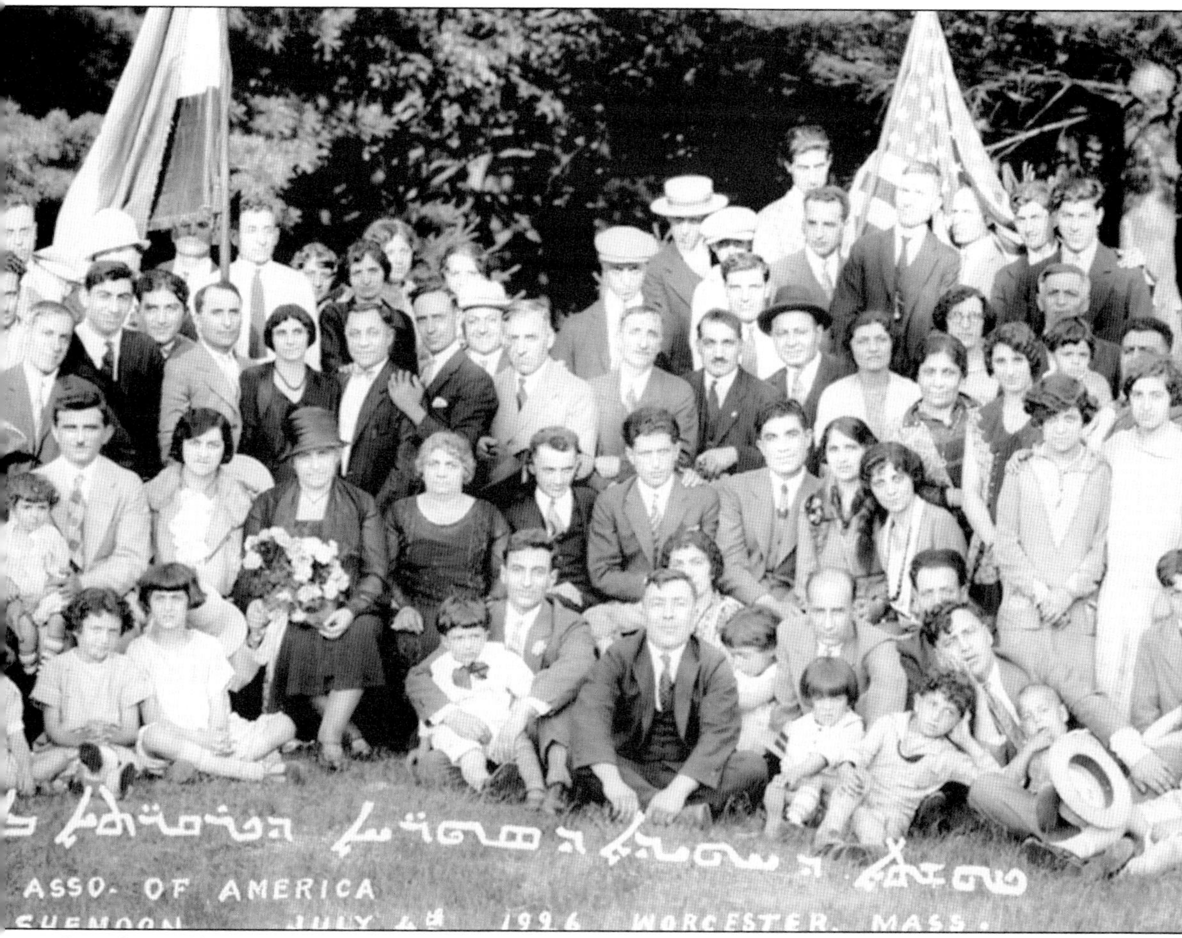

Josephine Ohan Forget, Lucia Ohan, Sartenig Arslen, Alice Perch, Nazli Hoyen, Mary Perch Andon, Yullita Elbag Perch, Mary Perch Andon, Sargon Hoyen, Gabriel Namen, Ibrahim Elbag, Elizabeth Johnson Manoog, Anne Hoyen Elbag, Albert Perch, Dave Johnson, Alice Alexander, Saliba Alexander, B. C. Manoog, Sahag Perch, Arthur Chavoor, Jacob Chavoor, Peter Hoyen, Albert Chavoor, Ashur Chavoor, Barsam Barsam, Emmanuel Perch, Zianna Donabed Perch, Ann Kurkjy, Francis Hoyen, and Mary Perch Manoog.

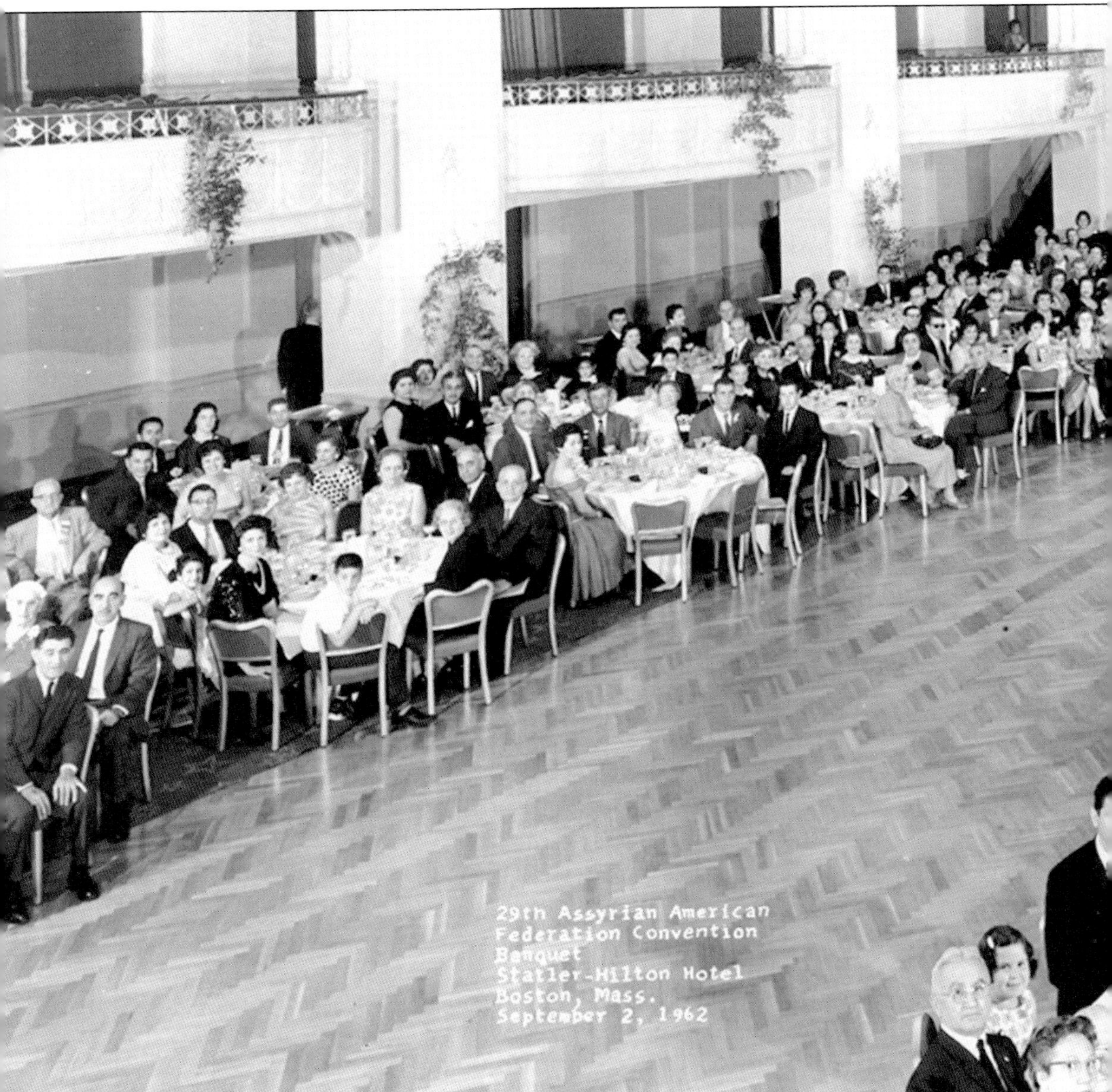

This photograph, taken on September 2, 1962, shows the Assyrian American National Federation (AANF) annual Convention Banquet at the Statler-Hilton hotel in Boston. The AANF president during the convention proceedings was Malcolm Karam. Seen in the image are George Donabed of Milton, Juliet Donabed, Helen Safer, Rose Deinha, Sadie Samuel, Sam Samuel, Bishara (Avidis) Donabed, Roumel Donabed, Helen Kazar, George Donabed

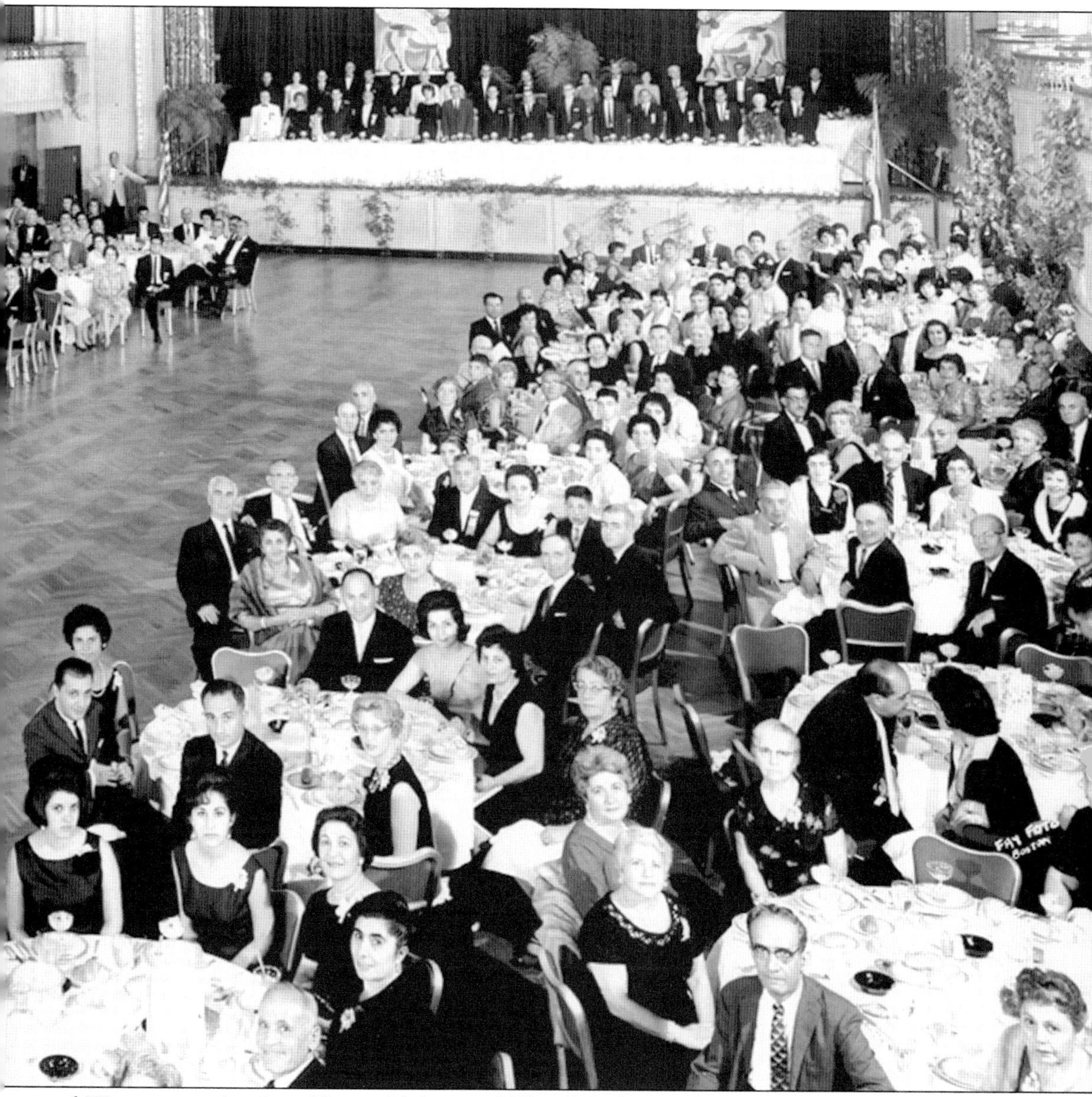

of Watertown, AnnLou Kazar, Abdenoor (Albert) Safer, Youhanna (John) Donabed, Janice Kazar Maritza Kashish, Jurjies Kashish, George Elbag, Ann Elbag, George Samuel family, Aram Donabed, Ann Donabed, Ralph Donabed, Aram Donabed Jr., Joe Kurkjy, Ann Kurkjy, Larry Kurkjy, Peters Family, Jacob Tashjy and wife, Kasper Saffer, George Ovannes, Ben Donabed, Albert Samuel, Francis Hoyen, and Charles Mannik and wife.

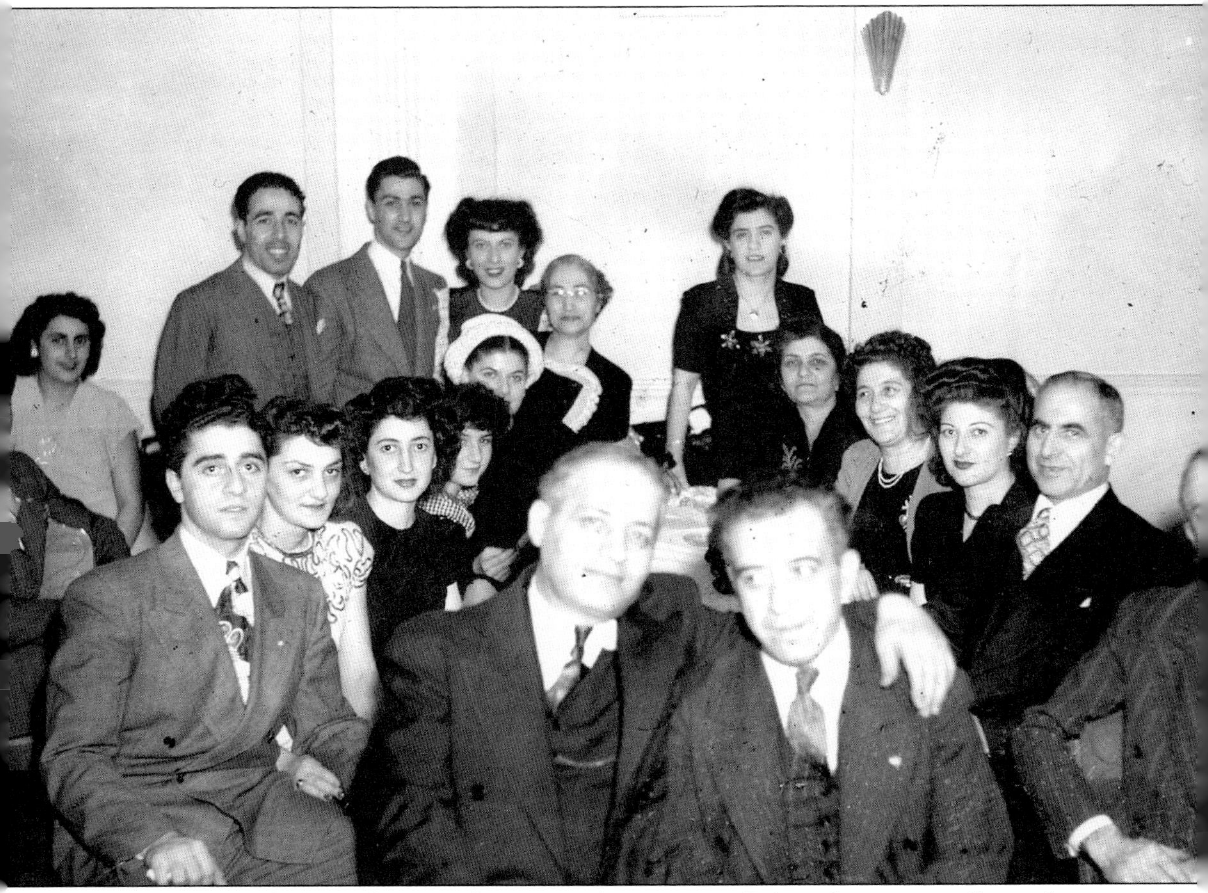

This photograph shows the United Assyrian Association of Massachusetts installation banquet in 1948. The United Assyrian Association of Massachusetts was an incorporation of the Assyrian Boston United Association, Harpoot United Association, Assyrian National Union, and the Assyrian American Progressive Union. Identified in the image are Youhanna Donabed (cut off on the far right), Bishara Donabed, Charlie Mannik (center), Sam Samuel, Henry Perch, and Rebecca Perch.

Five

RELIGIOUS INSTITUTIONS

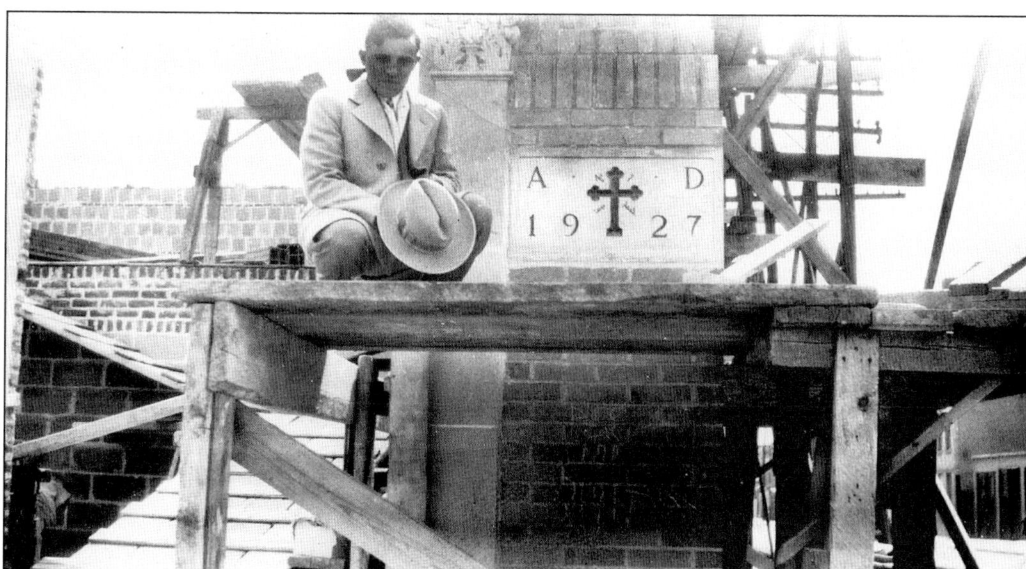

The laying of the foundation of St. Mary's Assyrian Apostolic Church of Antioch in 1927, at 17 Hawley Street in Worcester, was a momentous occasion. The Board of Trustees, which consisted of Charles Manoog, Aaron Saffer, Bishara Perch, Albert Chavoor, Mendoohie Ohan, Lucy Donabed, and Dr. Abraham K. Yousef, purchased the land for $1,200 in 1923. This structure was eventually sold and a new building was purchased at 1 Industrial Drive in Shrewsbury.

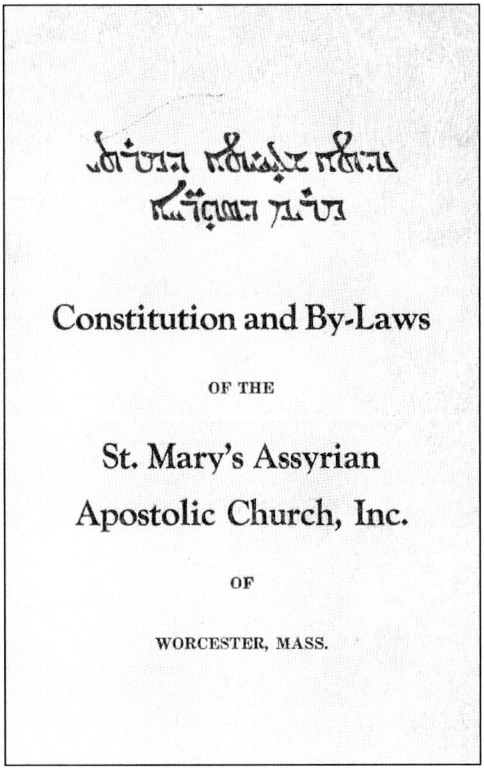

Constitution and By-Laws

OF THE

St. Mary's Assyrian

Apostolic Church, Inc.

OF

WORCESTER, MASS.

The Constitution and Bylaws of the St. Mary's Assyrian Apostolic Church, located in Worcester, are seen here. The church went through various changes of development and decay. In fact, the name of the church has even changed numerous times since its establishment in 1927. The church, originally called the Assyrian Apostolic Church of Antioch, was changed to the Assyrian Orthodox Church of Antioch. Sadly, the current name of the church is the Syrian Orthodox Church of Antioch. The final change came under pressure from Middle Eastern governments to eradicate the Assyrian identity.

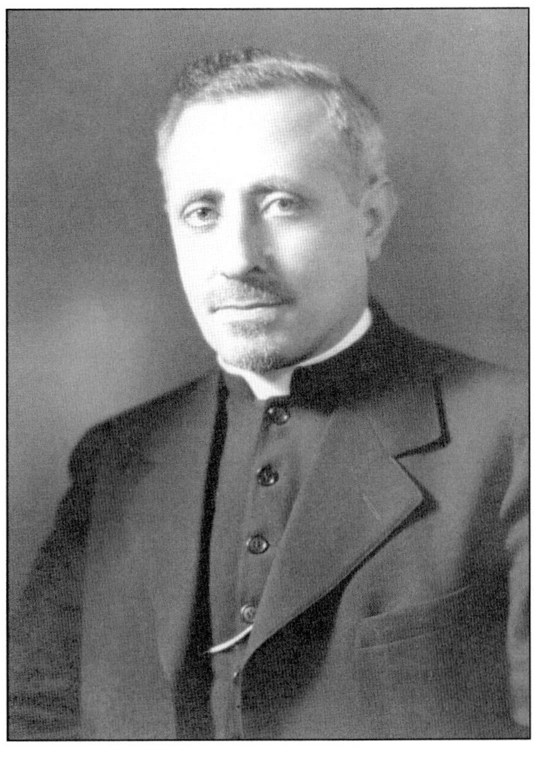

The Reverend Peter Barsoum, who filled the void left by the aging Rev. Favlos Samuel (served from 1927 to 1933), was at St. Mary's Assyrian Apostolic Church of Antioch in Worcester from 1933 to 1963.

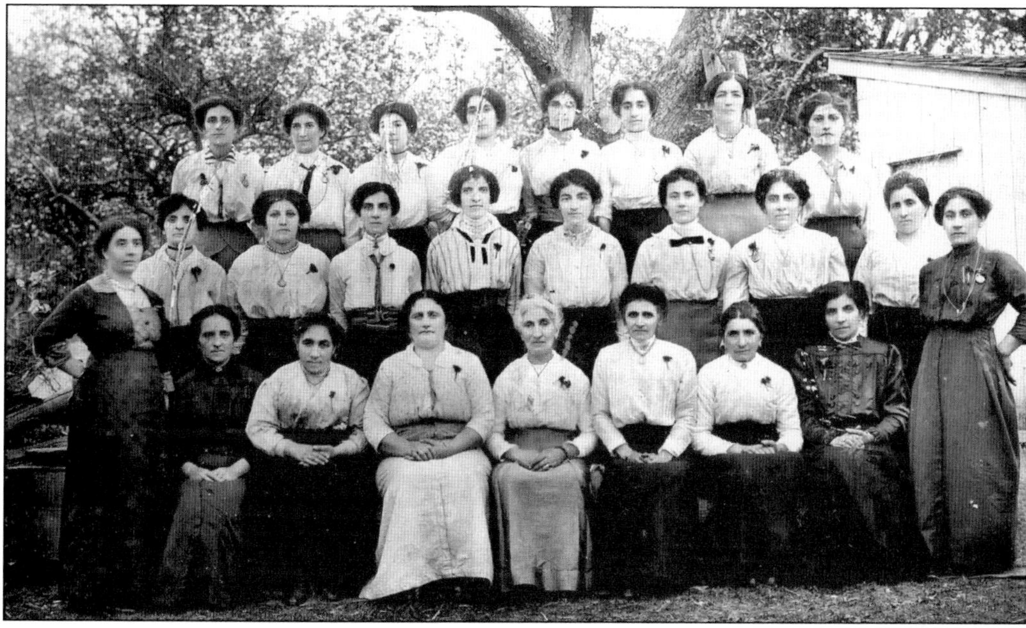

The Assyrian Ladies' Church Loving Association was established in 1908. This photograph, taken in 1915, shows Alice Saffer, Nazli Hoyen, Luciy Ohan, Mary Ilbag, Alice Saffer, Maritza Ohan, Ms. Eskander, Mary Chavoor Arslan, Mary Elbag, Mendoohi Ohan, Ms. Vakel, Sophia Arslan, Nazli Saffer, Lucia Donabed, Shamiram Hoyen, Ms. Arslan, Elizabeth (Yelsa) Chavoor, Alaper Johnson, Nazli Dasho, Mrs. A. Vakel, Mrs. Bedig, and Mrs. George.

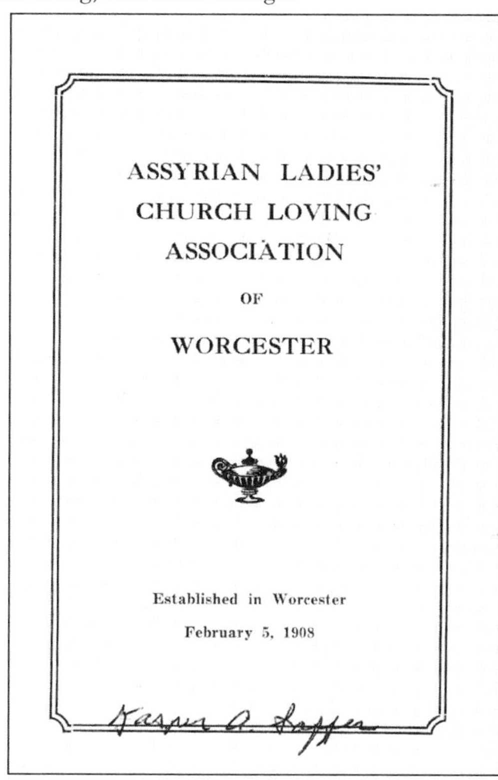

ASSYRIAN LADIES'
CHURCH LOVING
ASSOCIATION
OF
WORCESTER

Established in Worcester
February 5, 1908

Established in Worcester on February 5, 1908, the association's sole purpose as expressed in the bylaws was to "help the Assyrian Church and other benevolent enterprises." Any Assyrian woman was eligible to apply for membership.

Patriarch of Babylon Is Visitor in Brookline

The office of William Coltin & Co., in Brookline, was honored last seek by a visit from His Holiness, the Patriarch of Babylon, Mar Eshai Shimun XXIII, spiritual and temporal leader of the first Christian nation, the Assyrians, and Supreme Pontiff of the original Catholic Church of the East.

During his visit to the real estate and investment office His Holiness took the opportunity to open an account for his church with the Colonial Bank and Trust Company of Athol by handing a sizeable check to Barry Coltin, president of the bank.

Historically, the Assyrian Catholic Church has been heralded by scholars of all faiths as the greatest and most missionary church the world has ever seen. During the first and succeeding centuries it comprised the major portion of Christianity—reaching it's zenith in the eleventh century when it outnumbered both the Roman and Greek churches combined.

Aramic, the language spoken by Christ and the Apostles and the original language of the Hebrew Patriarchs is the compulsory language of the chanted Mass.

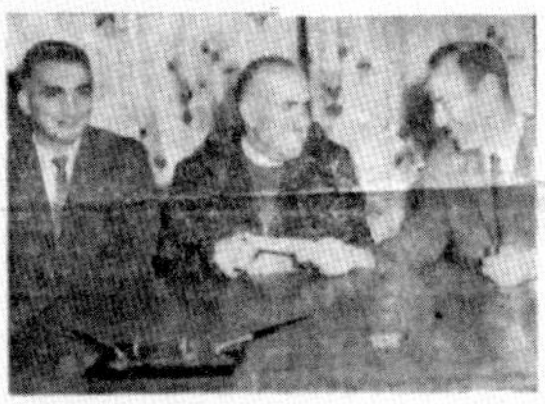

ASSYRIAN PATRIARCH, His Holiness Mar Eshai Shimun XXIII, center, hands check to open bank account to Barry D. Coltin, president of the Colonial Bank & Trust Co. of Athol. At left is Barson J. Kashish, salesmanager of William Coltin & Co.

Barsom J. Kashish and Mar Eshai Shimun, patriarch of the Church of the East, opened an account at the Colonial Bank and Trust Company in Brookline. Barsom is the husband of Margaret Kasab and father of Cindy and Lisa.

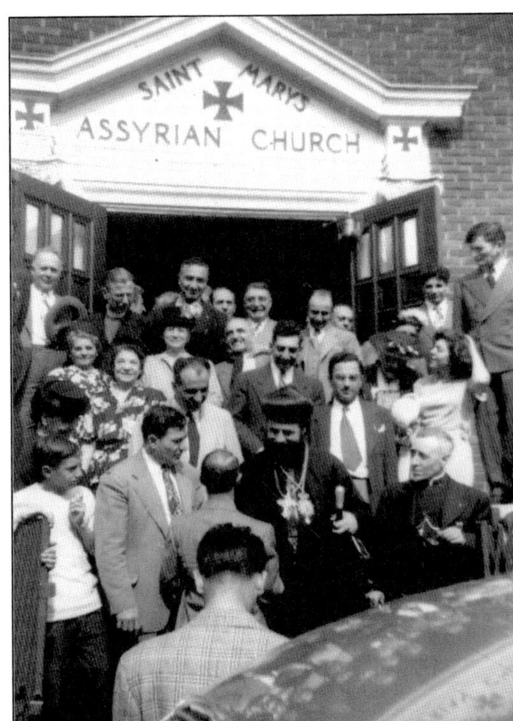

Though well known as Archbishop Severius Afrem Barsum, Patriarch Ignatius Afrem Barsum is seen leaving St. Mary's Assyrian Church with parishioners in 1949. Rev. Peter Barsoum, the church's second priest, was also in attendance.

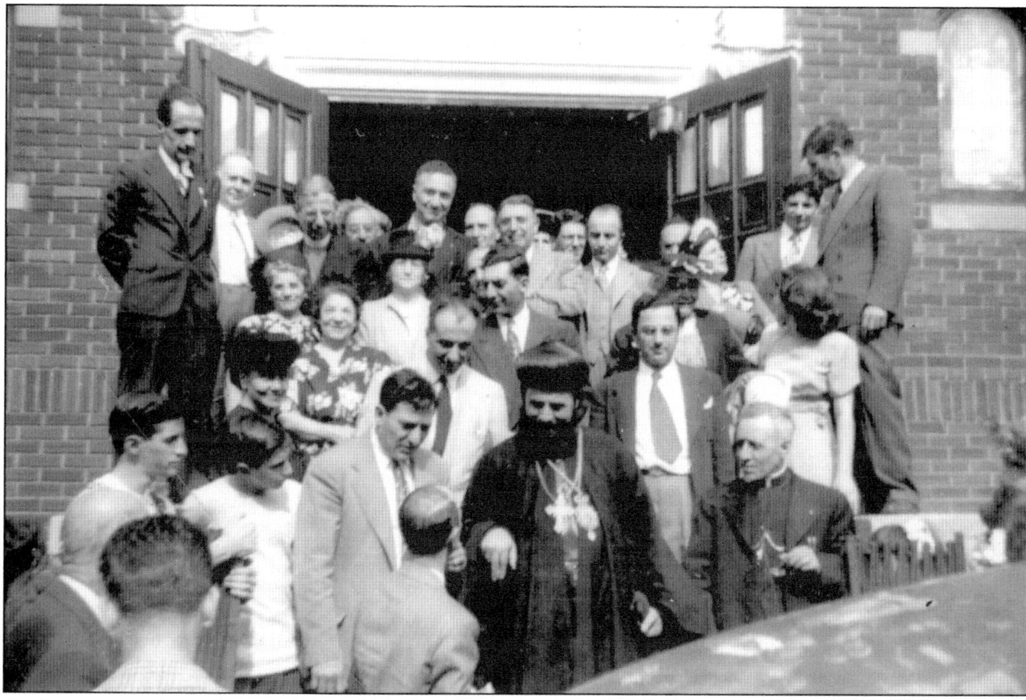

A closer view than the previous photograph is seen here, with the patriarch and various Assyrian Americans on the front steps of St. Mary's Assyrian Church.

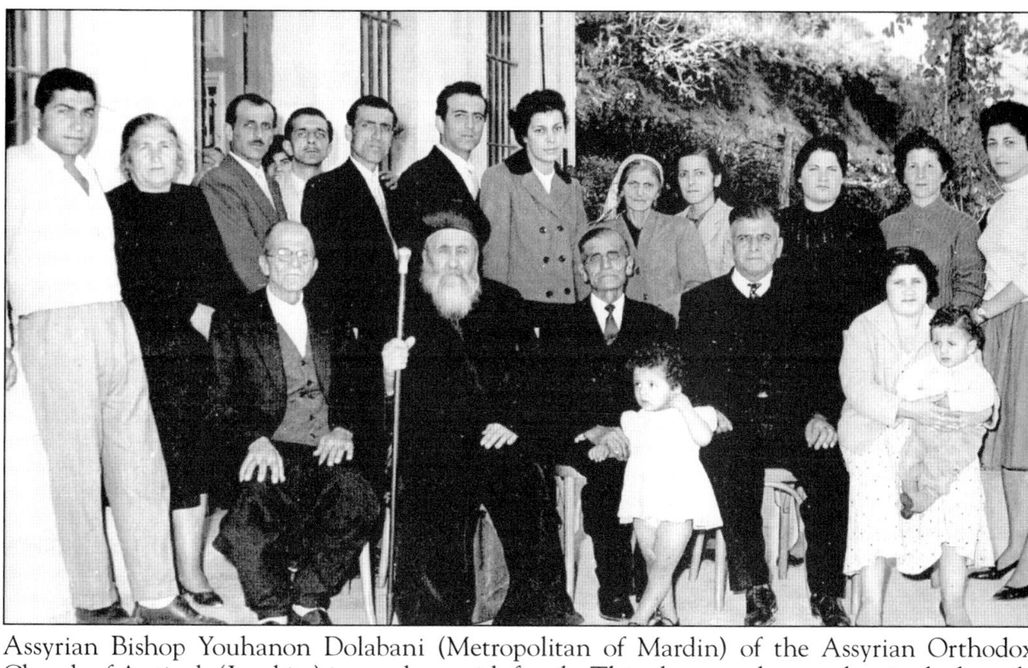

Assyrian Bishop Youhanon Dolabani (Metropolitan of Mardin) of the Assyrian Orthodox Church of Antioch (Jacobite) is seen here with family. This photograph was taken in the heavily populated Assyrian area of Zahle, Lebanon, around 1960. The Dawlabani family (spelled a variety of ways) settled in Boston where they helped to open St. Matthew's Church.

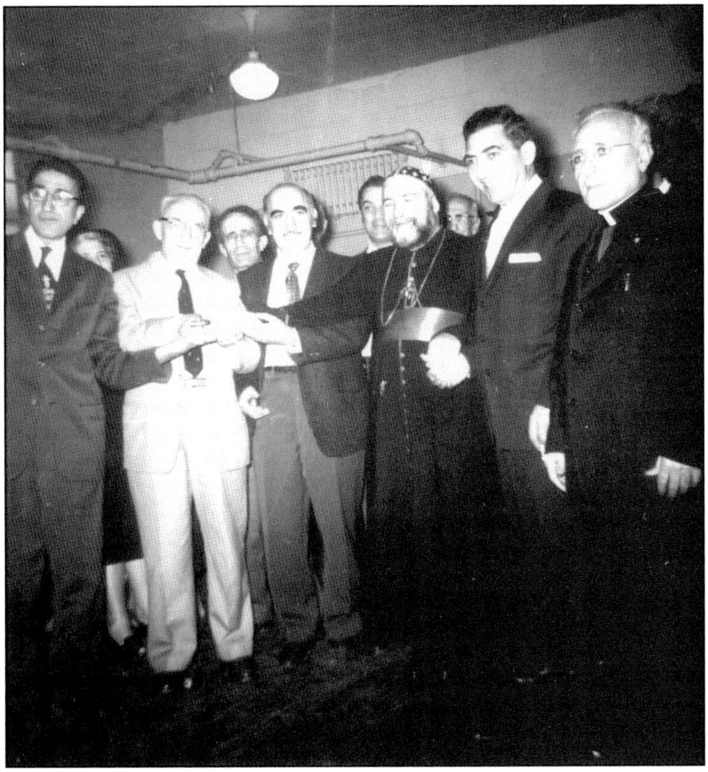

Identified here are Kasper Saffer, Rev. Peter Barsoum, and Henry Perch in attendance with Bishop Yeshue Samuel in the hall of St. Mary's Assyrian Church in Worcester. This meeting was prior to the upheaval that took place in the church when it was usurped by Arabized Assyrians.

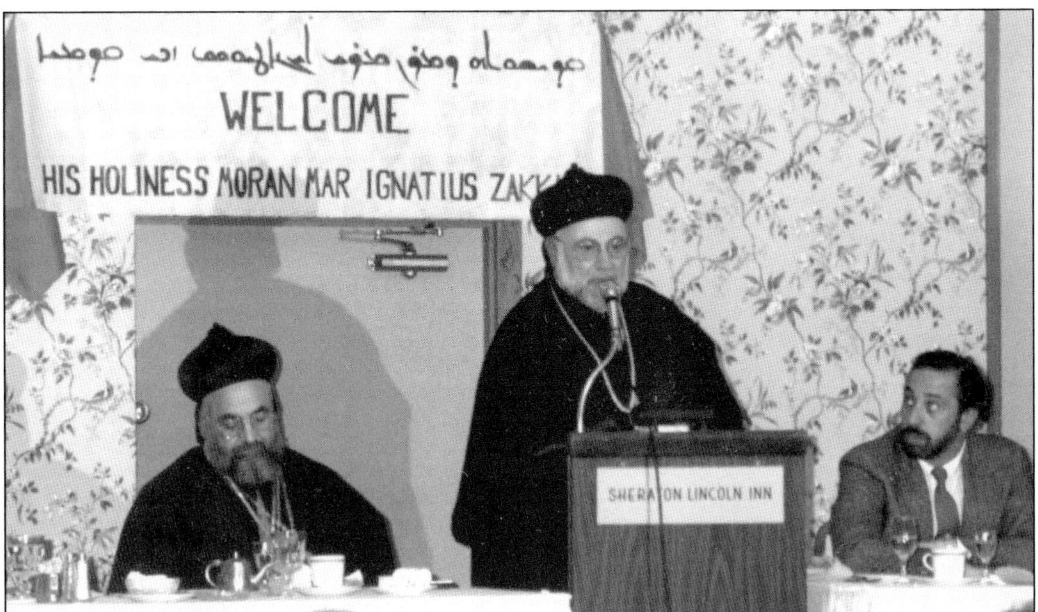

Seen here is a banquet held in the honor of Patriarch Ignatius Zakka Iwas seated to the left. The convention was held at the Sheraton Lincoln Inn located in Worcester from September 29 through October 6, 1981, and supported by the St. Mary's Assyrian Orthodox Church of Worcester. Mayor Jordan Levy of Worcester is present and is seated to the right of Archbishop Yeshue Samuel, who is speaking at the podium.

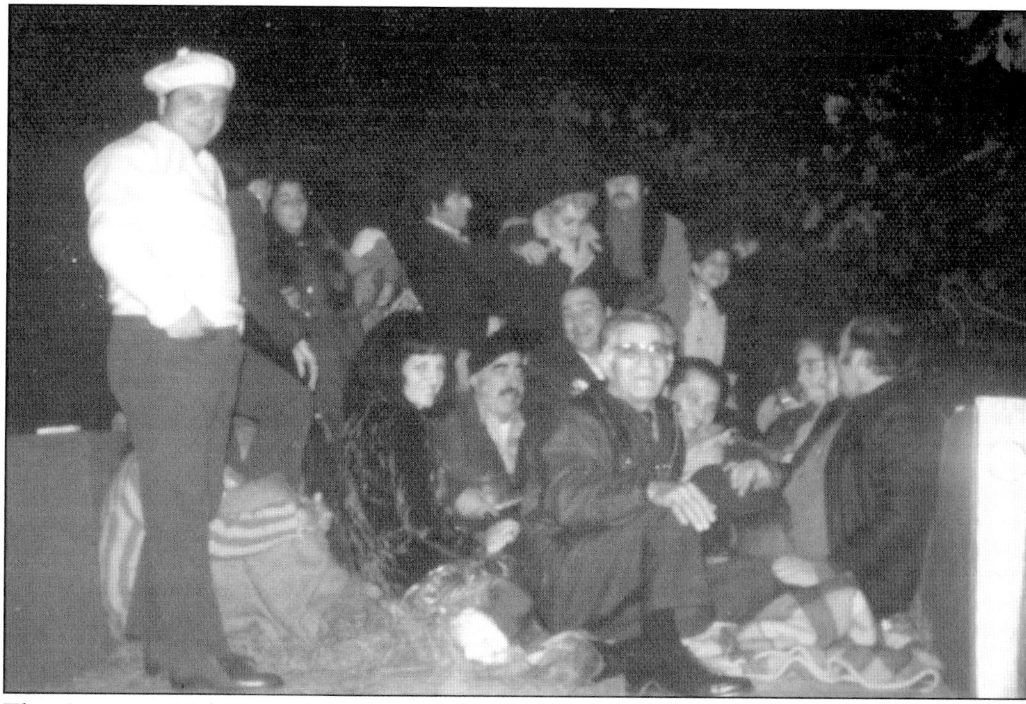

The Assyrian Orthodox Church of Antioch Hayride was held on October 21, 1972. Such gatherings were frequently organized to promote the unity of the Assyrian community in Massachusetts, regardless of religious denomination. In attendance are the Perch, Saffer, and Barsoum families.

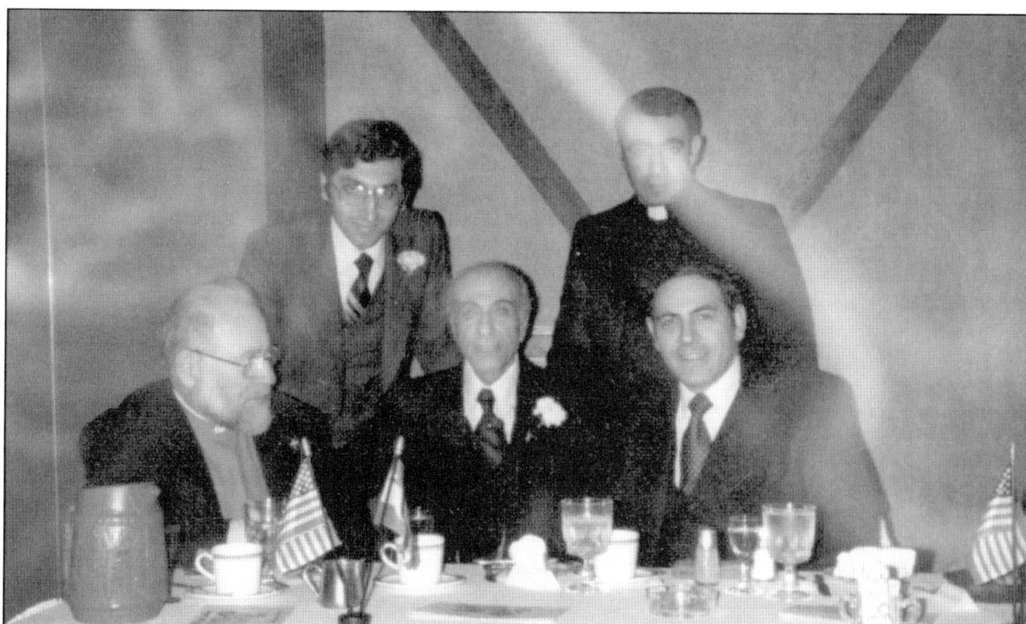

This Assyrian New Year's party, held on March 31, 1979, in Worcester, supported the local Assyrian community. Gabriel Namen, Dr. Elias Arous, and the Reverend Shamoun Asmar can be seen in the image.

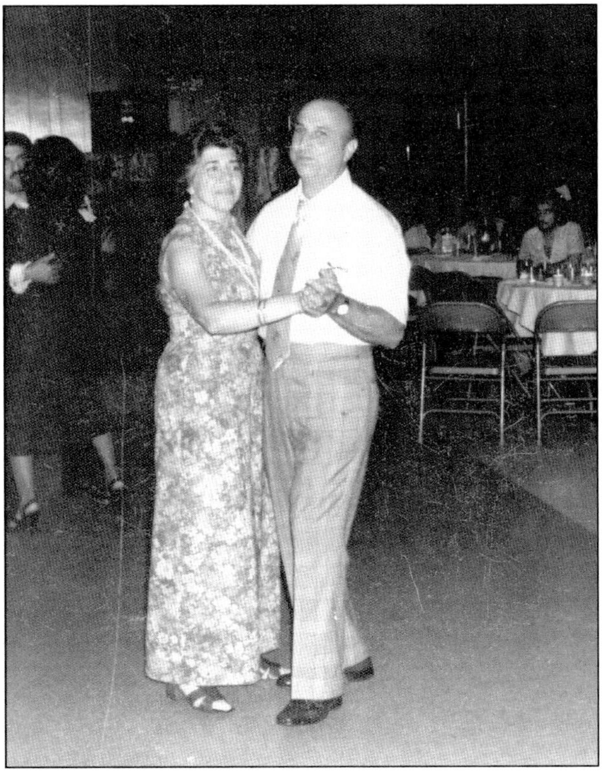

Harold and Mary Perch, two Massachusetts Assyrians, are seen dancing at the diocese convention held on August 27, 1976, in Paramus, New Jersey.

St. Mary's Assyrian Orthodox Church of Antioch

V. REV. SHAMOUN ASMAR, PASTOR
1152 PLEASANT STREET
WORCESTER, MA 01602
TEL: 508-753-7570

ONE INDUSTRIAL DRIVE
SHREWSBURY, MA 01545
TEL: 508-842-1003

October 6,1997

To whom it may concern:

As one of our main fund raising events, we are holding our Bazaar/Festival on Saturday and Sunday, November 22 and 23, 1997. We have been renovating our Church and are in need of funds.

In order to make this Bazaar a success, we must of necessity reach out to you for support and help. Needless to say, any consideration given will be greatly appreciated by our people and the community in general.

Appreciating your indulgence and consideration, we are

Most thankfully yours,

Marking an end to more than seven decades of cultural and religious prosperity, the name of the archdiocese was abruptly changed from the correct identifying term Assyrian to the erroneous name "Syriac."

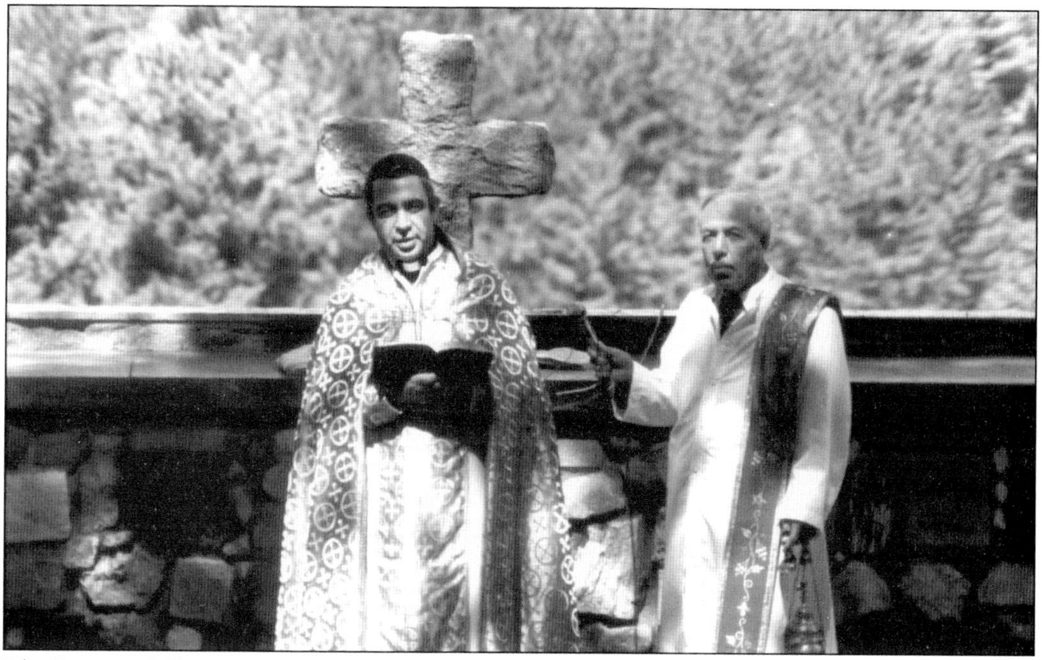

The Reverend Shamoun Asmar of St. Mary's church is seen here, holding mass at the Cathedral of the Pines in Rindge, New Hampshire, in August 1981. Also in the picture is the High Deacon Samuel Samuel. The Cathedral of the Pines is a frequent destination of many New England churches during the warm summer months when outdoor masses are held.

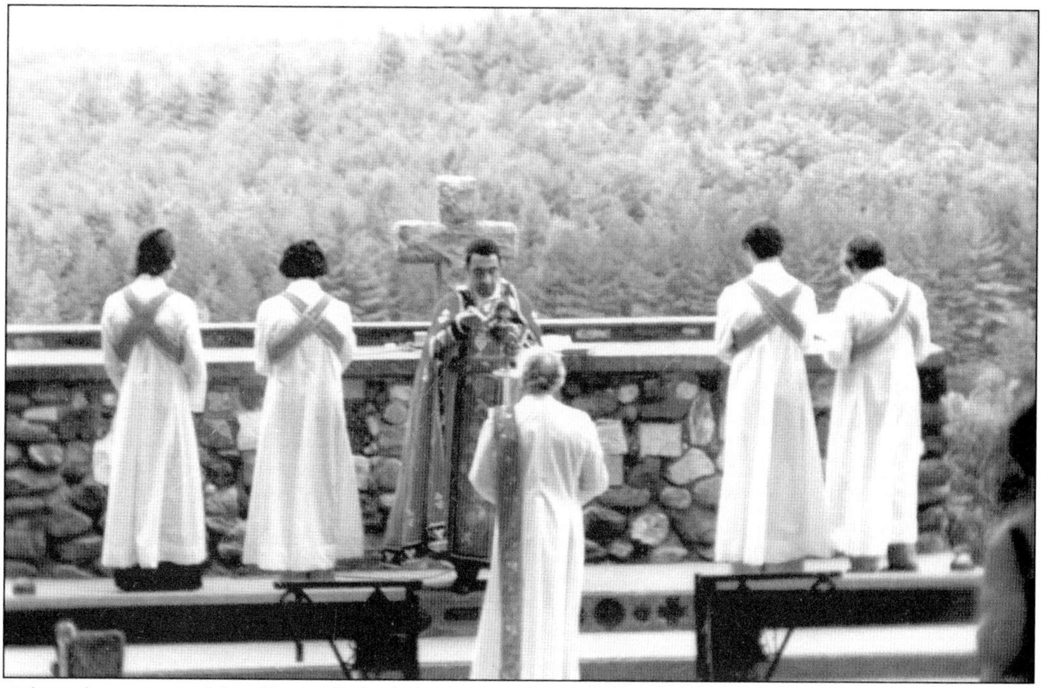

A broader image of the Cathedral of the Pines taken on June 6, 1976, shows the intricate beauty and vastness of the surrounding area. Many church communities have held services at the Cathedral of the Pines over several decades.

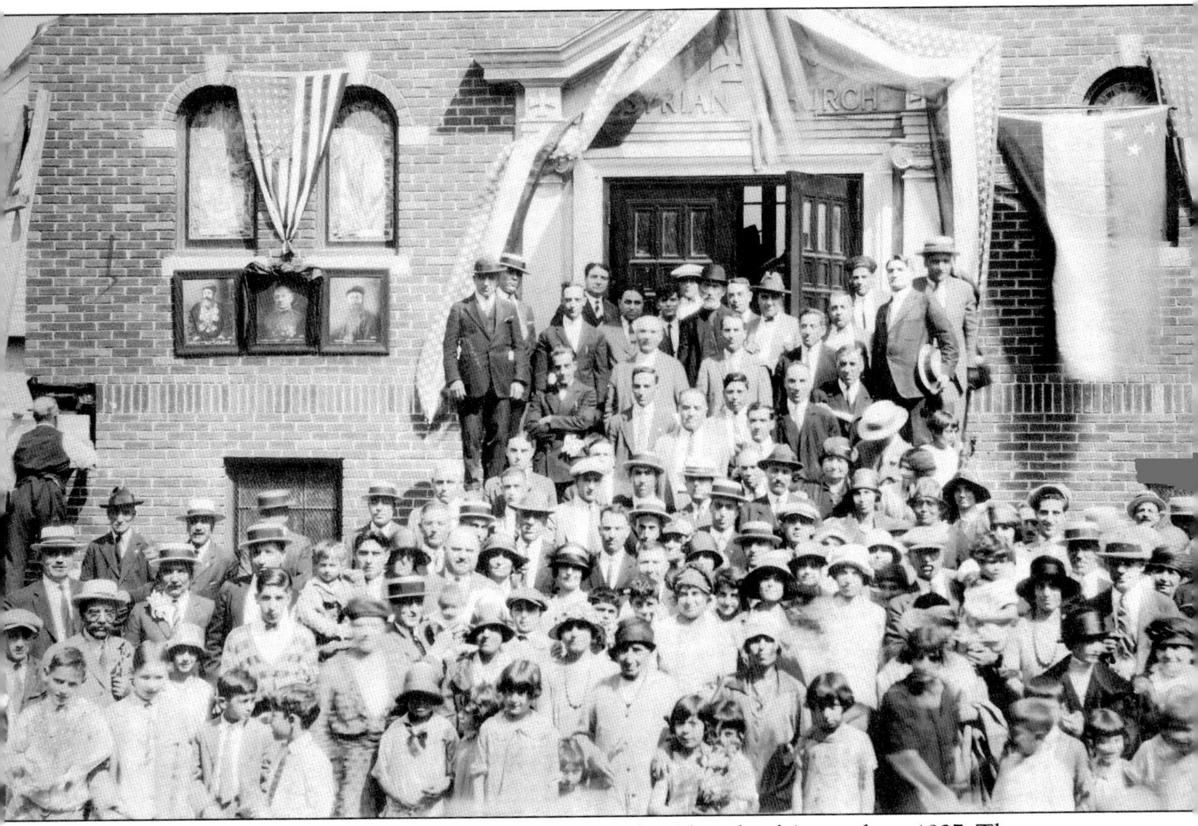

This is the grand opening of the Assyrian Apostolic Church of Antioch in 1927. The ceremony was celebrated by Rev. Naum Koorie, Rev. Nouri Koorie of New York, Rev. Gabriel Boyajy of Springfield, and the deacon G. E. Sugar of Worcester.

Six

Staying Together

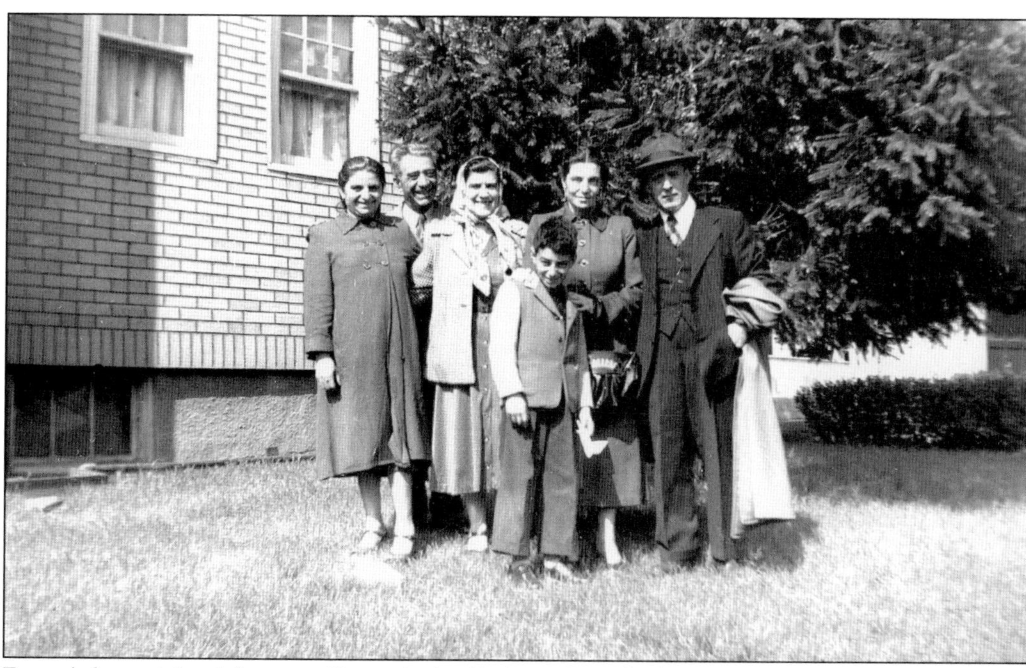

From left to right, Margaret Kazar Safer, Bishara Donabed, Sadie Donabed Samuel, George Donabed, Roumel Kazar Donabed, and Youhanna Donabed stand outside Sadie's 121 School Street home in Watertown. Young George was the only child born to Youhanna and Roumel.

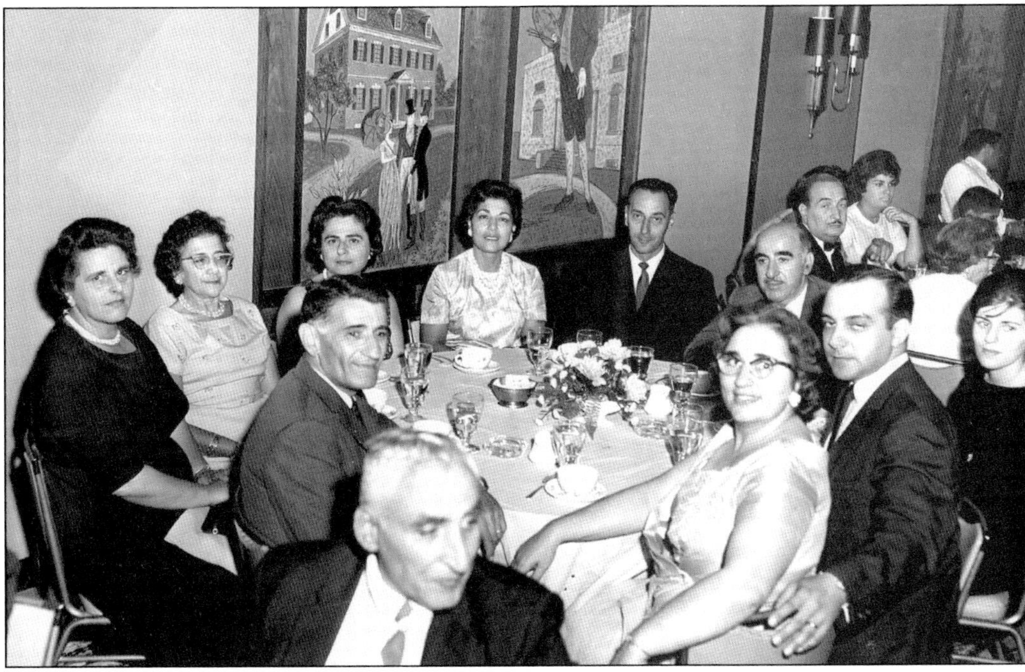

The Assyrian American Federation Convention was held in Philadelphia, Pennsylvania, in 1963. Massachusetts Assyrians in attendance and seated around the table in the forefront are Jurjies (George) Kashish (front center), to his rear are George and Anne Ovanes, Darius Baba, Barbara Baba, Kasper Saffer, Sargon Arslan, Shmooni Arslan, Phyllis Saffer, and Aram Donabed.

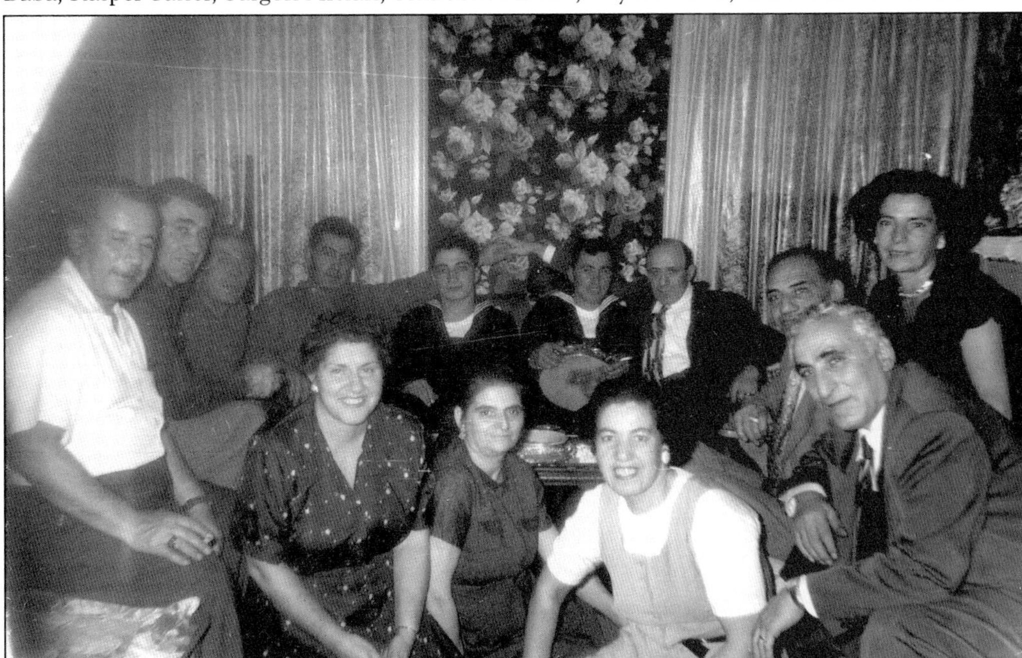

The Kashish, Donabed, Safer, and Kazar families are seen at a gathering in the Donabed residence in Dorchester, around 1950. The gathering was attended by Turkish sailors docked in the port of Boston.

Youhanna Behnam Donabed and Roumel Kazar Donabed pose in the early 1940s. Born in Harput, they immigrated to the United States on August 5, 1922, and November 30, 1927, respectively. Roumel worked in various factory jobs and a bakery, whereas Youhanna (John) continued his trade as a shoemaker while also serving in the United States military for a time.

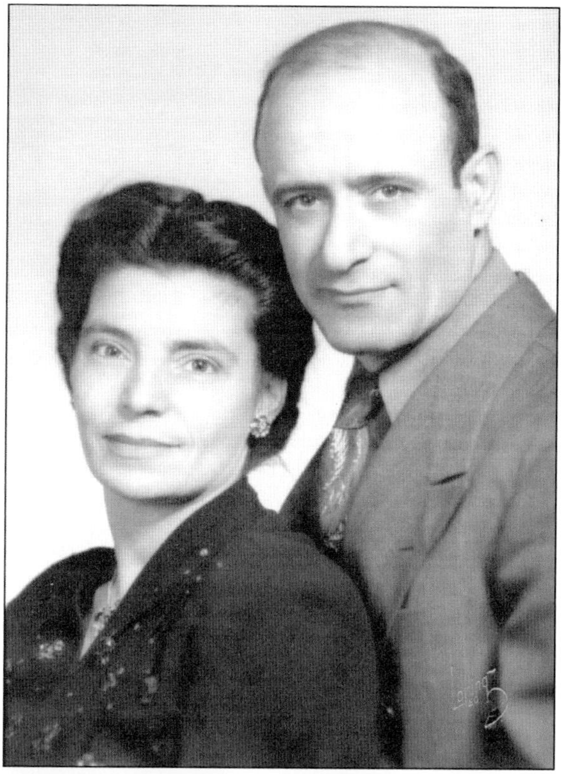

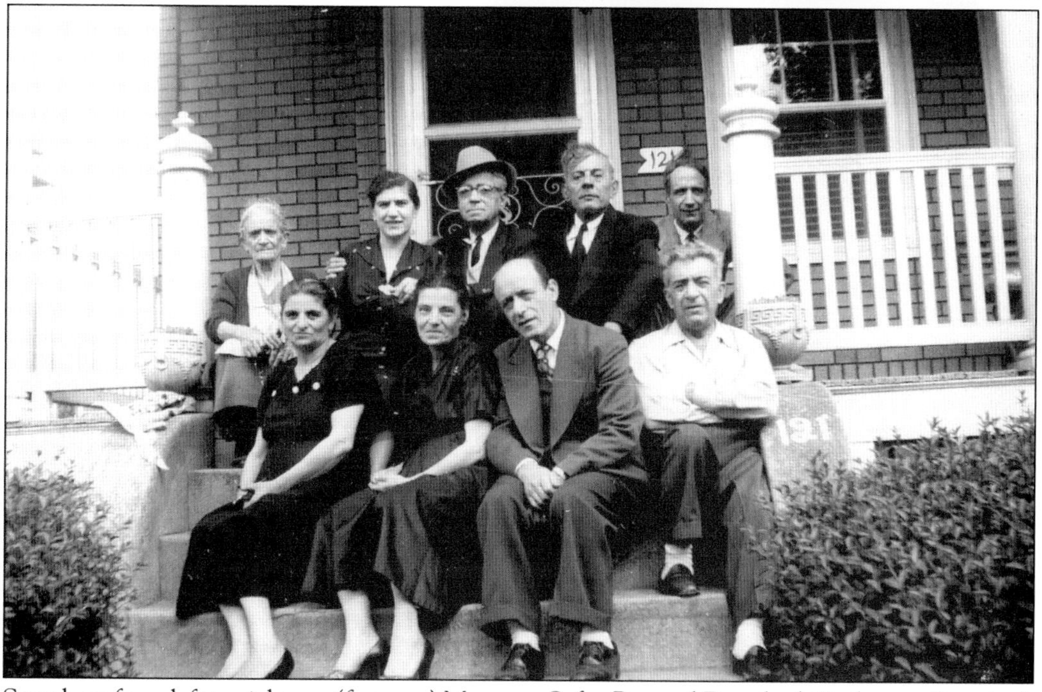

Seen here from left to right are (first row) Margaret Safer, Roumel Donabed, Youhanna Donabed, and Bishara Donabed; (second row) Maryam Donabed, Sadie Samuel, unidentified, Abdenoor Safer, and Elia Donabed. The photograph was taken around 1945.

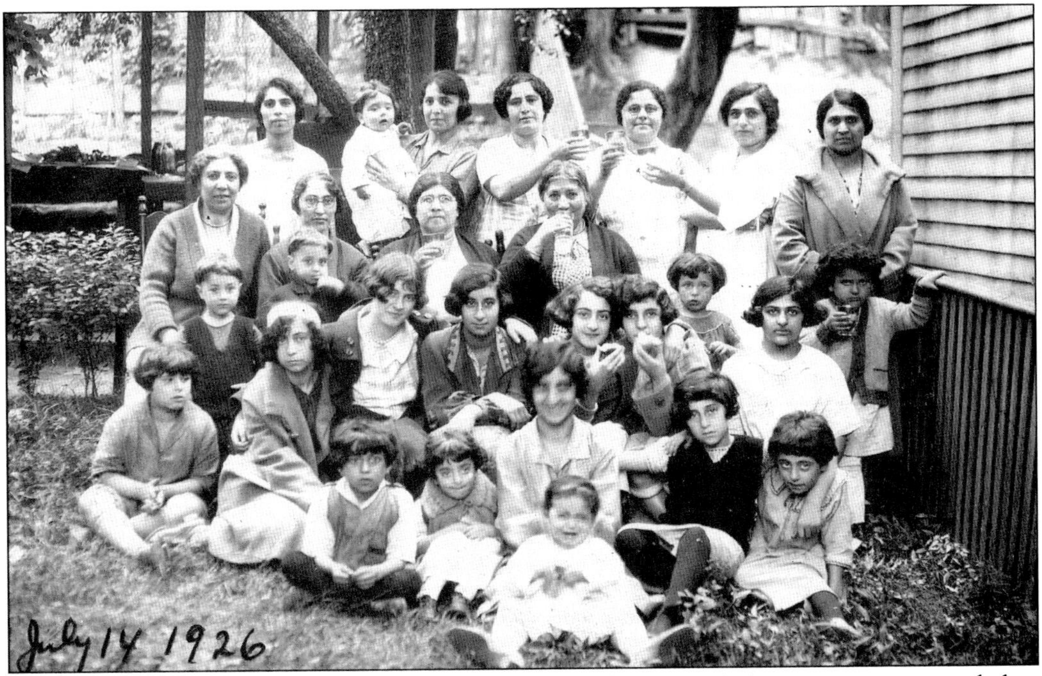

A gathering of women and children is seen here on July 14, 1926. Assyrian women tended to the children and worked the farms while some of their spouses worked a second factory job in the city.

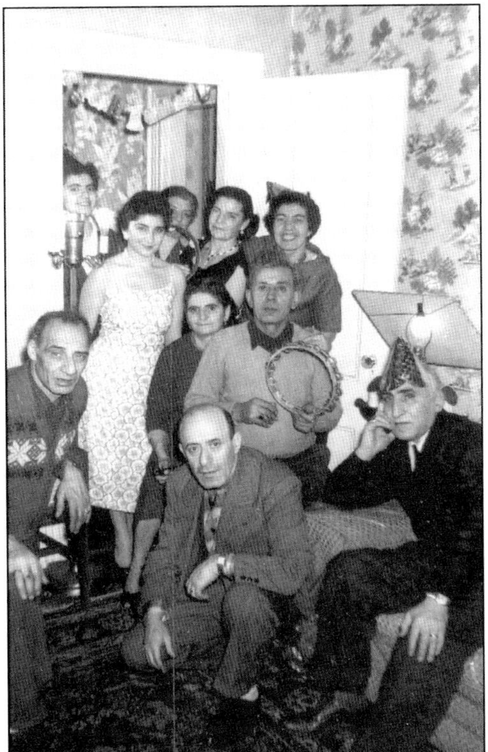

Peter and Helen Kazar entertain family and friends at their home in Boston on New Years Eve. Also seen in the picture are Jurjies and Maritza Kashish and their daughter Charlotte, Youhanna and Roumel Donabed, Margaret and Abdenoor Safer, and Peter and Helen's daughter AnnLou. Some audio recordings of such events were made by the Assyrians on old reel-to-reel tapes.

Many Assyrians who immigrated to the United States made regular trips back to the homeland. Roumel Kazar Donabed is seen above on her trip to her birth town of Harput in the late 1950s. Also seen in the picture are Afrem and Maryam, Roumel's cousins, residing at the time in Elazig, Turkey.

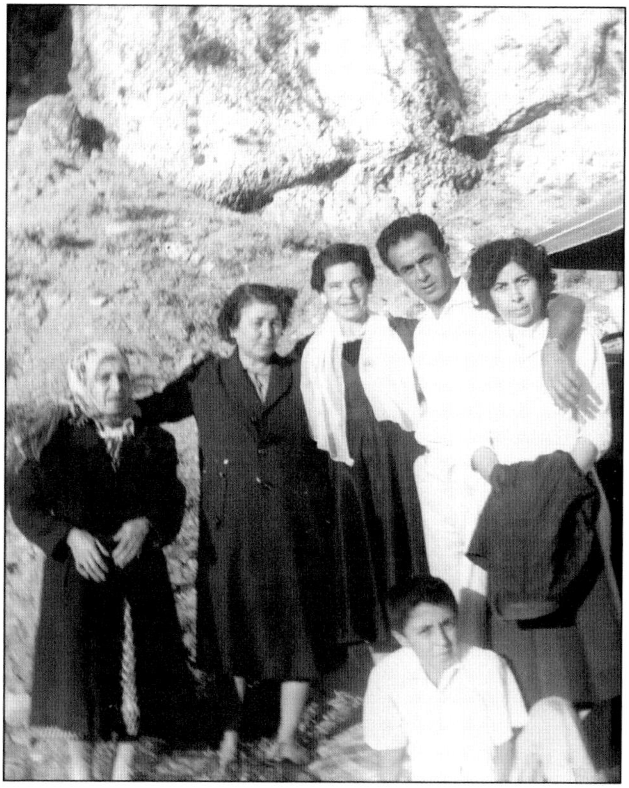

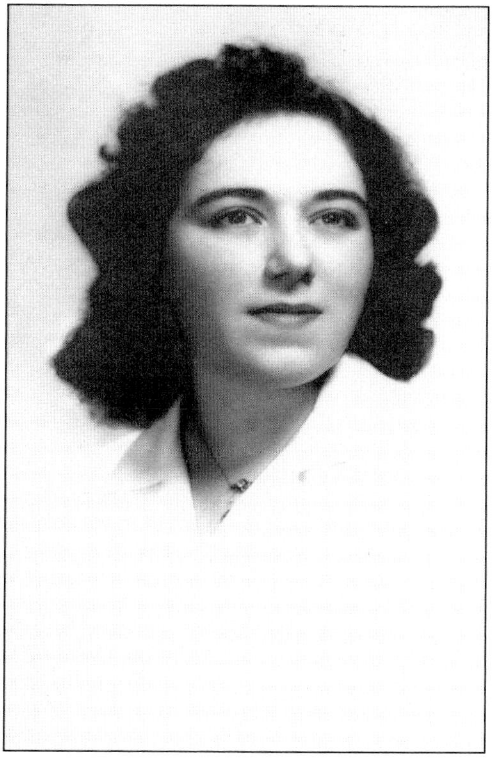

Shown here is Marion Atlas in 1944, sister of Dorothy Atlas. This picture was sent to Ann Kurkjy, mother of Larry Kurkjy. The Atlas family immigrated to the United States from Harput around the time of World War I.

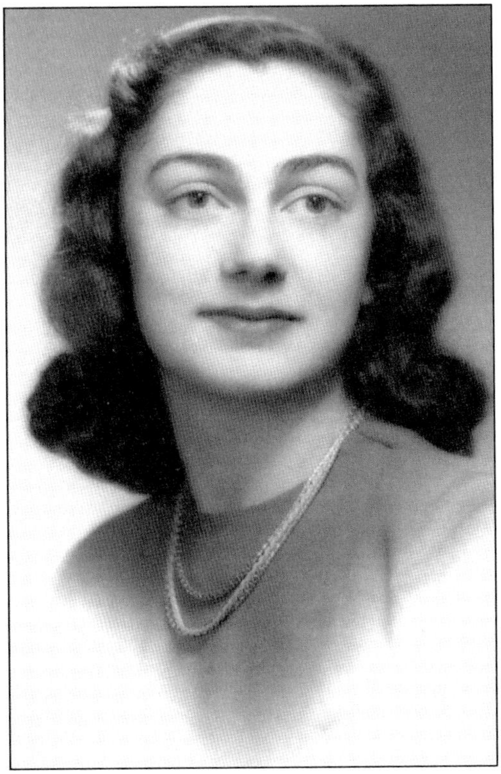

Shown here is Rose Deinha from 1945 at Armand Studio in Boston. The Rose's family is from Harput.

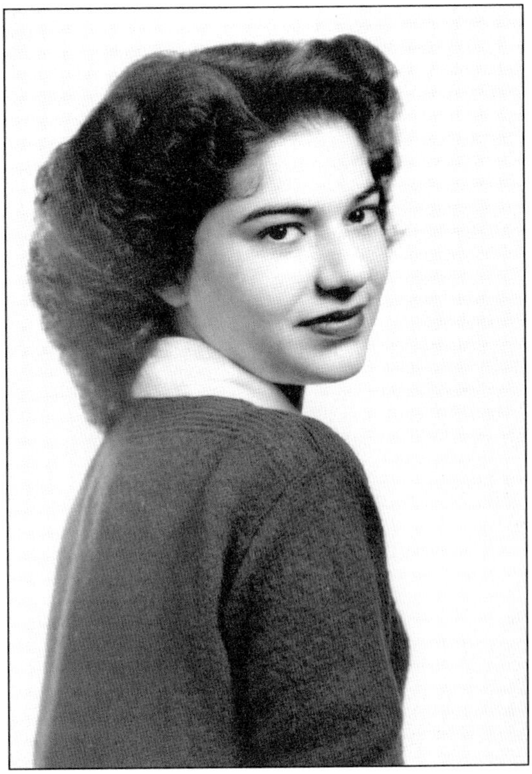

This is a picture of Dorothy Atlas, daughter of George and Lucy (Donabed) Atlas. She was born in Massachusetts, but in 1944, left with her family to reside in Los Angeles where her father was eventually employed by Technicolor Studios in Hollywood.

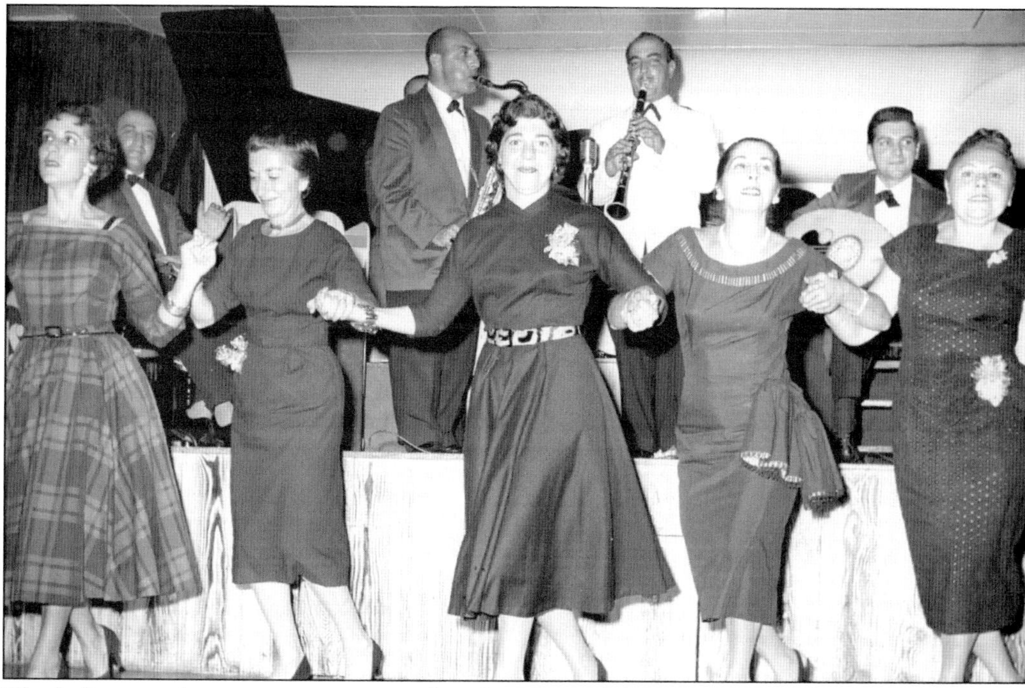

The ladies seen here are enjoying a night of traditional Assyrian song and dance. From left to right are Peggy Hoyen, Frances Manoog, Mary Perch, Hazel Balley, and Rose Deinha. Assyrian dances, like tanzara and halay, were popular among Assyrians from Harput and Diarbekir.

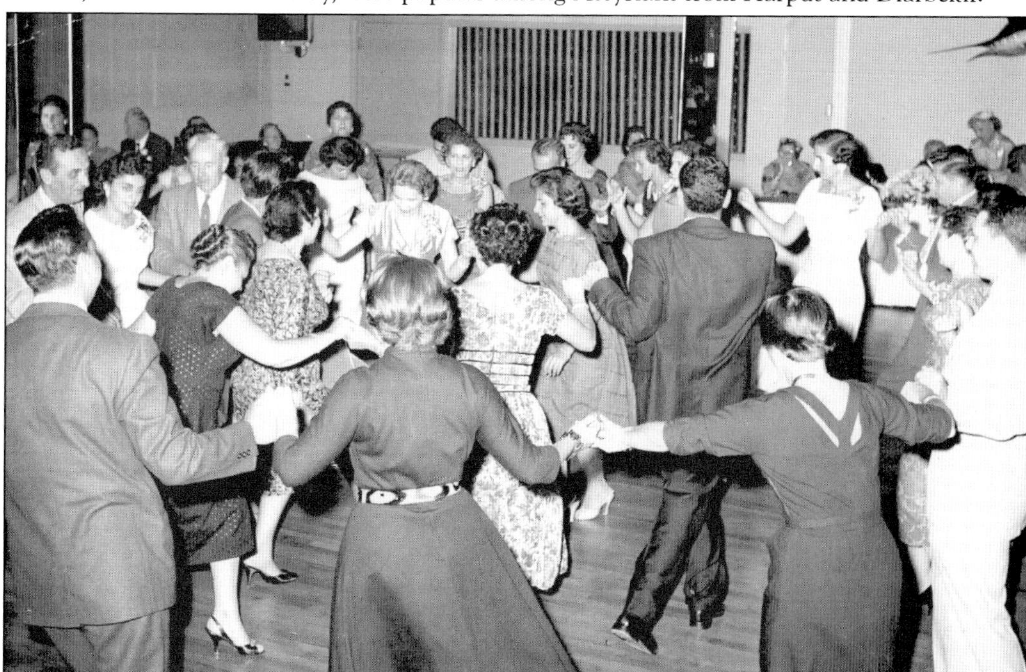

Dance through the years has helped preserve a unique aspect of Assyrian culture. Today, along with language and history, Assyrian dance has been a mechanism of self-preservation, especially amongst diaspora communities.

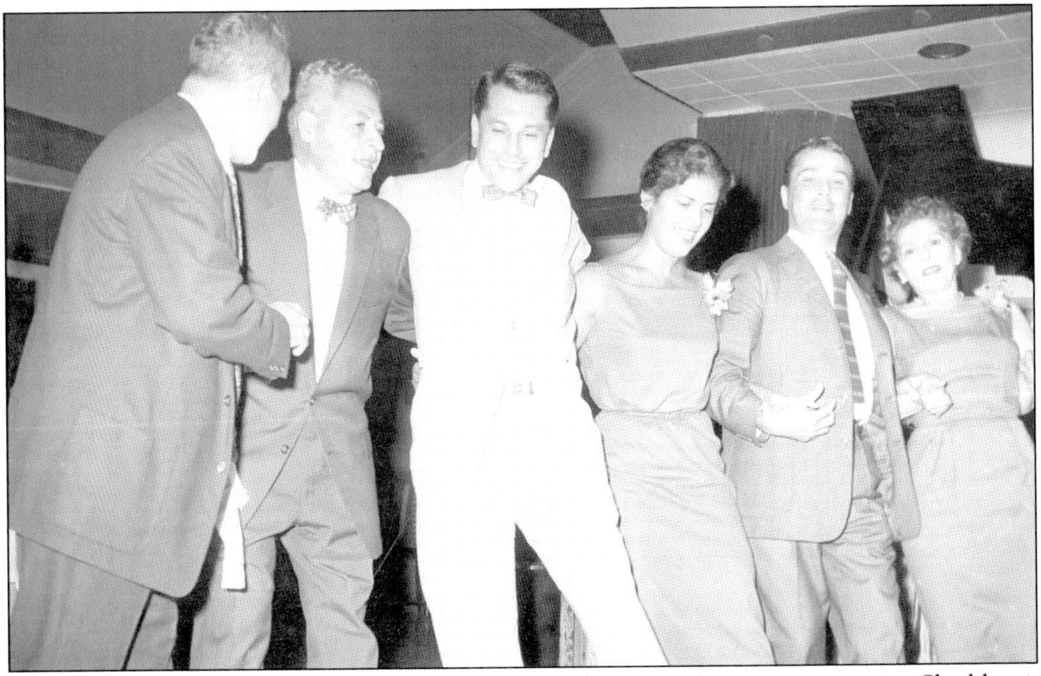

Assyrian line dances were the most beloved among the Massachusetts community. Sheikhani, Belati, Tanzara Halay, and (as seen above) Khigga Yaqora were among the favorites. Literally translated as "heavy dance," this particular jig is taken from an ancient war march. George Elbag, second from left, is seen dancing above.

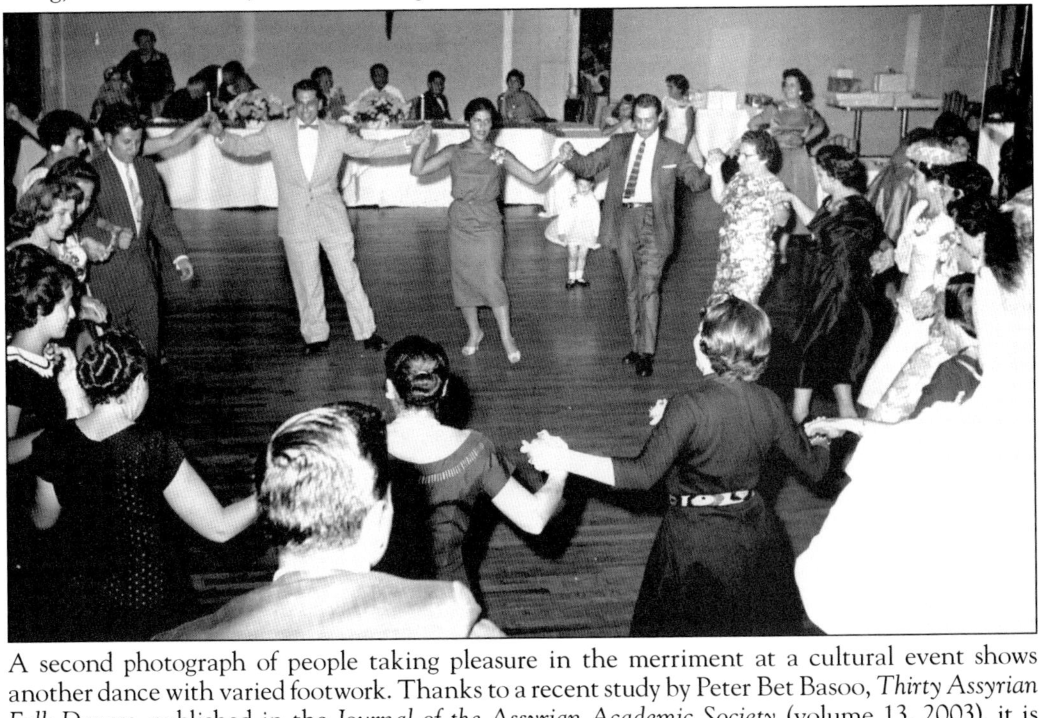

A second photograph of people taking pleasure in the merriment at a cultural event shows another dance with varied footwork. Thanks to a recent study by Peter Bet Basoo, *Thirty Assyrian Folk Dances*, published in the *Journal of the Assyrian Academic Society* (volume 13, 2003), it is evident that these dances were social expressions of culture, be it ceremonial, ritual, or other.

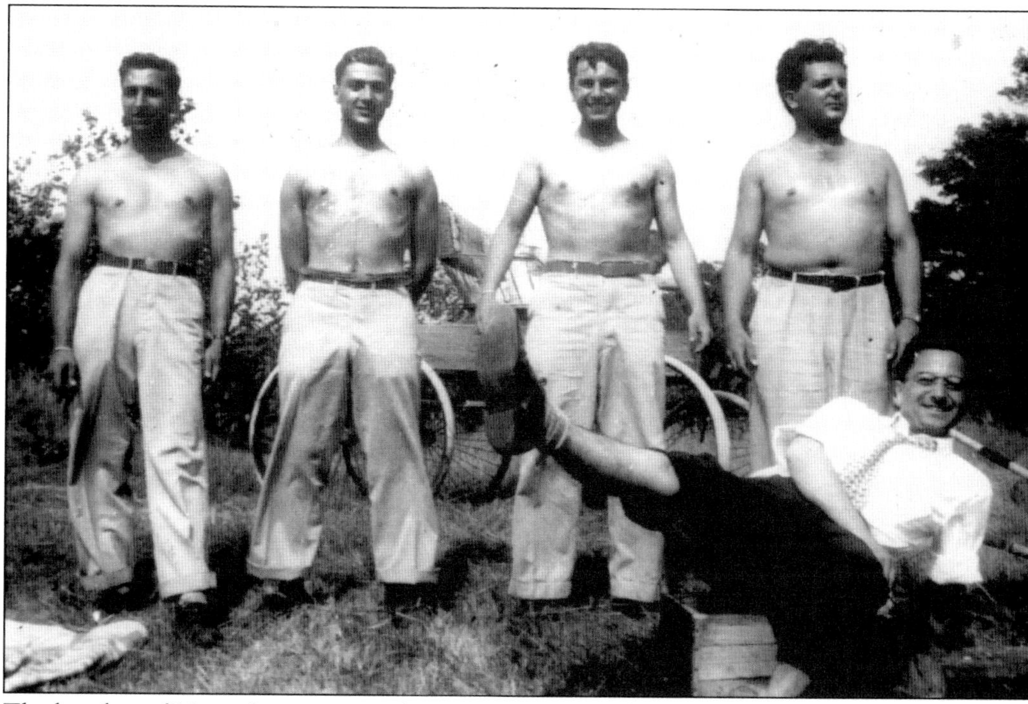

The beaches of Massachusetts were always a great retreat for Harold, Henry, Samuel, and Albert Perch. As young men desired to display their physical prowess to the ladies, these men did that and more while emulating bodybuilders in this entertaining photograph.

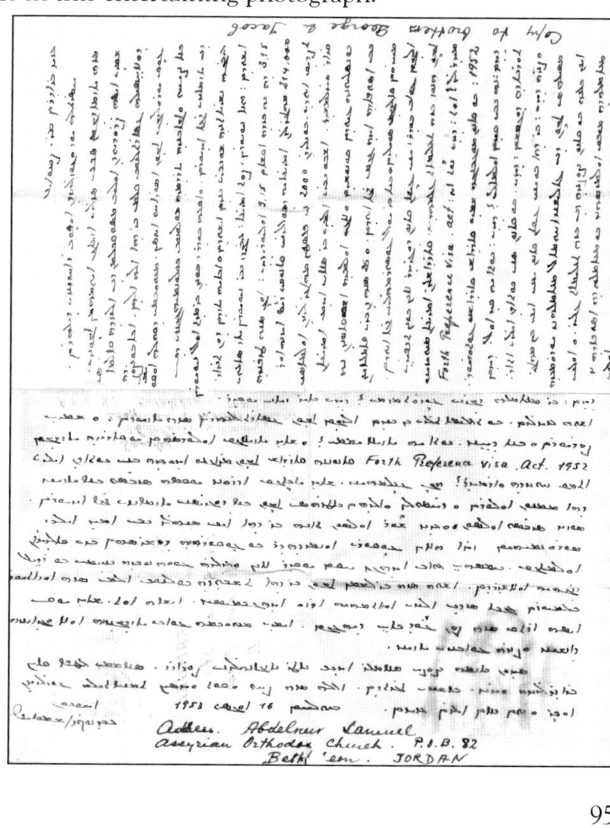

An Assyrian letter sent to Sam Samuel from Abdelnur Samuel in 1953 is seen here. Assyrians kept in close contact with relatives around the world, and the Samuel's were no exception. Notice the sender's address: Assyrian Orthodox Church, P.O. Box 82, Bethlehem, Jordan.

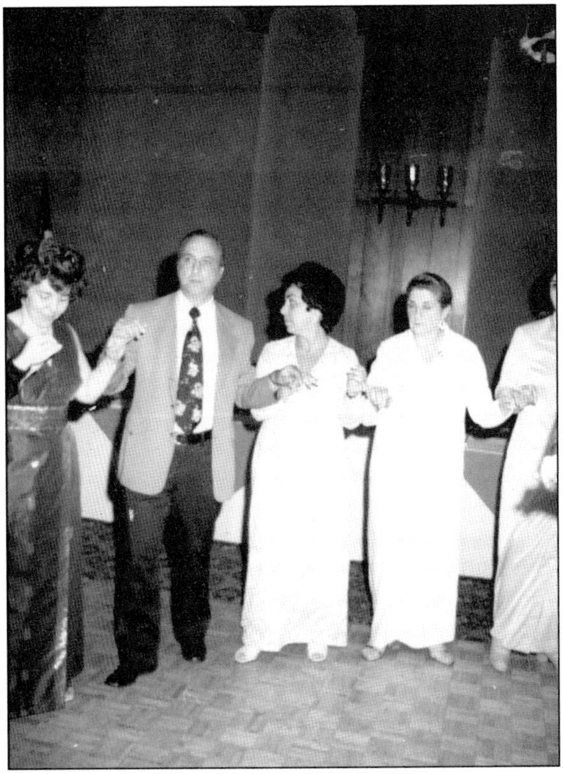

This is a banquet in honor of David Kashish Perley, a famous Assyrian activist and lawyer. Known for his poetry, activism, and philosophical works, Perley was honored numerous times by both non-Assyrians and his fellow Assyrians, as in this formal banquet in New Jersey in 1974. Assyrians from around the United States attended this event to thank Perley for his tireless activism.

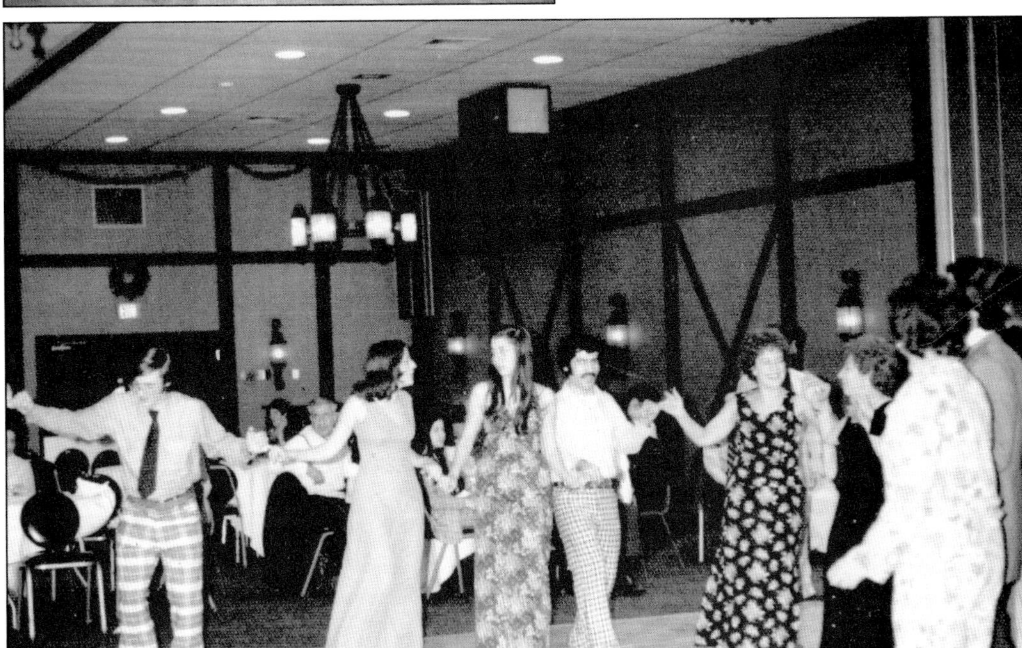

Debbie Perch and Ninos (now Reverend Efrem) Adde can been seen among the dancers of this Assyrian New Year celebration. Assyrian New Year, celebrated on April 1, is a millennia old ritual (Akitu) that began traditionally from the spring solstice, and ended 12 days thereafter with a merry celebration.

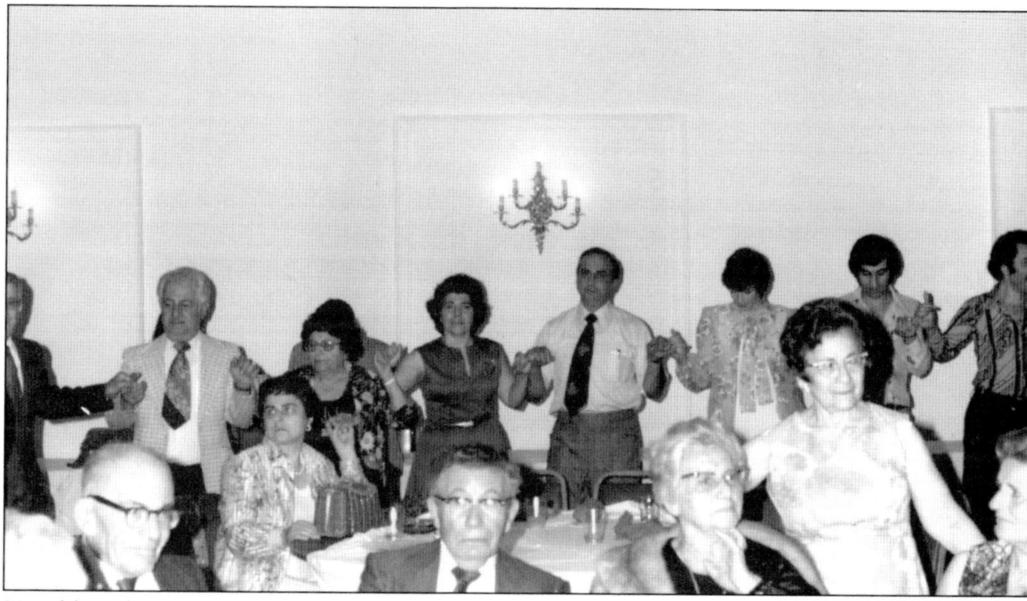

Harold and Mary Perch dance the night away in Waltham on May 24, 1975. This United Assyrian Association of Massachusetts banquet was also attended by the Saffer family (Phyllis is seen above) and George Ovanes and family.

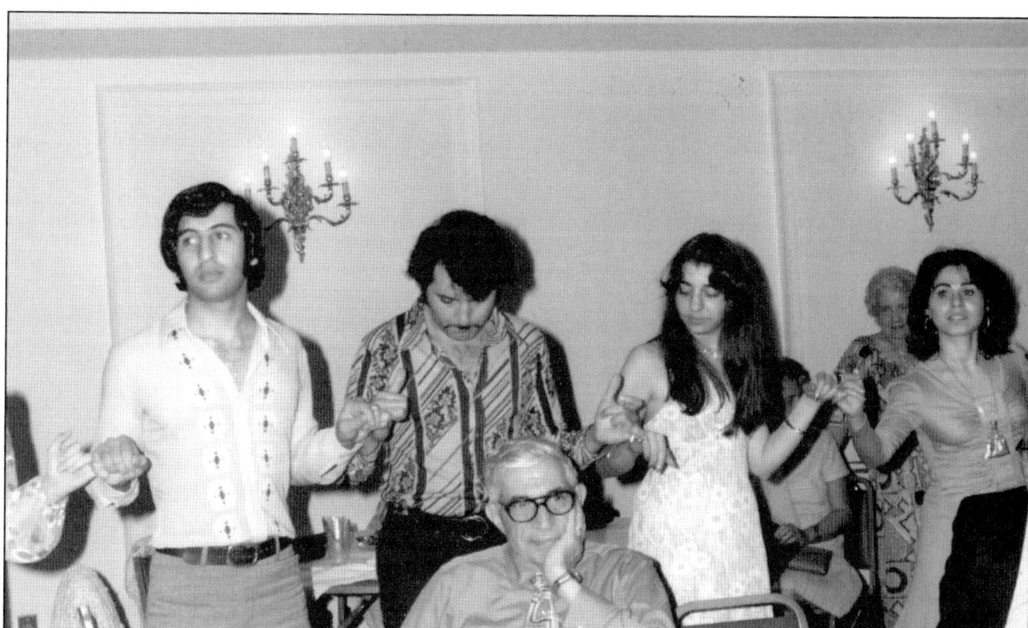

This is a second photograph of the May 24, 1975, party where Debbie Perch and Leslie Saffer (far right) are seen dancing. Barsam Deinha, a church deacon and resident oud player at Assyrian functions, sits in the front center.

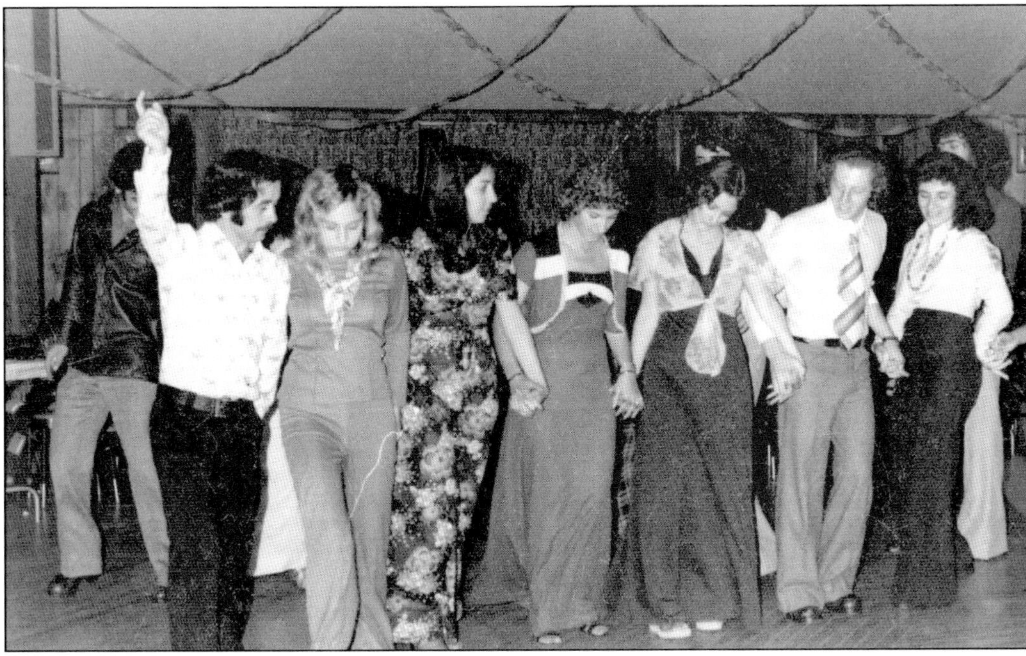

Above are Elias Hanna and Debbie Arslen dancing at Scandinavian Athletic Club Park in October of 1975. Years later, the two would wed and have three sons: Ashur, Ninos, and Sargon. Still residents of Grafton, the Hanna family owned and operated Hats On restaurant for many years. They are still active within the Assyrian community in Massachusetts and abroad.

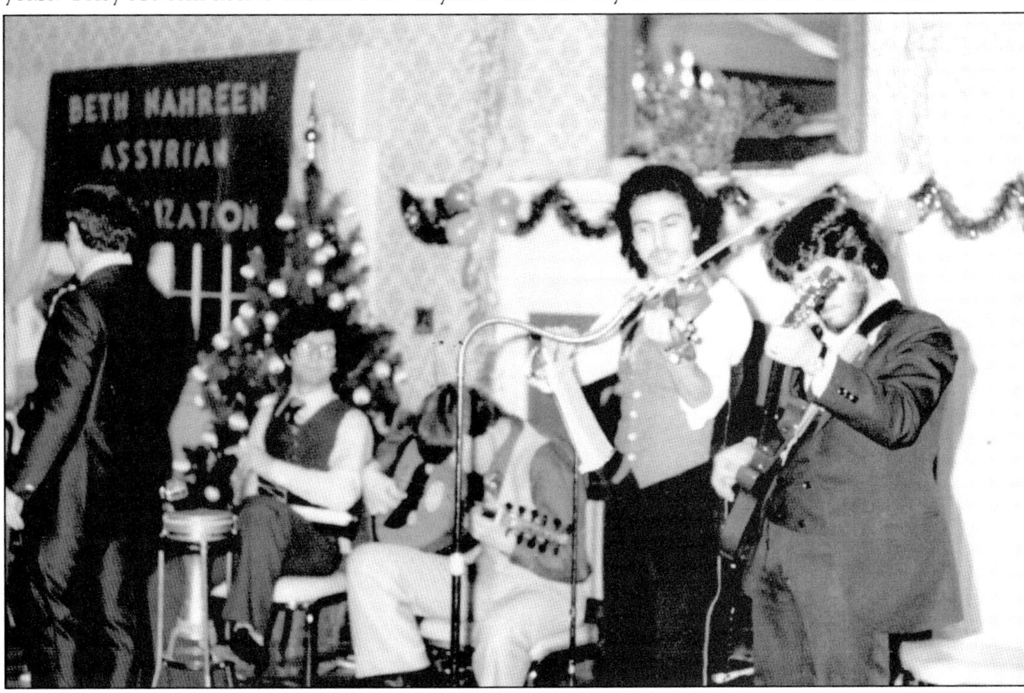

The Beth Nahreen Assyrian Organization was born out of the Assyrian Young Adults Association of Worcester. Members are seen here at the New Years Eve party in 1977 with Brad Perch on the oud and Senharip Tanoglu on violin.

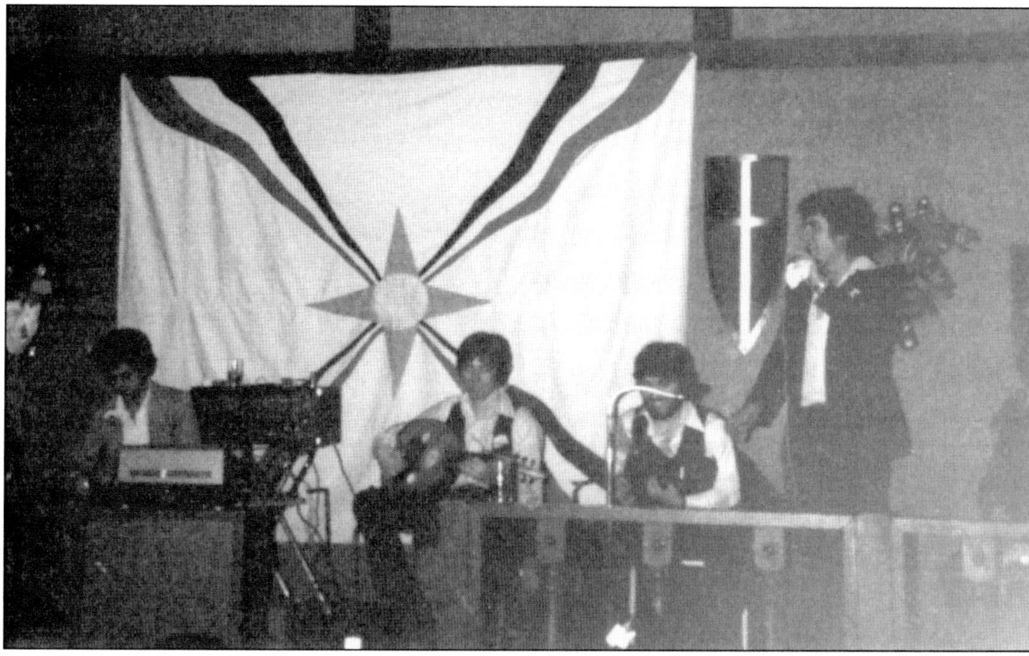

Another Assyrian New Year meant another celebration to the Assyrians of Massachusetts. The Sheraton ballroom in Lincoln was packed to capacity on March 31, 1979. The entertainment was provided by the famous oud player Brad Perch and Company. Brad is the son of Harold and Mary Perch, and brother of Debbie Perch Youkana.

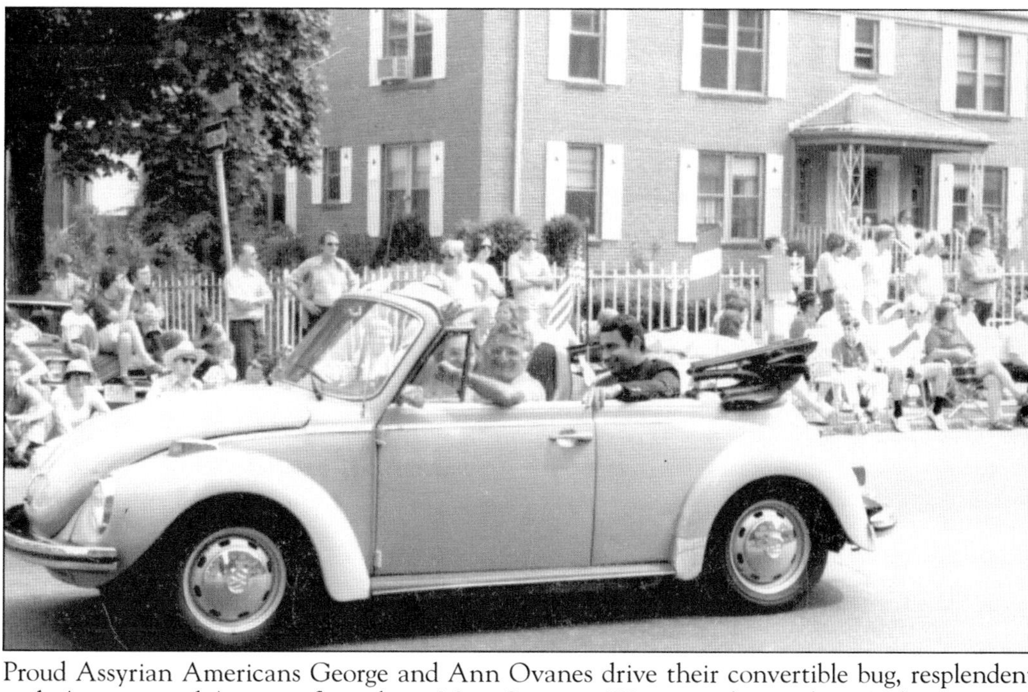

Proud Assyrian Americans George and Ann Ovanes drive their convertible bug, resplendent with America and Assyrian flags, down Main Street in Worcester during the 1976 bicentennial parade. As lifetime members of St. Mary's Assyrian Church, they brought along Rev. Shamoun Asmar who was highly regarded by the community at that time.

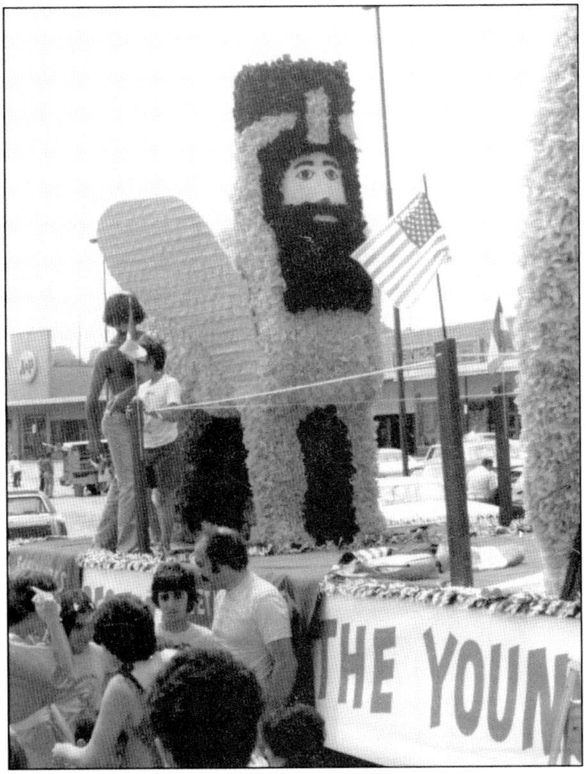

This is an image of an Assyrian winged bull float, which was unveiled during the bicentennial parade on July 11, 1976. The float was deigned by Robert Ovanes of Worcester. It was the first of its kind to be revealed at such a large Assyrian participated event in Massachusetts.

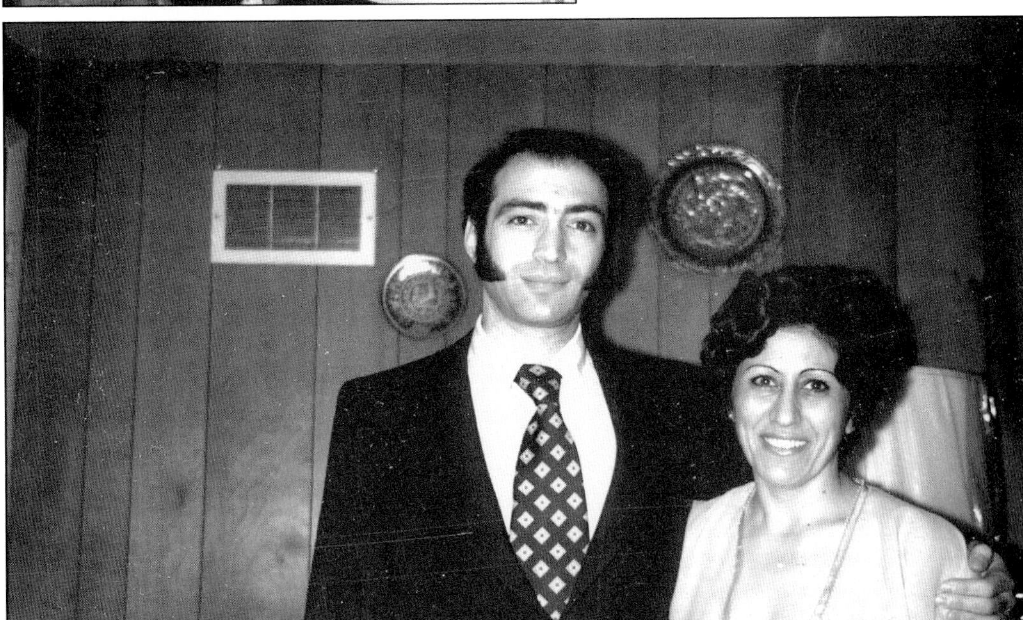

George Donabed was born and raised in Boston with parents from Harput, and has a Bachelors of Science degree in Electrical Engineering from the University of Massachusetts at Amherst. Elsie Odisho Youkhana was born in the Assyrian district of Baghdad, Iraq, and holds a Bachelors of Arts degree in Child Psychology from Central Connecticut State College. This picture was taken at the Donabed house in West Roxbury.

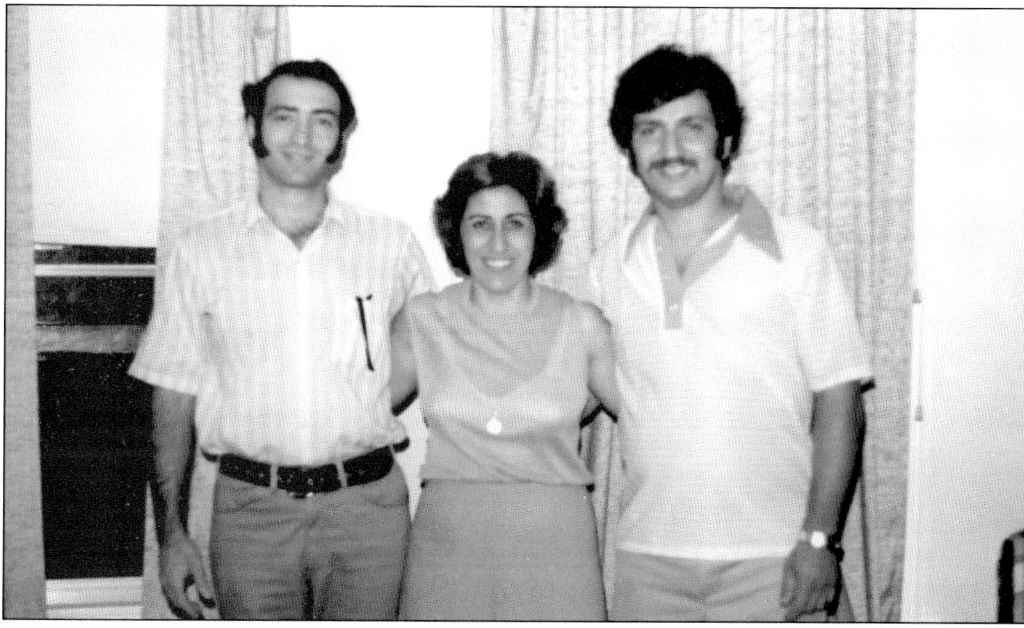

Edison Babella (right), like Elsie, was also born in the Assyrian district of Baghdad, Iraq. Like many others young men and women at the time, Edison left Iraq in pursuit of education and ethnic freedom, as was common amongst Assyrians who were persecuted for their religion and ethnic background. He settled in Chicopee where he owned and operated a gas station for many years prior to moving to California.

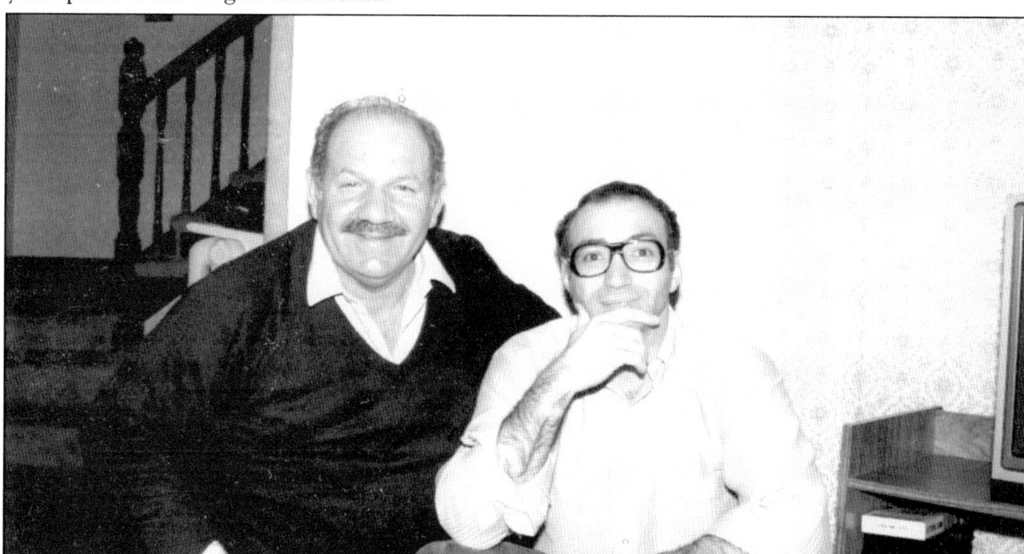

Shimshon Orahem Babella (left) visited relatives in Milton on occasion. Shimshon was born in Urmia on August 15, 1924, and later immigrated to Iraq where his two brothers Wilson and Johnson were born. Shimshon is married to Youlieh Khanisho and has five children (Dexen, Edison, Joanne, Charles, and Johnny) and six grandchildren (Ilbret, Patrick, Philip, Elvin, Danny, and Martin). The late Wilson Babella was married to Mariam and had four children (Sargon, Banipal, Nahrain, and Nadia) and three grandchildren (Nineveh, Natalie, and Ashur). The late Johnson Babella had one son, Frederick, who currently resides in Germany.

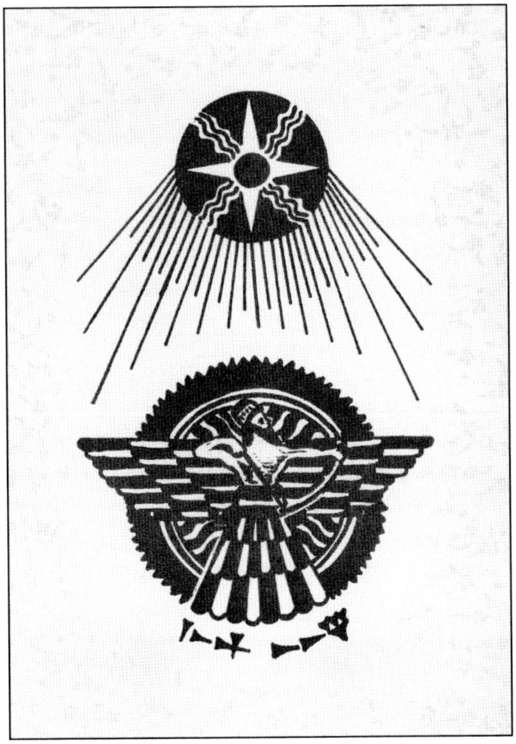

Shown here is the wedding invitation of George Donabed (son of Youhanna and Roumel of Kharput) and Elsie Youkhana (daughter of Odisho and Jerusha), to take place in New Britain, Connecticut, on January 15, 1977. Some second generation Harput Assyrians married Assyrian women from Syria, Lebanon, Iran, and in this case Iraq, showing the intermixing of Assyrian communities from various geographical locations as they adjusted to life in diaspora. Note both the Assyrian writing and Assyrian motifs on the front cover. The top image is a depiction of the Assyrian Star. The bottom symbol represents Ashur the ancient god of the Assyrians. This invitation was hand painted entirely by Andrew Bet-Shlimon.

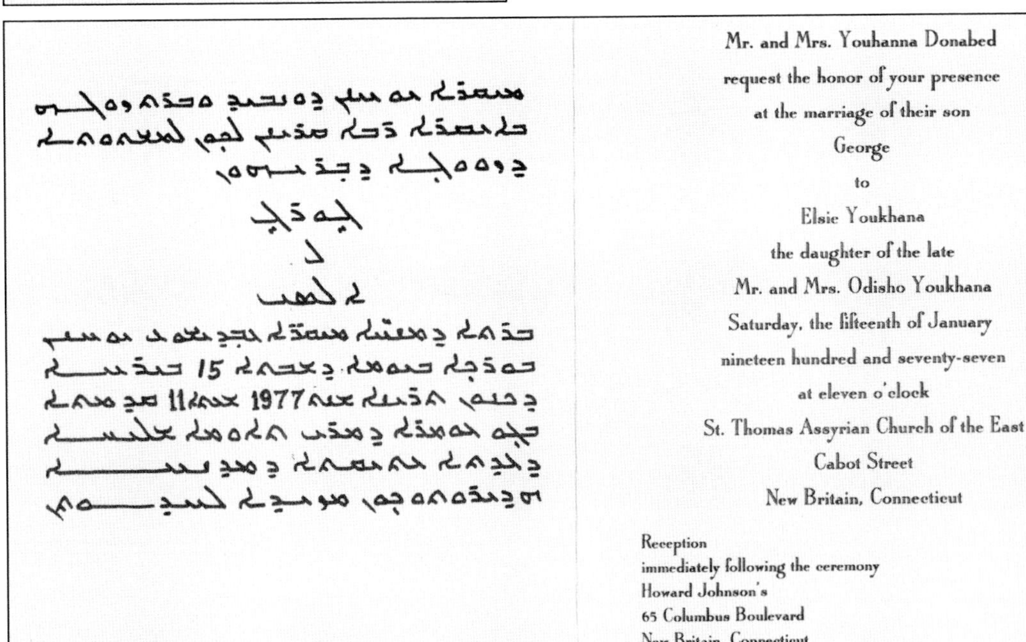

Mr. and Mrs. Youhanna Donabed
request the honor of your presence
at the marriage of their son
George
to
Elsie Youkhana
the daughter of the late
Mr. and Mrs. Odisho Youkhana
Saturday, the fifteenth of January
nineteen hundred and seventy-seven
at eleven o'clock
St. Thomas Assyrian Church of the East
Cabot Street
New Britain, Connecticut

Reception
immediately following the ceremony
Howard Johnson's
65 Columbus Boulevard
New Britain, Connecticut

The content of George and Elsie Donabed's wedding invitation is written in the classical Assyrian script. Note that Andrew Bet-Shlimon of Worcester designed and wrote both the inside and outside covers of the invitation. Andrew Bet-Shlimon was born in the Assyrian city of Qamishli, Syria. He is the current editor of the *Assyrian Star Magazine*, published on behalf of the Assyrian American National Federation.

Seven

GREAT ACCOMPLISHMENTS

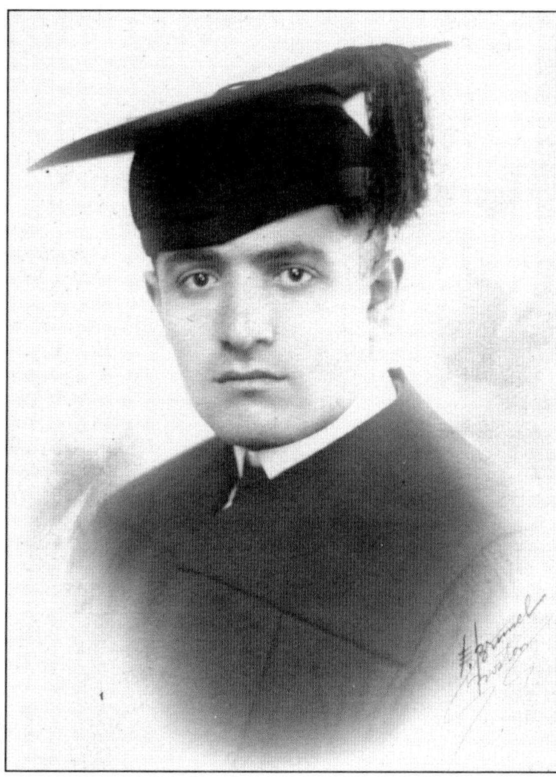

An attorney, writer, and Assyrian activist, David Barsum Perley (1901–1979) was a student of Ashur Yousef. During World War I, after his father had been killed, he fled with relatives and arrived in the United States in 1922. He attended Springfield International College, Boston University (Bachelors of Arts, 1928) and New York University (Doctor of Jurisprudence, 1933). That same year, yet another massacre of Assyrians occurred, this time in northern Iraq, at Simele. Perley wrote *Whither Christian Missions?* in 1944.

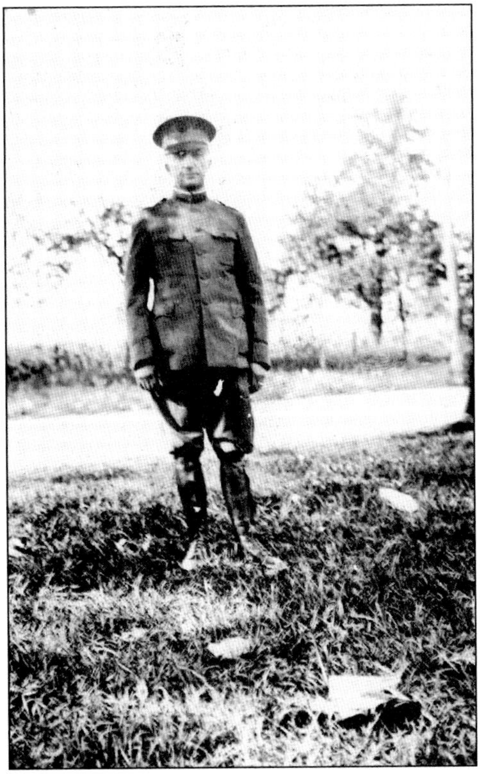

In 1912, Abraham K. Yousef studied post-graduate courses in London and Vienna. He graduated from Baltimore Medical College in 1895, and spent time in the Balkan wars as a medic. Interestingly, Yousef was decorated by Sultan Abdul Hamid (of the Ottoman Empire) himself for his great work during the cholera epidemic in Asia Minor.

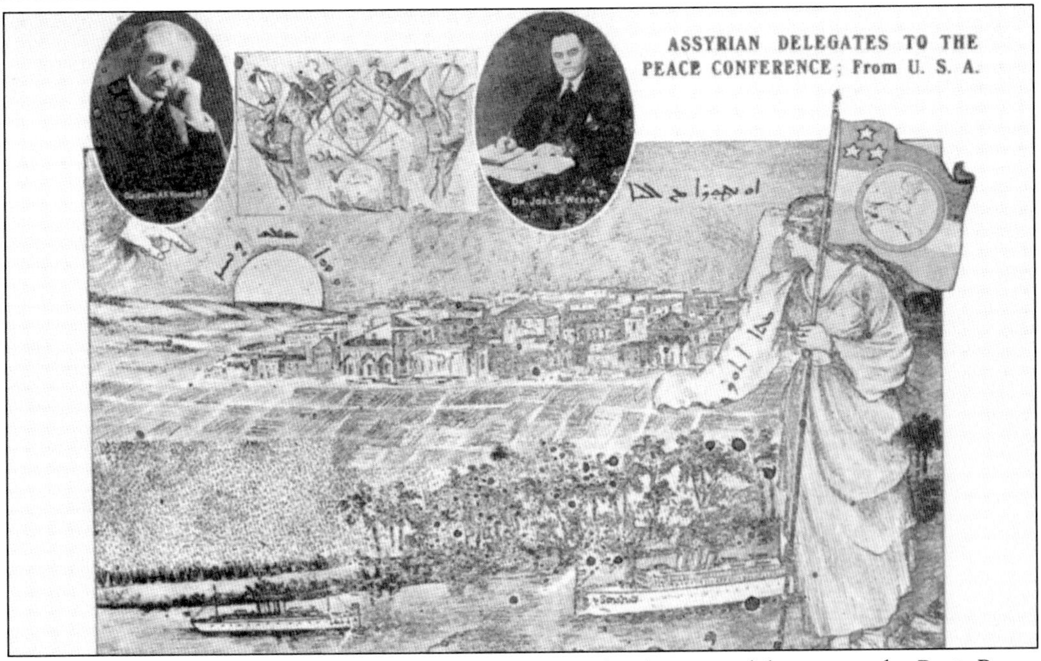

Dr. Abraham Yousef and Rev. Joel Werda were among the Assyrian delegates to the Paris Peace Conference in 1919 to demand an Assyrian homeland. Other Assyrians in attendance were Said Radji, Moussa Shukur, Bishop Severius Afrem Barsoum, Pierre Pacus, Brother Aram Abdelahad, Rustem Najib, Jean Zabony, and Said Anthony Namik.

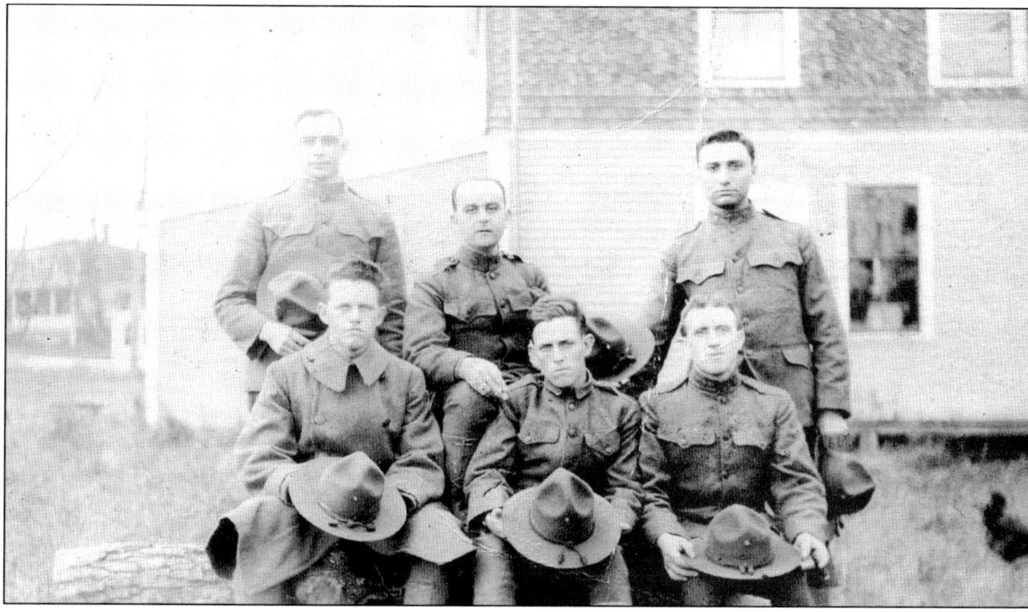

Charles Perch and fellow soldiers take a moment to pose for a photograph in 1918. Perch stands at the top right. Many Assyrians served proudly in the U.S. military. On November 17, 1997, the Assyrian American Veterans Monument was erected at Elmwood Park Cemetery in River Grove, Illinois, in remembrance of those who fought in World War I, World War II, Vietnam, Korea, and Desert Storm.

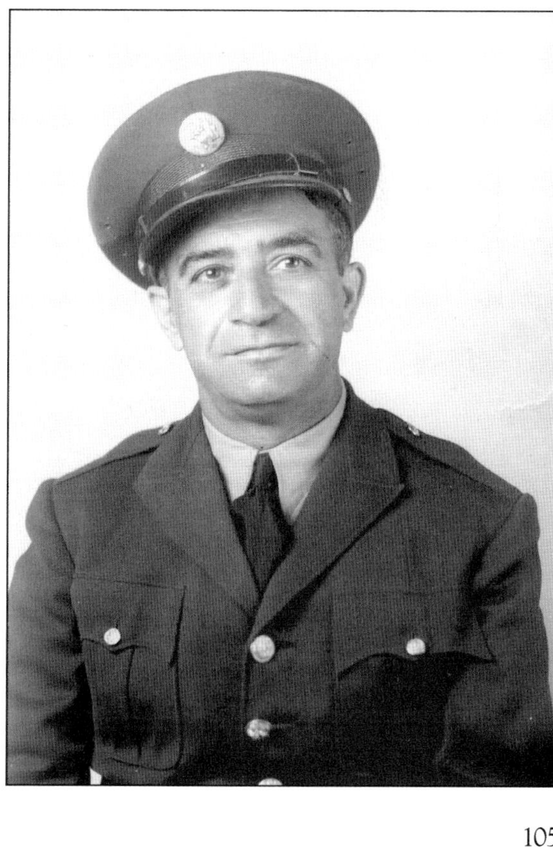

Bishara Donabed poses in military attire on September 20, 1942. Bishara was one of the first children of Assyrians from Harput who immigrate to the United States. He spent most of his life in Watertown, were he was married and later divorced.

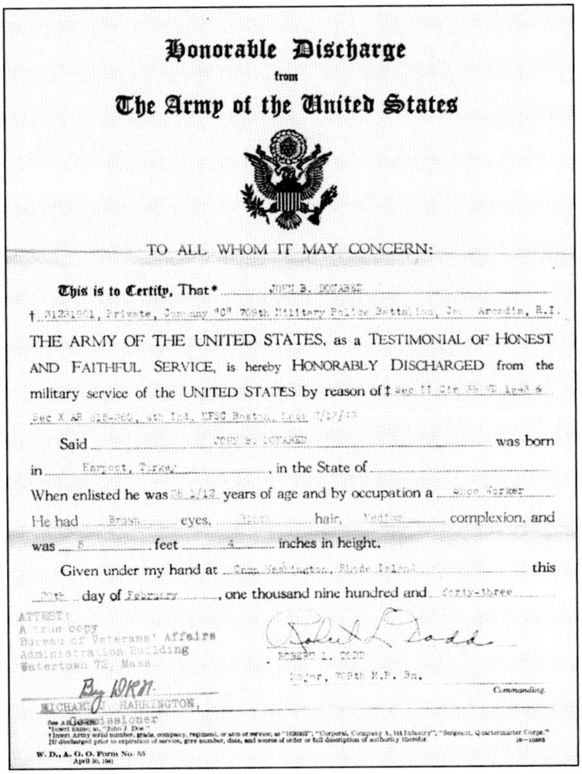

Honorable Discharge
from
The Army of the United States

TO ALL WHOM IT MAY CONCERN:

This is to Certify, That* JOHN B. DONABED
† 31231901, Private, Company "C" 709th Military Police Battalion, Camp Arcadia, R.I.
THE ARMY OF THE UNITED STATES, as a TESTIMONIAL OF HONEST AND FAITHFUL SERVICE, is hereby HONORABLY DISCHARGED from the military service of the UNITED STATES by reason of ‡ Sec II Cir [illegible] WD 1943 & Sec X AR 615-360, 4th Ind. UFSC Boston, Mass 2/13/43

Said JOHN B. DONABED was born in Harpoot, Turkey, in the State of
When enlisted he was 36 1/12 years of age and by occupation a Shoe Worker
He had Brown eyes, Black hair, Medium complexion, and was 5 feet 4 inches in height.

Given under my hand at Camp Washington, Rhode Island this 20th day of February, one thousand nine hundred and forty-three

ATTEST:
A true copy
Bureau of Veterans' Affairs
Administration Building
Watertown 72, Mass.

By [illegible]
MICHAEL J. HARRINGTON,
Commissioner

ROBERT L. TODD
Major, 709th M.P. Bn.
Commanding

See AR [illegible]
*Insert name; as, "John J. Doe."
†Insert Army serial number, grade, company, regiment, or arm of service; as "1620302"; "Corporal, Company A, 1st Infantry"; "Sergeant, Quartermaster Corps."
‡If discharged prior to expiration of service, give number, date, and source of order or full description of authority therefor.
16—10265

W. D., A. G. O. Form No. 55
April 30, 1941

Youhanna Donabed served his military service as a private in the U.S. Army. He was released in 1943 after entering at 36 years of age. He worked at the U.S. Military Arsenal in Watertown in lieu of military service.

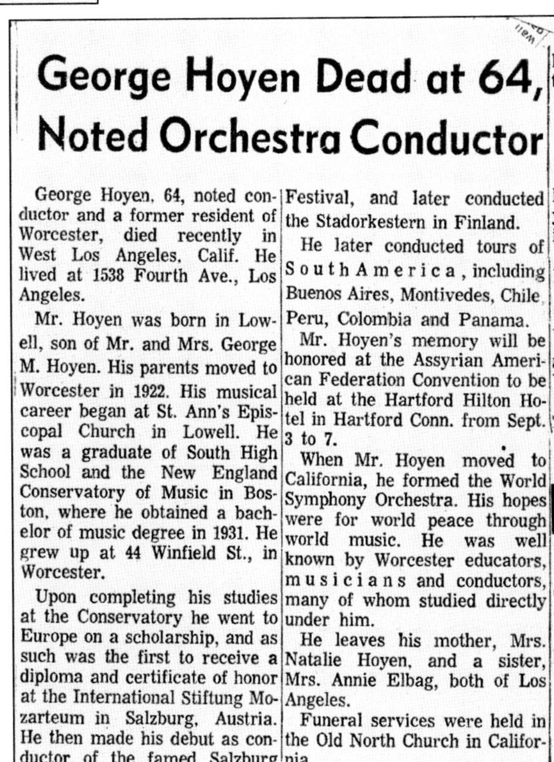

George Hoyen Dead at 64, Noted Orchestra Conductor

George Hoyen, 64, noted conductor and a former resident of Worcester, died recently in West Los Angeles, Calif. He lived at 1538 Fourth Ave., Los Angeles.

Mr. Hoyen was born in Lowell, son of Mr. and Mrs. George M. Hoyen. His parents moved to Worcester in 1922. His musical career began at St. Ann's Episcopal Church in Lowell. He was a graduate of South High School and the New England Conservatory of Music in Boston, where he obtained a bachelor of music degree in 1931. He grew up at 44 Winfield St., in Worcester.

Upon completing his studies at the Conservatory he went to Europe on a scholarship, and as such was the first to receive a diploma and certificate of honor at the International Stiftung Mozarteum in Salzburg, Austria. He then made his debut as conductor of the famed Salzburg Festival, and later conducted the Stadorkestern in Finland.

He later conducted tours of South America, including Buenos Aires, Montivedes, Chile, Peru, Colombia and Panama.

Mr. Hoyen's memory will be honored at the Assyrian American Federation Convention to be held at the Hartford Hilton Hotel in Hartford Conn. from Sept. 3 to 7.

When Mr. Hoyen moved to California, he formed the World Symphony Orchestra. His hopes were for world peace through world music. He was well known by Worcester educators, musicians and conductors, many of whom studied directly under him.

He leaves his mother, Mrs. Natalie Hoyen, and a sister, Mrs. Annie Elbag, both of Los Angeles.

Funeral services were held in the Old North Church in California.

George Hoyen was born and raised in Lowell and studied at the New England Conservatory of Music before traveling to Europe to pursue his music career. A famous composer, Hoyen spent time in Salzburg, Austria, where he conducted the Salzburg Festival before moving to Finland to head the Stadorkesteren. He also was the mastermind behind the formation of the World Symphony Orchestra.

The Assyrian journalist and scholar from Diarbekir, Naum Faik lived from 1868 to 1930. Faik was a great activist for his community in the United States. He published the *Beth Nahreen* periodical out of New Jersey up until his passing. There is also the "Naum Faik Assyrian Memorial Fund" at Columbia University. This particular portrait was found in the collection of the Kurkjy family in Watertown.

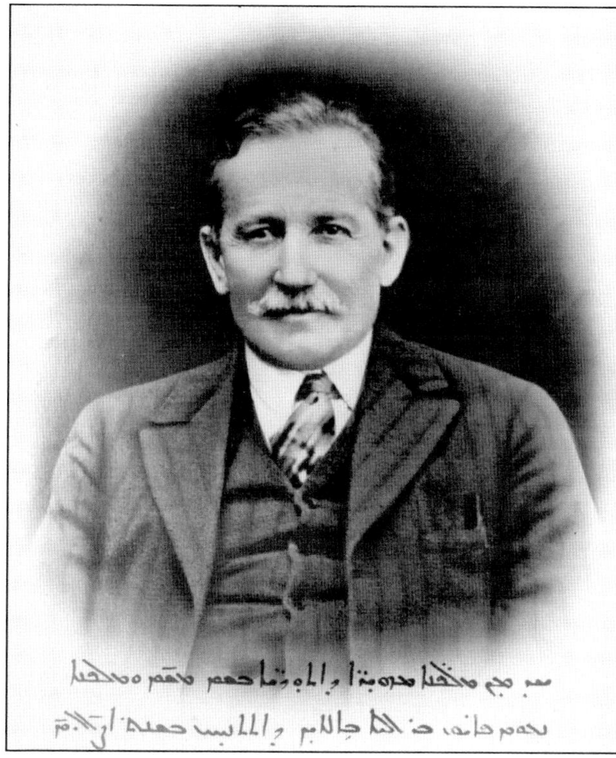

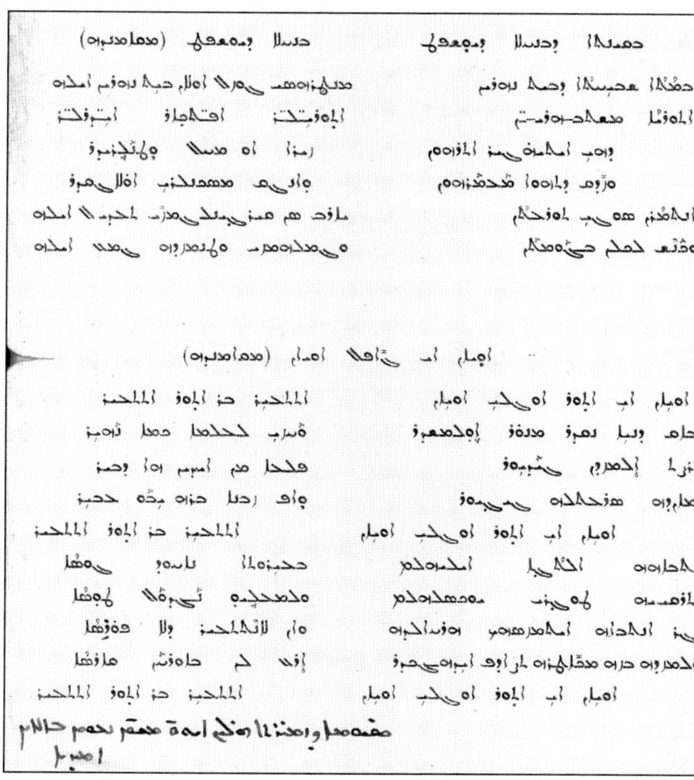

Here are two songs written by Naum Faik that were part of Sam Samuel's collection of Assyrian material. The songs are written in the Assyrian language. Each set is translated into Turkish using the Assyrian script. Since some Assyrians were well versed in Turkish, they used such translations as a means to spread such poetry to a wider reaching audience.

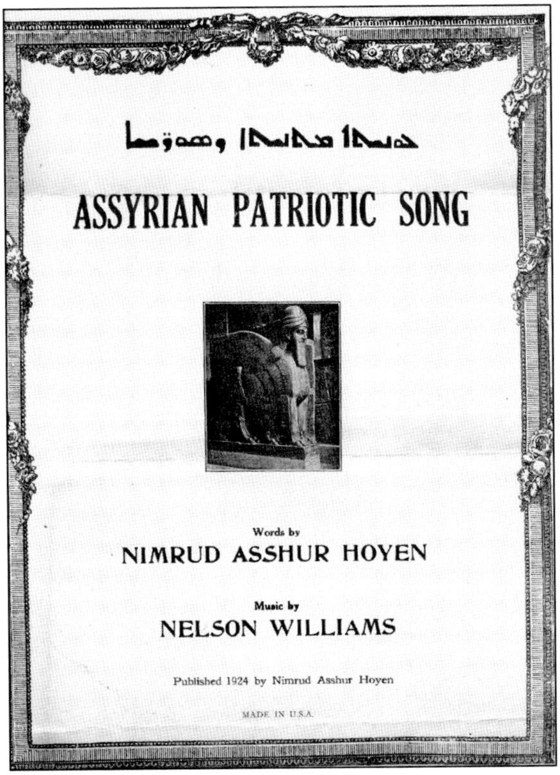

A three page score entitled "Assyrian Patriotic Song" was written in 1924 by Nimrud Asshur Hoyen, brother of Francis Emmanuel Hoyen of Worcester. The music was composed by Nelson Williams and appealed to the psyche of a people that suffered greatly during the Assyrian Genocide from 1914 through 1919.

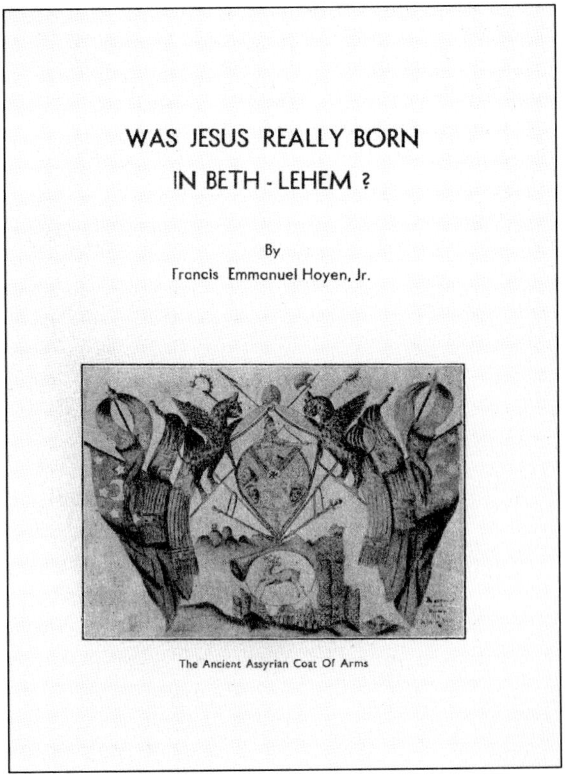

Was Jesus Really Born in Beth-lehem? was the title of this self published work by Francis Emmanuel Hoyen Jr. The book, which was published in May 1954, and was purchasable for $1 from the author, argued that Jesus was of the blood of Assyrian Galileans who were transplanted from Assyria proper. It was published by Samia Printing Press in Beirut, Lebanon.

The Hoyen family produced some of the most influential poets, musicians, and nationalist philosophers the Assyrian Nation had seen. The poem on the right, published in *The New Assyria* periodical, was written by Francis Emmanuel Hoyen Sr., and dedicated to Assyrians who still struggled for survival in the lands of Assyria.

An Assyrian Song

ASSYRIAN SONG

Oh! sons of Asshur arise and do
your share,
The glorius hours are nigh, we must
be there;
Worthy of such ties, we must now
conquer and guide
The enemy's leaders and ambitious
pride.

CHORUS

Joined in arms, boys, ahead we must
go,
And clean our world of such scan-
dalous foes;
By doing it now a good lesson we
will give,
Which they will neve forget as long
as they live.
Let us break the chains, and break
them today,
And free our country and open the
way
To see our historical Nineveh as it
was before,
And all its beautiful surroundings
that we so adore.
Onward let us go until we get to
Assyria,
For joy and happiness will follow
our Victoria;
We will have some tough fighting,
but will not mind,
To destroy our enemy for mankind.
By Son of Asshur,
FRANCIS EM. HOYEN.

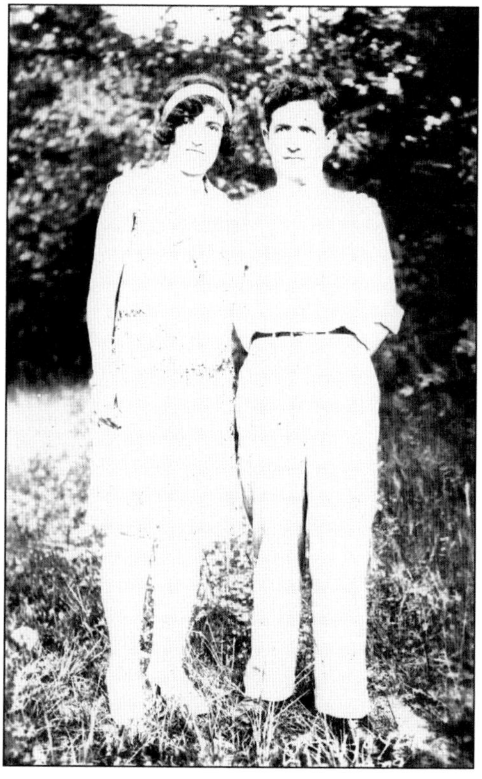

This is a picture of a young David Perley and his sister Shmuni. The six children of Barsam and Vatar Kashish were born in Harput. Unfortunately, David and Shmuni's father was martyred at the hands of the Kurds and Ottomans during the genocide. Harvard College Library has an endowment in the name of David Perley, set up by the family and the Assyrian community.

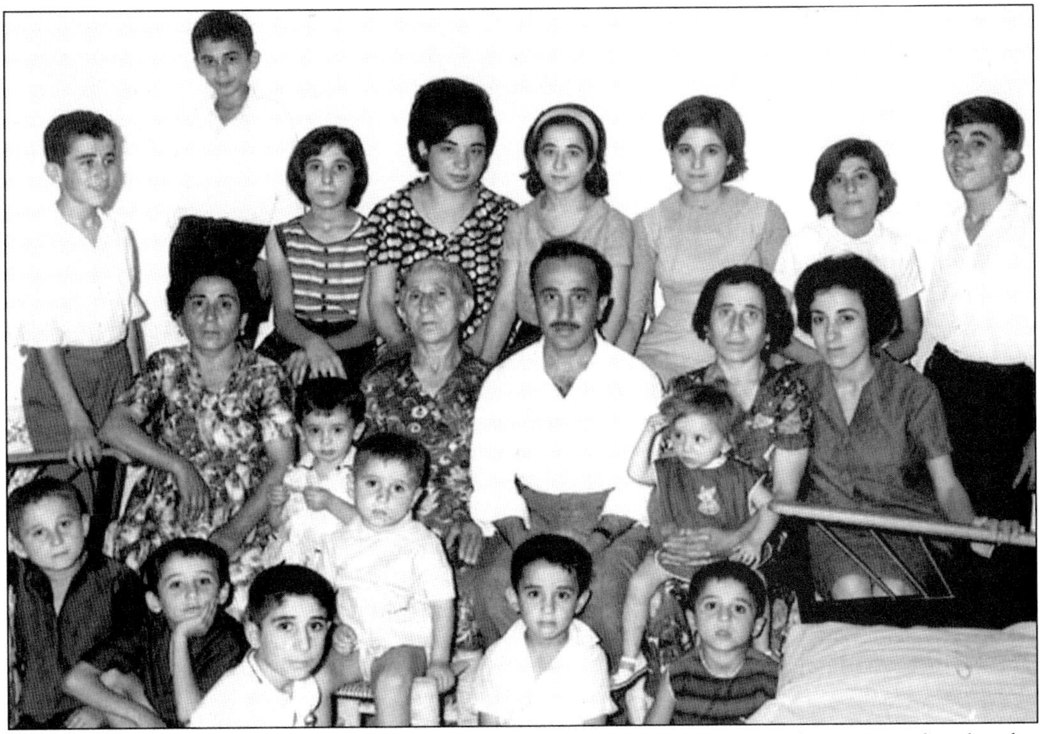

The Hanna family, from the city of Qamishli, Syria, is the quintessential Assyrian family who immigrated to Massachusetts for education purposes and has since become successful engineers and business owners. They have given back to both Assyrian and American communities tremendously. Seen in the *c.* 1967 photograph are brothers Elias, Morris, Gabriel, Raymond, Wade, and sister Khatoon.

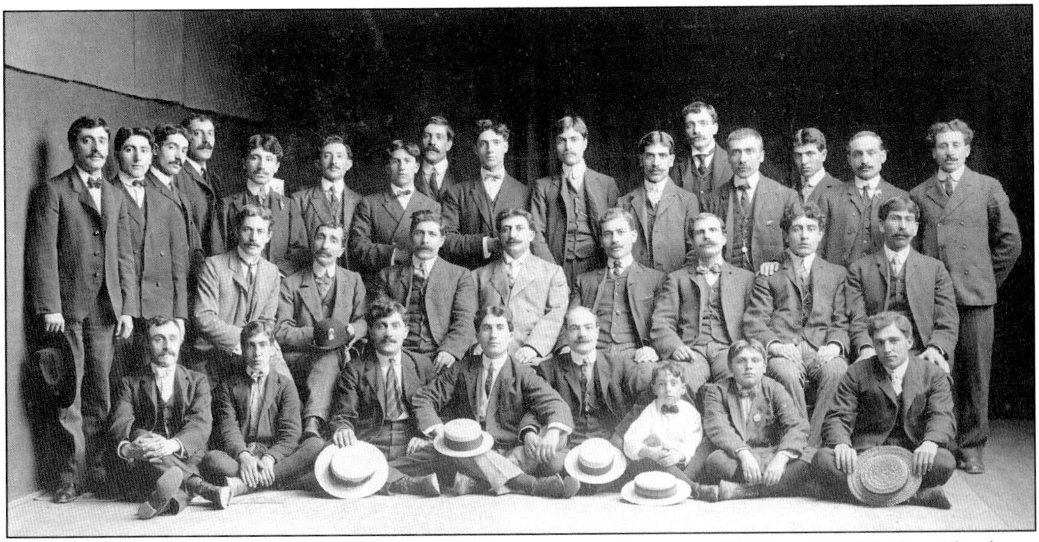

This photograph, of Assyrian men, was taken sometime between 1905 and 1907. Dr. Abraham K. Yousef, medic, captain, poet, and philosopher, is seated in the second row, forth from the left. Also pictured here are Peter Elbag and Charlie Bedig along with other Assyrians who helped establish the new Assyrian community in New England.

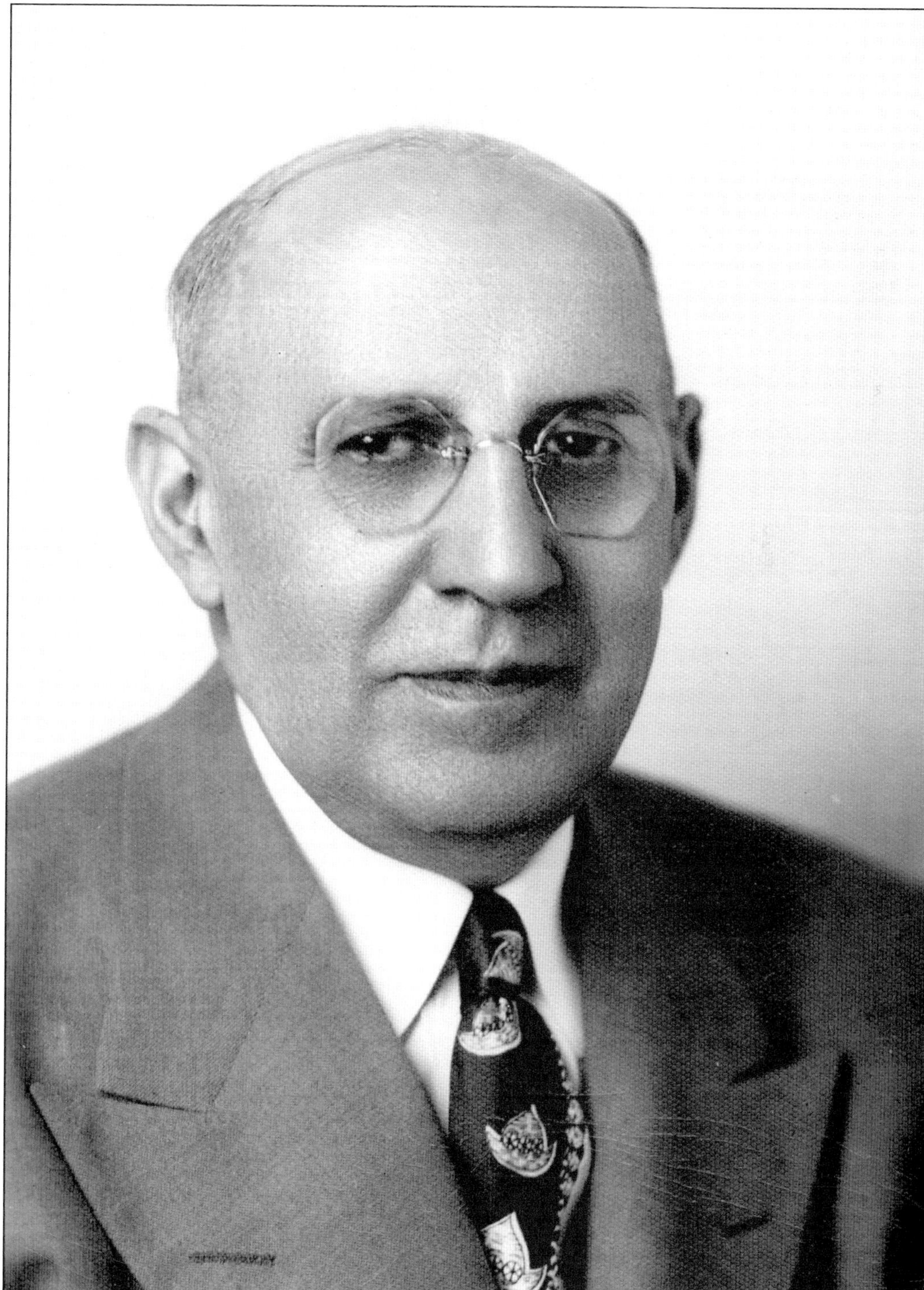

Dr. Edward Esa was a famous Boston medical doctor of Assyrian heritage. Esa was a pillar of the community and was instrumental in aiding the spread of the Assyrian people and culture to the public and private sectors of Boston.

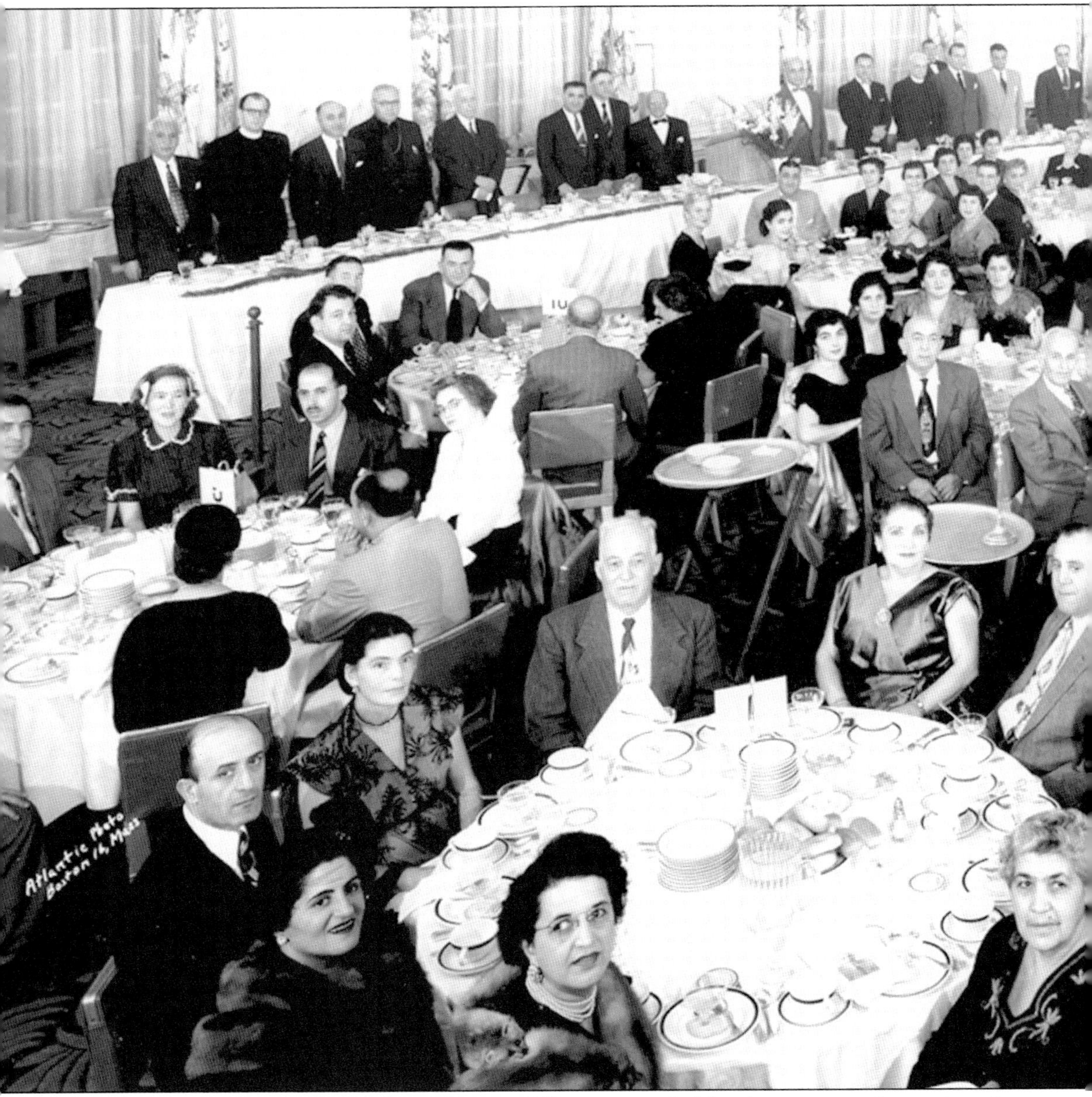

A banquet in honor of Dr. Edward Esa in 1953 was attended by Assyrians and non-Assyrians alike. Dr. Esa was a well known figure in the Middle Eastern communities in and around Boston.

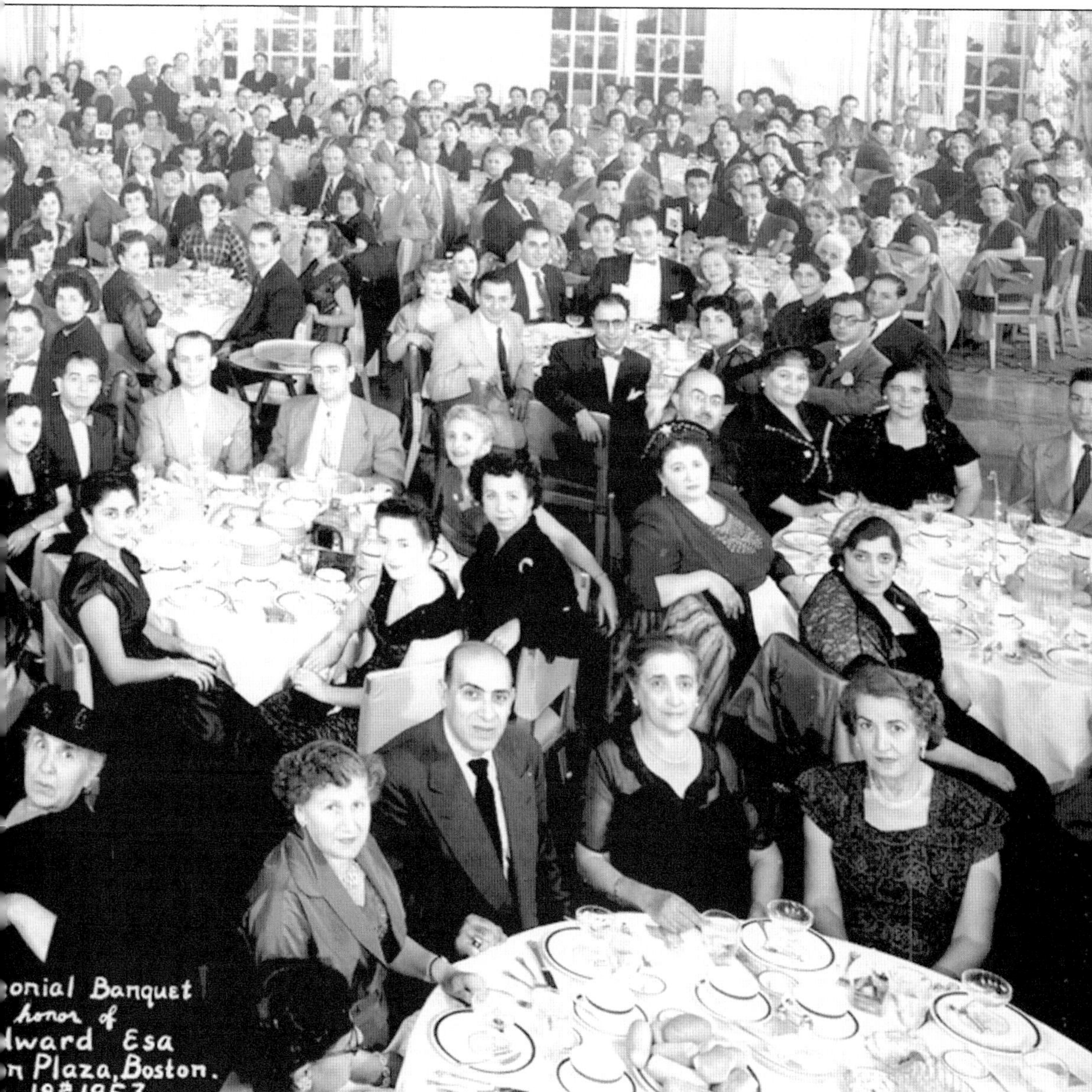

He had particularly good relations with the Syrian Christian community and the Lebanese Maronite and Orthodox sects.

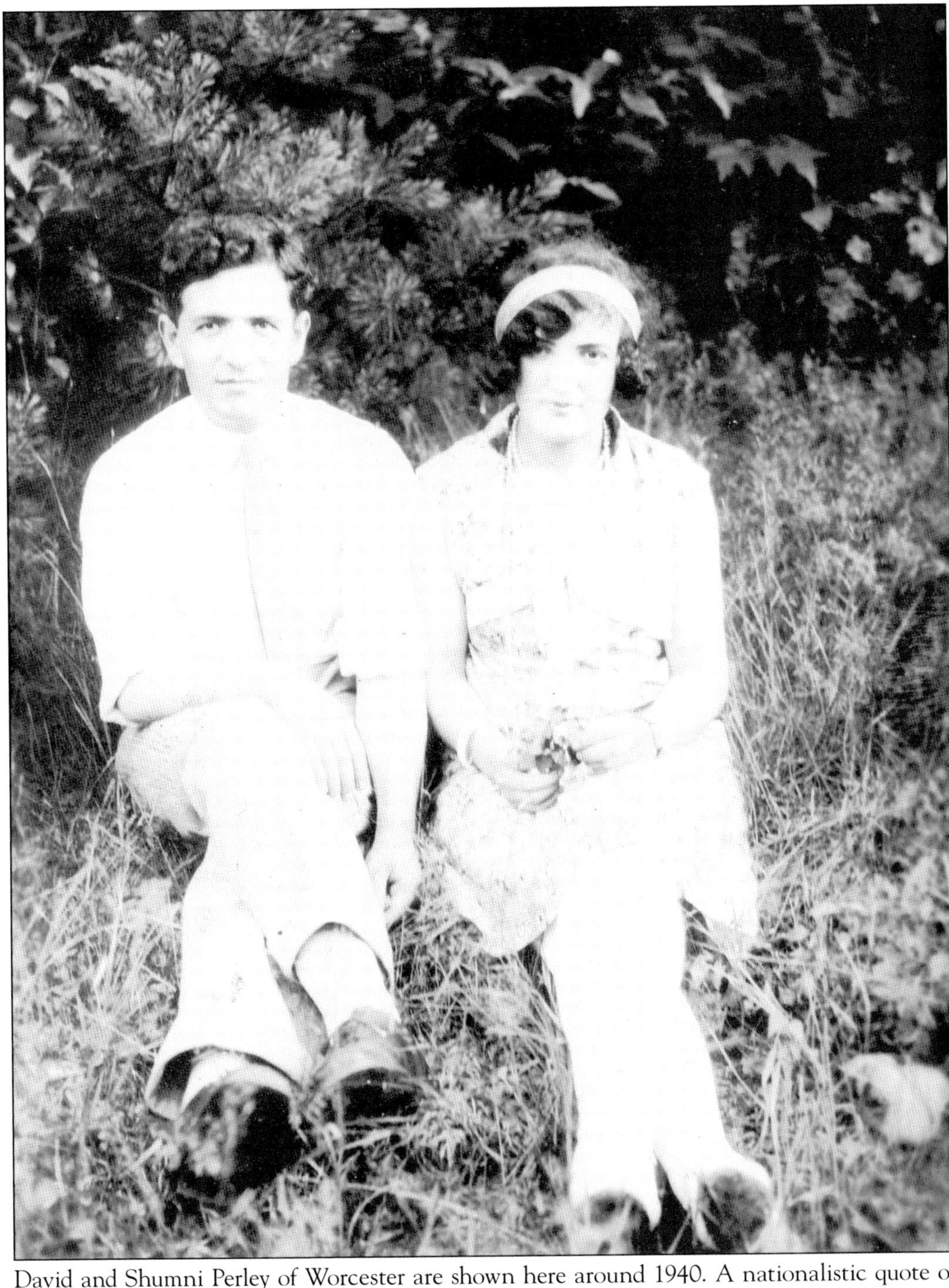

David and Shumni Perley of Worcester are shown here around 1940. A nationalistic quote of David Perley's is, "When a person is of Assyrian blood, he retains his birthright, self-esteem, and the heritage of his fathers. The term Assyrian is one single unity. The approach of this oneness of all Assyrians regardless of their religious adherence is through the avenue of blood, and through the majesty of common memories. Religion is a faith acquired and is changeable. Nationality is one's flesh and blood, it is his total nature. Even death cannot undo it."

Eight

The Next Generation and Massachusetts Assyrians Today

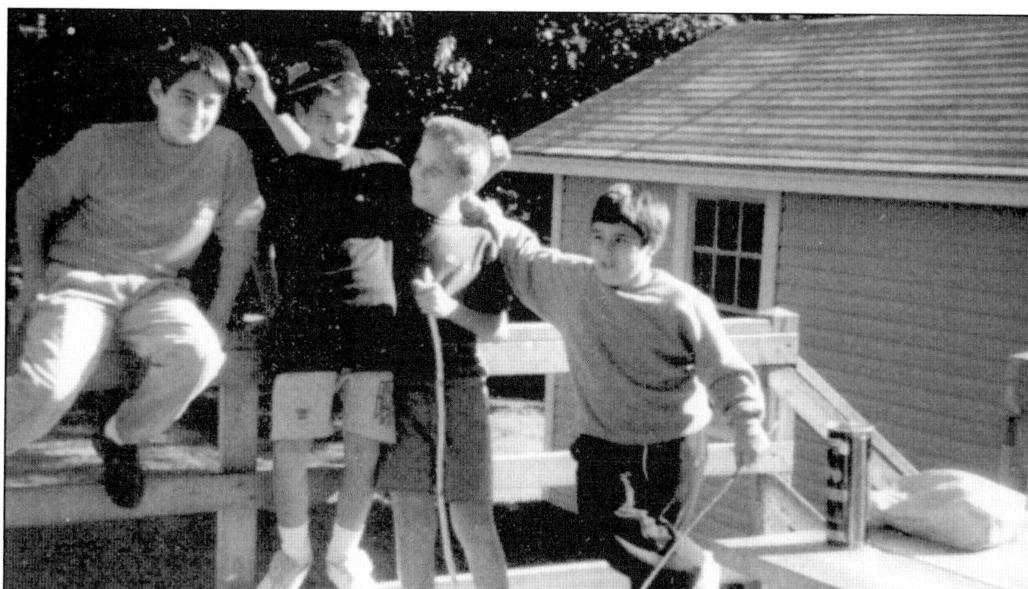

Assyrians also settled in the suburbs of Boston such as Milton. Seen here as children from left to right are coauthor Sargon Donabed, Matt Hooper, Ken Hooper, and coauthor Ninos Donabed. The early Assyrian community stressed integration of themselves into American society. Assyrian Americans have played an active role in maintaining their culture, heritage, and language and becoming an integral part of American society.

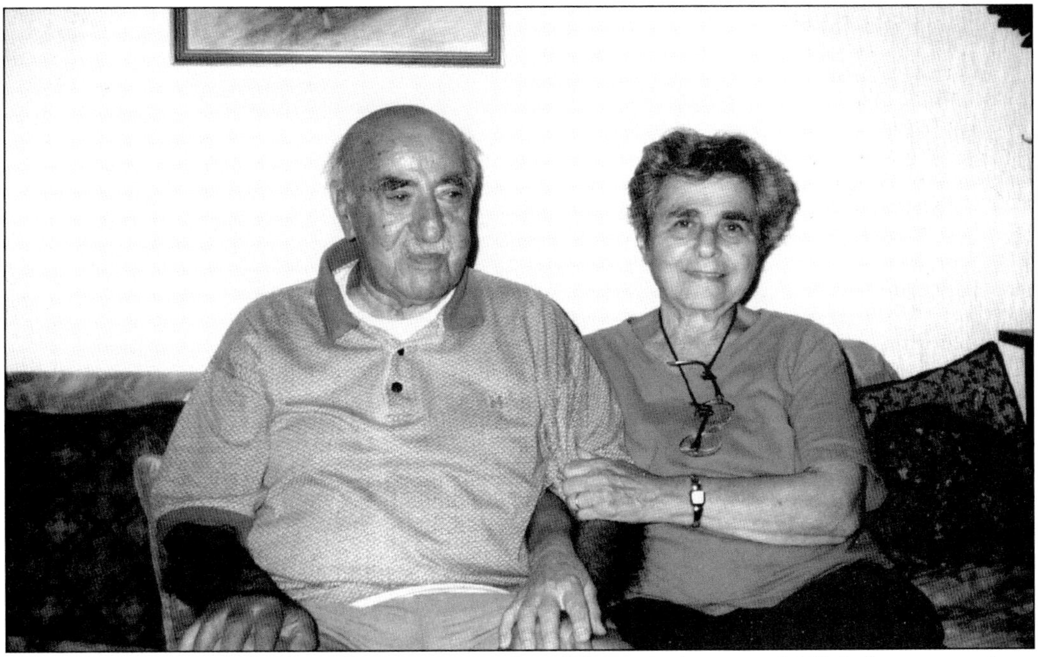

Kasper A. Saffer and Phyllis Saffer are seen at their Worcester home in 2001. Lifetime members of the United Assyrian Association of Massachusetts, Kasper "Kay" Aaron Saffer, 94, with his wife of 62 years, Phyllis (Arslen) Saffer, had two daughters, Pam and Leslie, also of Worcester. The Saffers are a testament to Assyrian American heritage in Massachusetts.

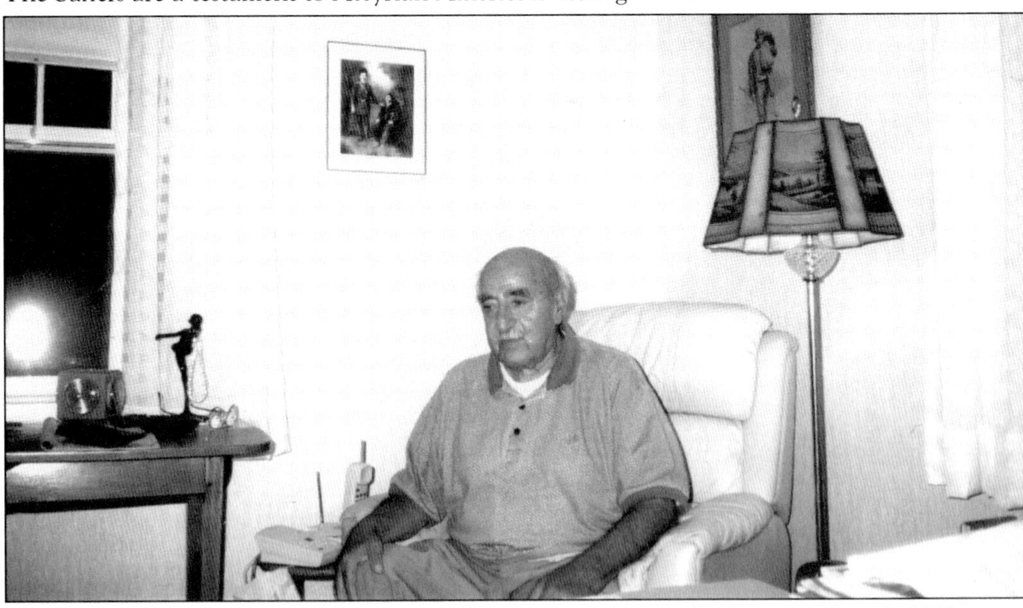

Born in Watertown, the son of Aaron and Sophie (Atlas) Saffer, Kasper attended Worcester and West Boylston Schools. He was a Navy veteran of World War II. Kasper was the owner and operator of Kay's Barber Shop on Park Avenue from 1950 until his retirement in 1978. He was a member of the former St. Mary's Assyrian Apostolic Church, Disabled American Veteran's Association, and the National Association of Watch and Clock Collectors Incorporated, a professional percussionist and speed skater.

Assyrian poet and nationalist Ninos Aho is seen speaking at the 41st Assyrian American National Federation Convention held in Chicago, Illinois, in 1974. On August 7, 2005 (Assyrian Martyrs Day), along with fellow Assyrian poet Yosip bet Yosip, Ninos Aho, representing "Occupied Assyria," took home awards in different categories at the 25th annual meeting of the World Congress of Poets organized by the World Academy of Arts and Culture in Los Angeles, California.

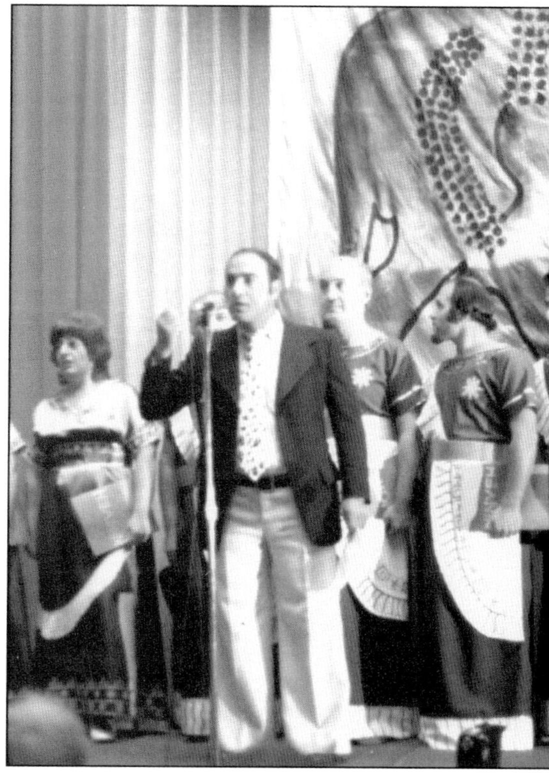

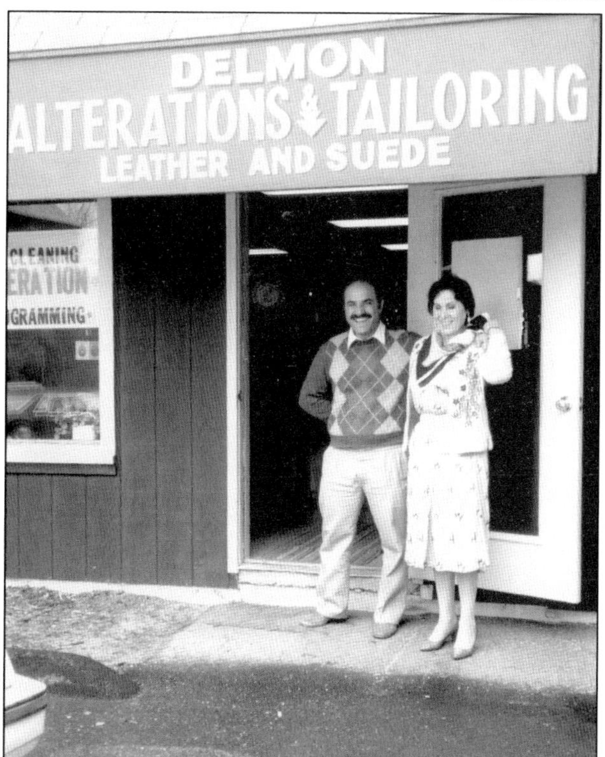

Ninos and sister Mansoura Aho stand outside their store in Sturbridge on May 2, 1988. Delmon (which comes from the ancient Assyrian word for paradise) Alterations and Tailoring, was a family run business. Family run businesses were common amongst first generation Assyrian immigrants from both Turkey and Syria. Business ownership offered stability to an immigrant population and also allowed the second generation the opportunity to become professionals, such as lawyers, doctors, and engineers.

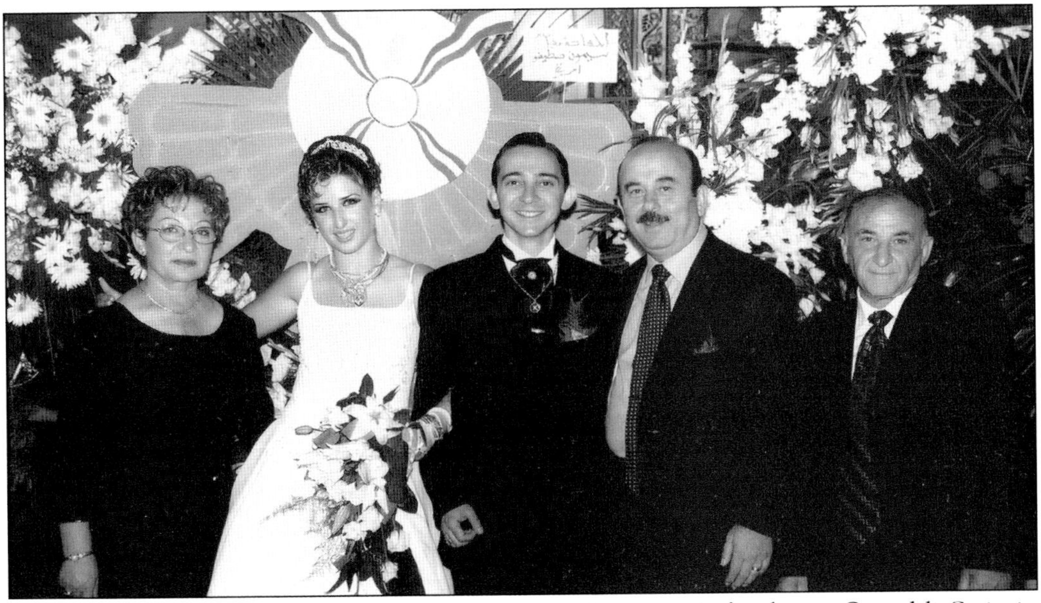

This is the wedding photograph of George Stifo and Stella Asmar Stifo taken in Qamishli, Syria, in the fall of 2003. The marriage of diaspora and non-diaspora Assyrians is a common practice as the forced immigration of Assyrians continues. The need for a common identity, a common heritage and culture, and a common language is prevalent in these types of marriages. They also help connect diaspora Assyrians with those living in their ancestral homeland. Elias Hanna (second from right), Malik Stifo (far right), and Khatoon Stifo (far left) are also present in the photograph.

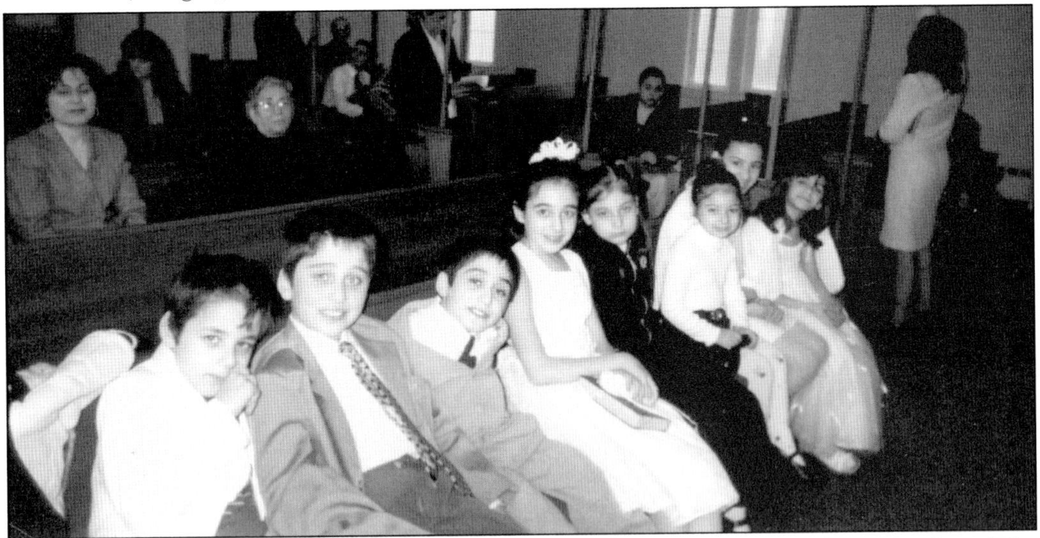

These young Assyrians attended mass at the Assyrian National Church in Grafton. The Assyrian National Church was started in 2002, in response to the underhanded name change of Assyrian Orthodox Church of Antioch in Worcester to "Syriac." The Assyrian National Church incorporates all three main Assyrian denominations (Jacobite, Nestorian, and Chaldean) with Assyrian nationalism (language, history, and culture). It has a congregation of both Eastern and Western Assyrians originating from the United States, Turkey, Syria, Iraq, and Iran. From left to right Michael Hanna, Mathew Hanna, Brian Hanna, Ninwa Hanna, Shana Solomon, Alexis Solomon, Ramtha Lahdo, and Dorin Lahdo are the youths present in the image.

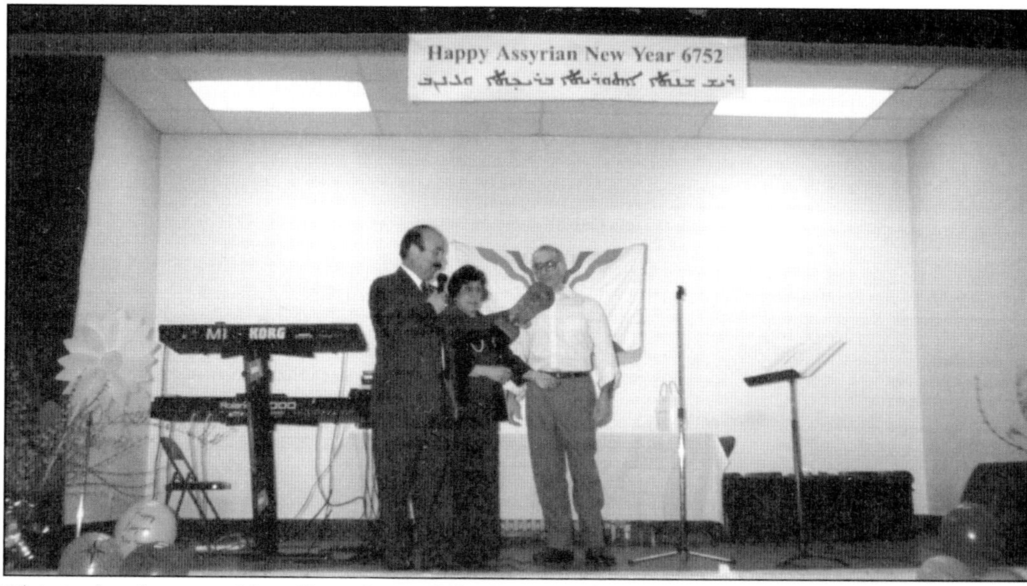

This is the Assyrian New Years Party (*Kha B' Nissan*), Assyrian year 6752, held in Sturbridge in April 2002. Assyrian New Year's is celebrated on April 1 (originally March 21), around the world, marked by the beginning of the spring season. In Assyria, New Years is the most important holiday of the year consisting of a 12 day festival. Seen in the image are Elias Hanna (left) and Elsie and George Donabed, all members of the United Assyrian Association of Massachusetts.

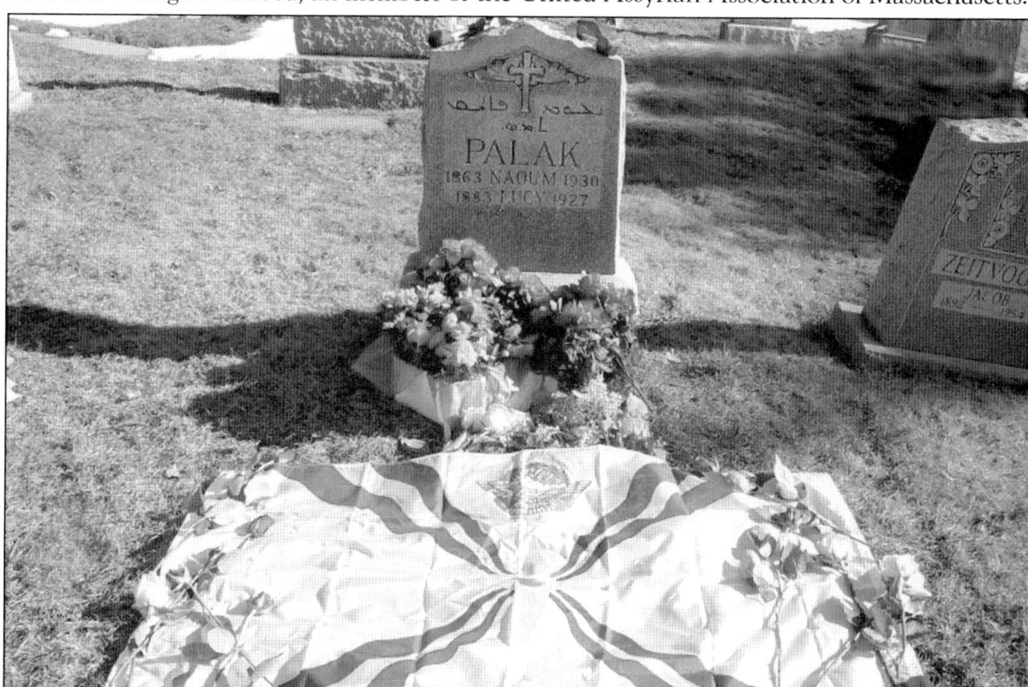

The Third Annual Naum Faik Commemoration held at his grave site located in New Jersey on February 6, 2002, was organized by the United Assyrian Association of Massachusetts. Naum Faik started the journal entitled *Beth Nahreen* in 1916, mainly written in Assyrian. The Assyrian *Hujådå* magazine (published in Sweden) is a continuity of Faik's *Beth Nahreen*.

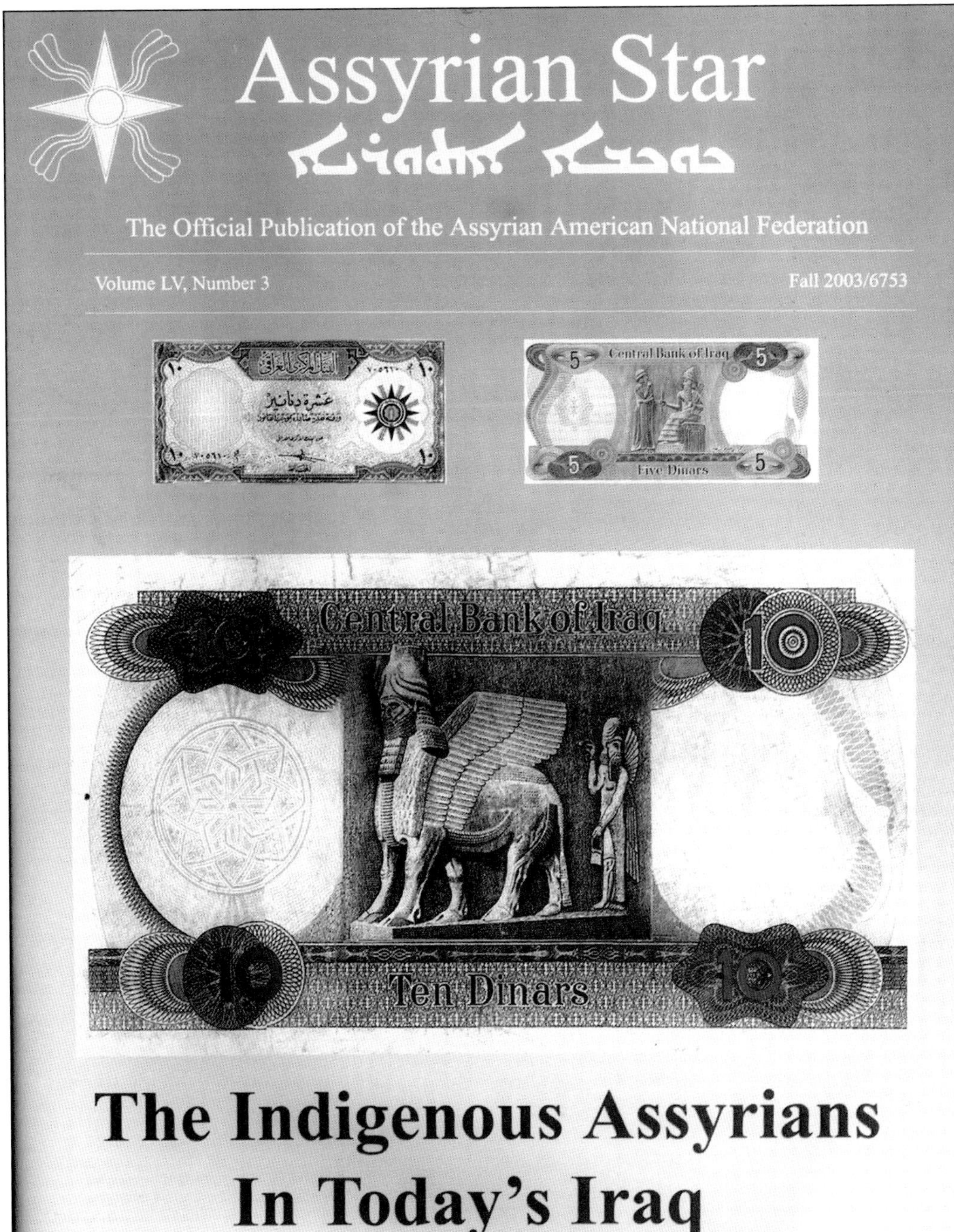

The *Assyrian Star* magazine was founded in 1952, and is the official publication of the Assyrian American National Federation and is produced quarterly by the United Assyrian Association of Massachusetts in Worcester. Andrew Bet-Shlimon, the editor-in-chief, and George Stifo, technical editor, along with Ashur Bet-Shlimon, Dr. Ramina Jajoo, Dr. Eden Naby, George Donabed, Debbie Hanna, Sargon Hanna, and coauthor Ninos Donabed, as well as other members of the United Assyrian Association of Massachusetts, help create the magazine.

PROGRAM

Third Mishael & Lillie Naby Assyrian Lecture

Assyrian History, Poetry & Music

Sunday, April 29, 2001

Lamont Forum
Lamont Library, Harvard University

Sponsored By

The Department of Near Eastern Languages and Civilizations Harvard University
&
The Beth Nahrin Assyrian Organization of Worcester, Massachusetts

Assyrian History, Poetry and Music was held on April 29, 2001, in the Lamont Library at Harvard University. It was sponsored by the Department of Near Eastern Languages and Civilizations and the Beth Nahrain Assyrian Organization of Worcester. The program consisted of a prayer and a song by Senharib Lahdo and Andrew Bet-Shlimon, a poem by Ninos Aho with an English translation by George Stifo, a poem by coauthor Sargon Donabed, and a lecture by the Assyrian Professor Michael Abdalla from Poland. It was the third Mishael and Lillie Naby Assyrian lecture.

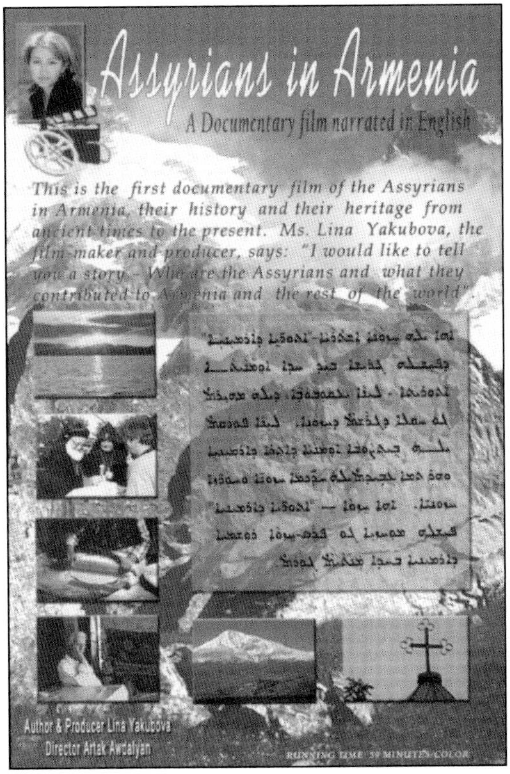

Assyrians in Armenia created and produced by Lina Yakubova, was presented at Harvard University by the Department of Near Eastern Languages and Civilizations, and the Mishael and Lillie Naby Assyrian Lecture Fund on October 10, 2004, in Cambridge. The United Assyrian Association of Massachusetts was actively involved in the event as it has concerned itself with cultural as well as educational activities of Assyrians.

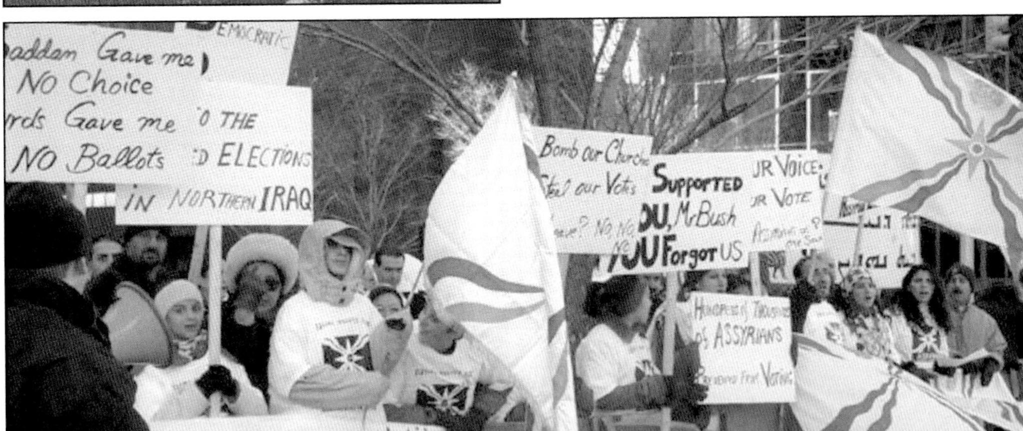

Assyrians protest against the lockout of Assyrian voters in the January 2005 Iraqi election at the United Nations in New York City in February 2005. Participants demanded: fair and equal National Assembly representation for the indigenous Iraqi Assyrian population; the formation of a special UN committee to investigate fraud during the recent Iraqi elections; an immediate end to the Kurdish Democratic Party terror campaign against Assyrians in Northern Iraq, including Mosul and Kirkuk; the creation of a self-administrated region on the Nineveh Plains to preserve and protect the history, language, and culture of the indigenous Assyrian Christians; and constitution protection for the Assyrian language, the oldest language of the Middle East. Included here are members of the United Assyrian Association of Massachusetts.

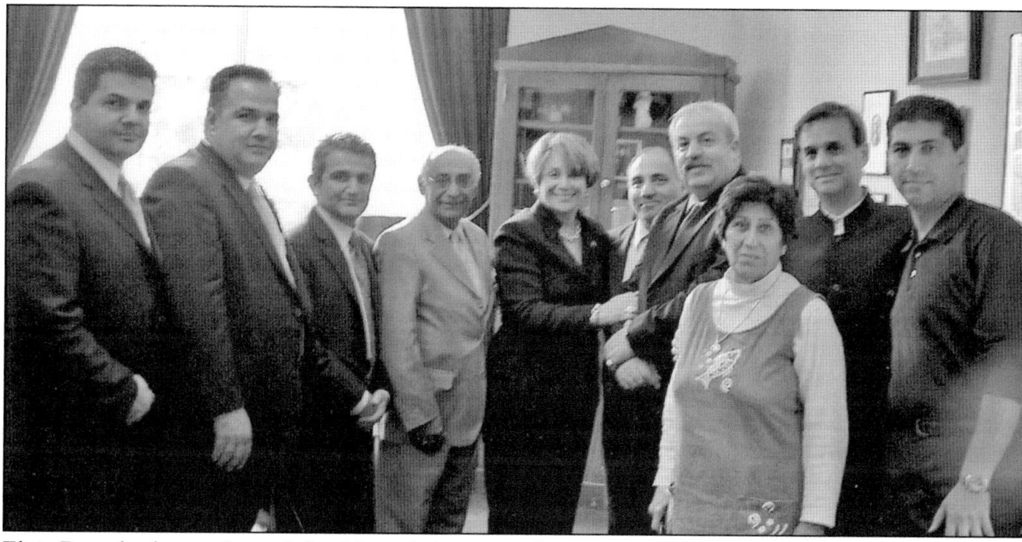

Elsie Donabed, member of the United Assyrian Association of Massachusetts, is seen here at a meeting with Assyrian U.S. Congresswoman Anna Eshoo (center) of California in Washington, D.C., in September 2005. Also present from left to right are Firas Jatou, vice president of the Assyrian Academic Society; Carlo Ganja of the Assyrian Universal Alliance; Dr. John Michael, president of the Assyrian Academic Society; Pierre Toulakhany, Assyrian American National Federation board of advisors; Anna Eshoo; unidentified; Aladin Khamis, president of the Assyrian American National Federation; Elsie Donabed; Assyrian activist Rev. Ken Joseph; and Ramin Daniels, board of directors of the Assyrian Aid Society.

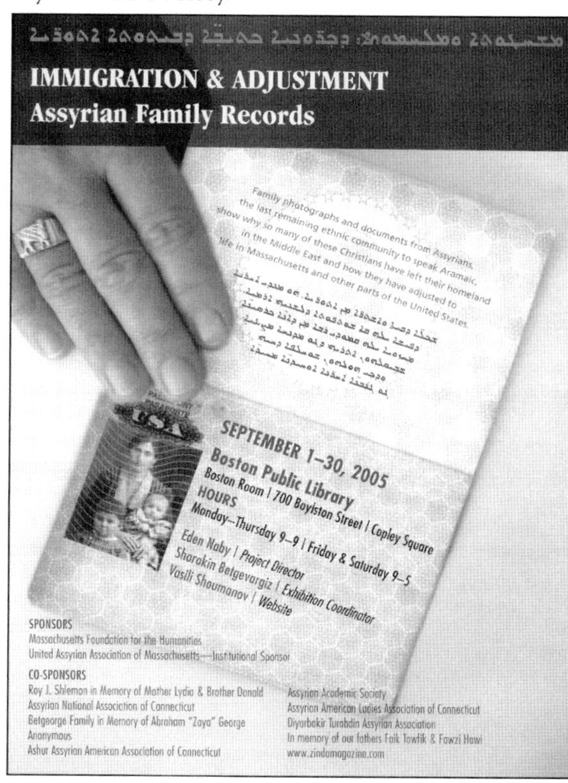

The catalog for the Immigration and Adjustment: Assyrian Family Records exhibit, held at the Boston Public Library from September 1 through September 30, 2005, in Boston is seen here. "The exhibit consisted of family photographs and documents from Assyrians, the last remaining ethnic community to speak Aramaic, show why so many of these Christians have left their homeland in the Middle East and how they have adjusted to the life in Massachusetts and other parts of the United States." The project director was Eden Naby and the exhibit coordinator was Sharokin Betgevargiz.

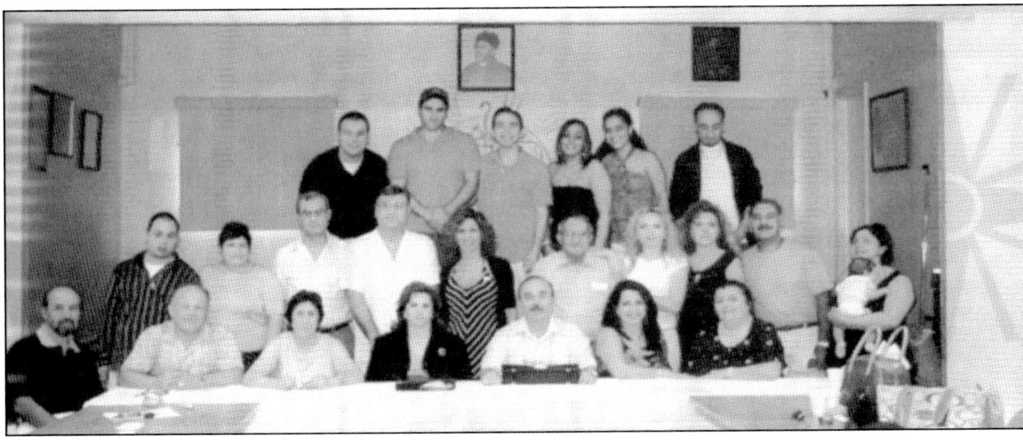

The 72nd Assyrian American National Federation Annual Convention committee is seen here during a planning meeting in New Britain, Connecticut, in the summer of 2005. Seen here from left to right are (first row) Andrew Bet-Shlimon, John Yousefzadeh, Elsie Donabed, Janey Golani, chairman Elias Hanna, Josephine Moreno, Madlein Abruscato, and Zeena Tawfik holding son Tomas; (second row) Ashur Hanna, Sharlette Toma, Ogin Lahdo, Senharib Lahdo, Agnes Pireh, Wilson Baba, Bella Dooman, Caroline Bet Oushana, and Johnny Ovraham; (third row) Ninos Hanna, coauthor Ninos Donabed, George Stifo, Lorissa Ovraham, Elaine Hagverdi, and Simon Stifo. The convention was held in Boston over Labor Day weekend. (Photograph taken by Sargon Hanna.)

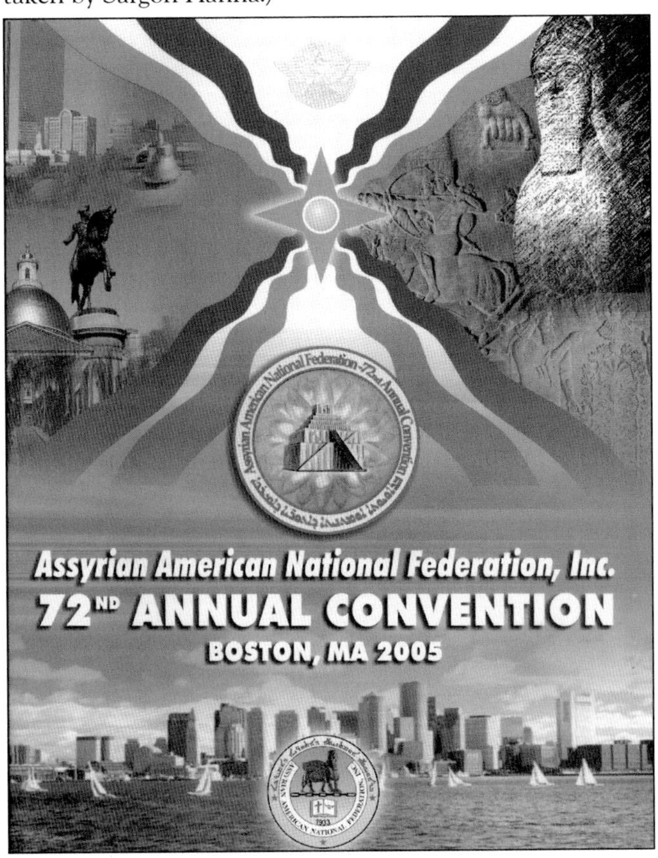

The 72nd annual Assyrian American National Federation Convention was held in Boston from September 1 through September 5, at the Sheraton Copley hotel. The convention program consisted of seminars, a youth excellence pageant, a youth camp, athletics, parties, a banquet, and a picnic. Assyrians and non-Assyrians alike traveled from far and wide, from all over North America, Europe, Australia, and the Middle East, to attend the most extensive Assyrian American annual cultural event.

This c. 2004 photograph is of the Mar Tishmoni Jacobite (Syrian Orthodox) Church in the Assyrian town of Bartilla, Nineveh, in north Iraq. The majority of Assyrian immigrants of eastern Massachusetts originated from modern-day Turkey (mainly Harput) and Northeast Syria. However, the most recent wave of immigration, due to persecution, has been Assyrians from north Iraq. During the Iraqi Elections held in January 2005, Bartilla, along with other Assyrian towns in the region (including Bakhdida, Karemlesh, Shekhan, Ain Sifne, and Bahzan) were blockaded by the Kurdish Democratic Party, thus preventing hundreds of thousands of Assyrians from voting in northern Iraq alone.

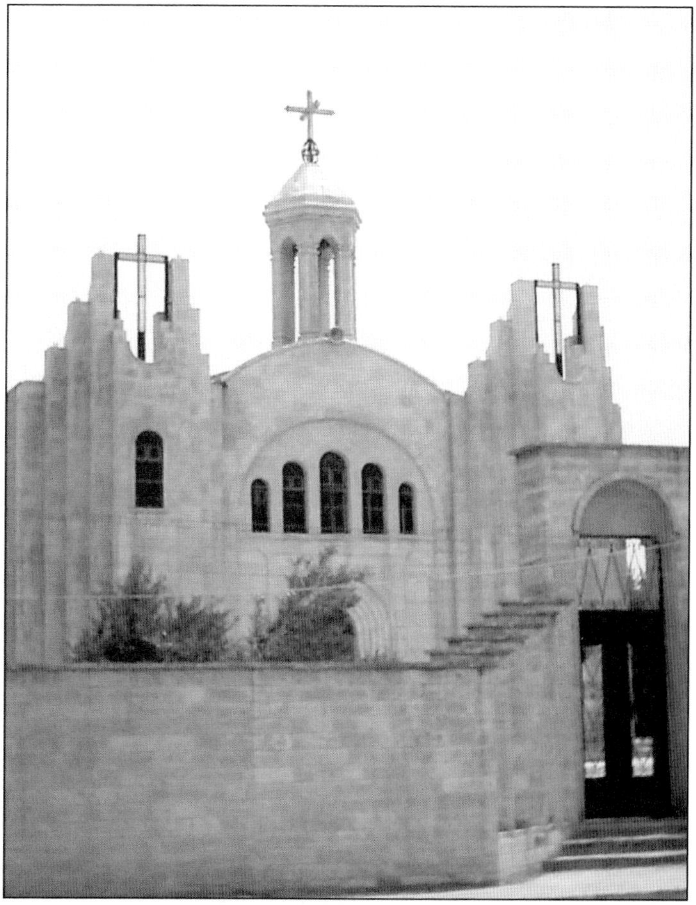

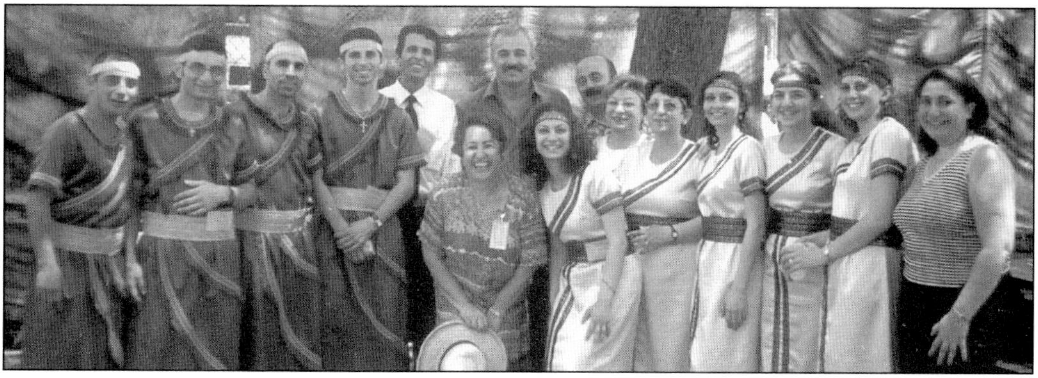

This photograph was taken during the 36th annual Smithsonian Folklife Festival entitled The Silk Road: Connecting Cultures, Creating Trust, 2002, which explored the cultures of the lands of the ancient Silk Road. Assyrians contributed singers and musicians, as well as the famous calligrapher Issa Benyamin. Seen in the photograph are members of the Urhoy Group II from Quamishly, Syria, the late John Karat (group leader), Shamiram Steifo, Edward Danho, Adnan Aziz, Ezla Karat, George Kentar, Fadi Karat, Eelona Danho, Maya Stifo, Khatoon Stifo, and Sandy Amsih. Also seen are members of the United Assyrian Association of Massachusetts Elias Hanna and Dr. Eden Naby; along with representative of the Assyrian Democratic Movement Younan Hozaya; and Maysoon Tawfik of Connecticut. (Courtesy of Bethsuryoyo.com.)

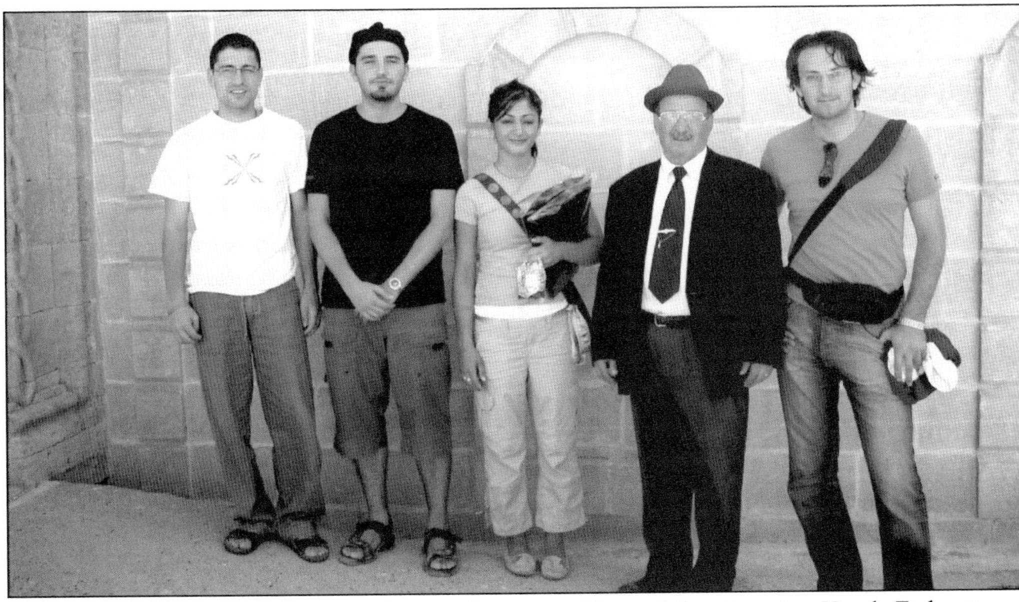

Ninos Poli and Aryo Makko, president and vice president of the Assyrian Youth Federation of Sweden; Shamiran Mako, liaison of the Council for Assyrian Research and Development; Fr. Toma Begtas of the Assyrian village of Hassana in the Bohtan region, and Dr. Matay Beth-Arsan are seen here. The picture was taken by coauthor Sargon Donabed at the Mor Gabriel Assyrian Monastery outside of the city of Midyat on his research trip to southeast Turkey (part of the Assyrian homeland) in 2005.

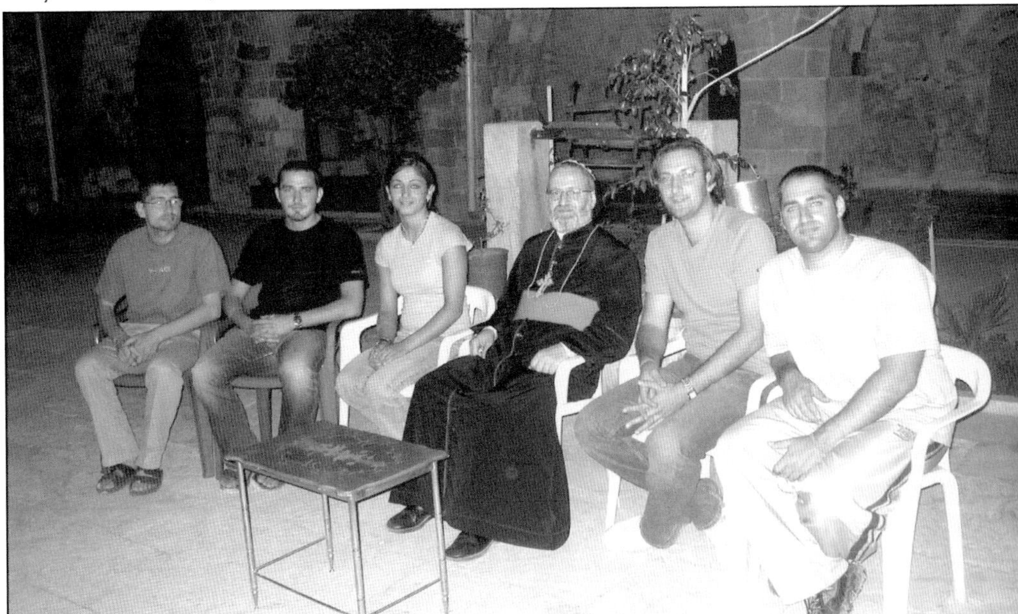

From left to right are Ninos Poli, Aryo Makko, Shamiran Mako, Bishop Saliba Ozmen of Deiro Du Zafaran (the Saffron Monastery) in the Mardin district of southeast Turkey, Dr. Matay Beth-Arsan, and coauthor Sargon Donabed. Once a bastion of Assyrian Christian culture and religion, not many Assyrians remained in Mardin following the genocide and Kurdification of the region. This picture was taken in 2005.

BIBLIOGRAPHY

Annemasse. *The Assyrian Tragedy*. 1934.

Aprim, Fred. *Indigenous People in Distress*. Chicago: Assyrian Academic Society Press, 2003.

Assyrian National Federation. *The Assyrian National Directory in the US for 1960*. New Jersey: Assyrian National Federation, 1960.

Donabed, Sargon. *Remnants of Heroes: The Assyrian Experience*. Chicago: Assyrian Academic Society Press, 2003.

Dadesho, Sargon O. *The Assyrian National Question at the United Nations*. California: Bet Nahrain Press, 1987.

http://www.aas.net/aasmain.htm

http://www.aina.org

http://www.cardonline.org

Korbani, Agnus. *The Political Dictionary of the Modern Middle East*. Maryland: University Press, 1995.

Lamsa, George. *The Oldest Christian People*. New York: AMS Press, 1970.

Malek, Yusuf. *The British Betrayal of the Assyrians*. Chicago: the Assyrian National Federation and the Assyrian National League of America, 1935.

The New Assyria, Periodical. Jersey City, New Jersey: New Assyria Publishing Company.

Nissan, Mordechai. *Minorities in the Middle East*. Second Edition. McFarland and Company, 2002.

Rosie Malek-Yonan. *The Crimson Field*. California: Pearlida Publishing, 2005.

Discover Thousands of Local History Books Featuring Millions of Vintage Images

Arcadia Publishing, the leading local history publisher in the United States, is committed to making history accessible and meaningful through publishing books that celebrate and preserve the heritage of America's people and places.

Find more books like this at
www.arcadiapublishing.com

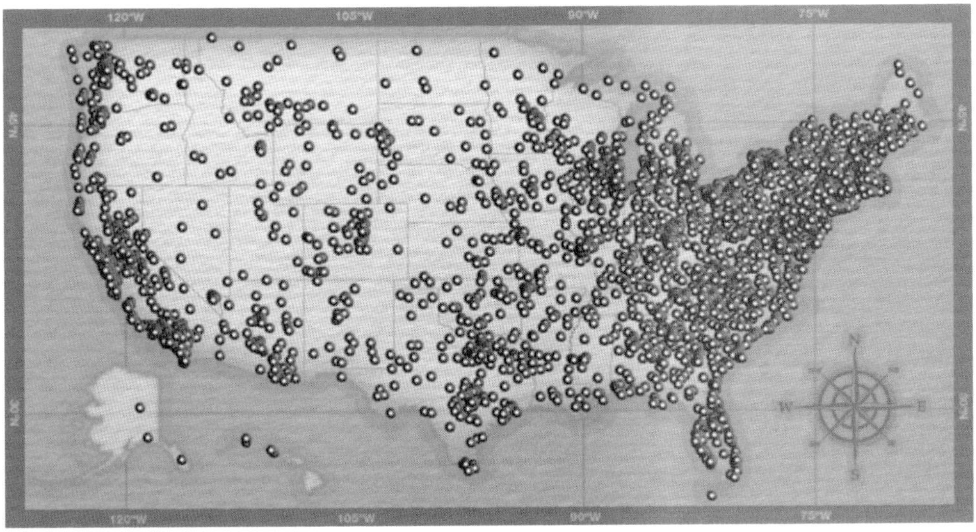

Search for your hometown history, your old stomping grounds, and even your favorite sports team.

Consistent with our mission to preserve history on a local level, this book was printed in South Carolina on American-made paper and manufactured entirely in the United States. Products carrying the accredited Forest Stewardship Council (FSC) label are printed on 100 percent FSC-certified paper.

MADE IN THE USA